SmartWatch Design Fundamentals

WatchFace Design for Samsung Galaxy SmartWatches

Wallace Jackson

Apress®

SmartWatch Design Fundamentals: WatchFace Design for Samsung Galaxy SmartWatches

Wallace Jackson
Lompoc, CA, USA

ISBN-13 (pbk): 978-1-4842-4368-8   ISBN-13 (electronic): 978-1-4842-4369-5
https://doi.org/10.1007/978-1-4842-4369-5

Library of Congress Control Number: 2019935493

Managing Director, Apress Media LLC: Welmoed Spahr
Acquisitions Editor: Natalie Pao
Development Editor: Matthew Moodie
Coordinating Editor: Mark Powers

Cover designed by eStudioCalamar

Cover image designed by Freepik (www.freepik.com)

Distributed to the book trade worldwide by Springer Science+Business Media New York, 233 Spring Street, 6th Floor, New York, NY 10013. Phone 1-800-SPRINGER, fax (201) 348-4505, e-mail orders-ny@springer-sbm.com, or visit www.springeronline.com. Apress Media, LLC is a California LLC and the sole member (owner) is Springer Science + Business Media Finance Inc (SSBM Finance Inc). SSBM Finance Inc is a **Delaware** corporation.

For information on translations, please e-mail editorial@apress.com; for reprint, paperback, or audio rights, please email bookpermissions@springernature.com.

Apress titles may be purchased in bulk for academic, corporate, or promotional use. eBook versions and licenses are also available for most titles. For more information, reference our Print and eBook Bulk Sales web page at http://www.apress.com/bulk-sales.

Any source code or other supplementary material referenced by the author in this book is available to readers on GitHub via the book's product page, located at www.apress.com/9781484243688. For more detailed information, please visit http://www.apress.com/source-code.

Printed on acid-free paper

This Smartwatch Design Fundamentals book is dedicated to everyone in the open-source community who is working so diligently to make professional new media application development software and content development tools freely available to rich application developers to utilize to achieve our creative dreams and our financial goals. Last, but not least, I dedicate this book to my father, Parker Jackson, my family, my lifelong friends, and my Point Concepcion Peninsula production ranch neighbors, for their constant help, assistance, and those stimulating, late night BBQs.

Table of Contents

TABLE OF CONTENTS

About the Author

Wallace Jackson has been writing for several leading multimedia publications about groundbreaking multimedia content development industry work since the advent of the *Multimedia Producer* magazine, when he wrote about advanced computer processing architectures, for the issue centerfold (a removable "mini-issue" insert) distributed at one of the first SIGGRAPH trade shows. Since then, Wallace Jackson has written for a large number of popular new media publications, about his work in interactive 3D and new media advertising campaign design. These include *3D Artist* magazine, *Desktop Publishers Journal*, *CrossMedia* magazine, *Kiosk* magazine, *AVvideo/Multimedia Producer* magazine, *Digital Signage* magazine, and many other vanguard publications. Wallace Jackson has authored two dozen Apress books, including several books in the popular Pro Android series, several Java (JavaFX) game development books, digital image compositing books, digital video editing books, digital audio editing books, special effects (VFX) books, and new media content design and production books.

This *Smartwatch Design Fundamentals* book focuses on the new media genres which are supported in Samsung's new Galaxy Watch Designer and the concepts, terminology, work processes, and data footprint optimizations, which will be needed to make great Samsung Galaxy Watch Face multimedia for your Tizen 3.0 and 4.0 smartwatch application designs.

Wallace Jackson is currently the founder and CEO of Mind Taffy Design, a new media content production and digital new media campaign design and development agency which is located in the Northern Santa Barbara County, halfway between their clientele in Silicon Valley to the North and Hollywood, "The OC," West Los Angeles, and San Diego to the South.

ABOUT THE AUTHOR

Mind Taffy Design has created open-source technology-based (HTML5, JavaScript, CSS4, Java, JavaFX, Tizen, and Android) digital new media i3D content deliverables for more than a quarter century (since 1991) for a significant number of major international branded manufacturers, including Sony, Tyco, Samsung, IBM, Dell, Epson, Nokia, TEAC, SGI, KFC, Sun Microsystems, Micron, KDS USA, EIZO, CTX International, Nanao USA, Techmedia, EZC, Adobe, and Mitsubishi.

Wallace Jackson received his undergraduate BA degree in Business Economics from the University of California, Los Angeles (UCLA). He received his graduate degree in MIS Design and Implementation from the University of Southern California (USC), also in Los Angeles. Mr. Jackson received his postgraduate degree in Marketing Strategy from USC, and he also completed the famed USC Graduate Entrepreneurship Program. The two USC degrees were completed while he was at USC's nighttime Marshall School of Business MBA Program, which allowed Mr. Jackson to also work full-time in the day as an RPG-2 and COBOL programmer while he completed his USC graduate and postgraduate MIS business information systems design and marketing degrees at night.

About the Technical Reviewer

Fabio Claudio Ferracchiati is a senior consultant and a senior analyst/ developer using Microsoft technologies. He works for BluArancio (`www.bluarancio.com`). He is a Microsoft Certified Solution Developer and Microsoft Certified Application Developer for .NET, a Microsoft Certified Professional, and a prolific author and technical reviewer. Over the past ten years, he's written articles for Italian and international magazines and coauthored more than ten books on a variety of computer topics.

Acknowledgments

I would like to acknowledge all my fantastic editors and their support staff at Apress, who worked those long hours and toiled so very hard on this book, making it the ultimate Image Compositing Fundamentals book currently on the market.

Natalie Pao, for her work as the Acquisitions Editor for the book and for recruiting me to write development books at Apress covering widely popular open-source new media content development platforms (Galaxy Watch Designer, GIMP, Fusion, Resolve, Blender).

Matthew Moodie, for his work as the Development Editor on the book and for his experience and guidance during the process of making it one of the leading Image Compositing books.

Mark Powers, for his work as the Coordinating Editor for the book and for his constant diligence in making sure that I either hit my chapter delivery deadlines or far surpassed them.

Fabio Claudio Ferracchiati, for his work as the Technical Reviewer on the book and for making sure that I didn't make technical mistakes.

Finally, I'd like to acknowledge Linus Torvalds and his Tizen 4 team for continuing to enhance Linux and Tizen 4.0 so that these desktop and mobile operating systems will remain the premiere open-source operating systems and so that open-source multimedia content will continue to take this expanding industry to the next level.

Introduction

Smartwatch Design Fundamentals is designed for budding smartwatch designers, programmers, multimedia producers, application designers, Tizen user interface or user experience designers, and anyone interested in developing custom watch faces using new media supported by Tizen 4.0 and Galaxy Watch Designer 1.6.2 or later software.

Chapter 1 covers smartwatch history, terms, fundamentals, and software installation for the tools that we will be learning about and using during the course of this book. We cover many of the Samsung smartwatches which have come out and are supported by the open-source Samsung Galaxy Watch Design (currently Version 1.6.2) software package.

Chapter 2 covers how to acquire free for commercial use or Creative Commons Zero (CC0) assets which we can use to create smartwatch face designs. We look at how to find the popular sites which contain these assets as well as how to download and acquire them.

Chapter 3 covers smartwatch face design types such as analog, digital, and hybrid watch face designs and other considerations regarding the watch faces you will design over the course of this book.

Chapter 4 covers watch face design states such as Active Mode, Low-Bit Color Always-On Mode, and High Color Always-On Mode, as these modes exist across all Samsung Galaxy and Gear Watch models. These different modes exist to allow battery power to be saved by watch face designs, so that models that use Always-On technology to save power allow watch face designers to customize the colors used in their watch faces. When a user rotates their wrist to view the watch face using millions of colors (called Active Mode), when in this mode a smartwatch is using all of the watch's battery power.

Chapter 5 covers the fourth dimension of watch face design, that is, motion-capable or animated watch faces. In this chapter, we show you how to create watch face designs that feature animated elements, as well as how to create the motion assets used in such a design using digital image compositing software such as GIMP 2.10.8.

Chapter 6 takes a look at the various ways to test your watch face design, including the **Run (emulator) Icon** in the Galaxy Watch Designer 1.6.2 software package, the **Samsung Remote Testing Lab** (aka RTL) online in South Korea, the United States, and Poland, and on actual smartwatch devices, such as the Galaxy Watch, Gear Fit, Gear Fit 2, Gear S, Gear S2, Gear S3, or the Gear Sport or Frontier.

Chapter 7 covers how to design watch faces outside of the Galaxy Watch Designer 1.6.2 software package using open-source software packages such as Inkscape and GIMP 2.10.8. It covers the use of layers in GIMP 2.10 to create watch face designs in a way that allows you to export all of the "assets" needed in the Galaxy Watch Designer (GWD) software.

Chapter 8 then shows you how to create an all-original watch face design using the assets which were created in Chapter 7 using GIMP 2.10.8.

Chapter 9 covers Battery Charge Percentage conditional statement implementation, so we can turn the watch face design from a black pinwheel into a red pinwheel as the battery power runs out, giving the user a visual indication of battery power usage.

Chapter 10 covers how to add, design, and modify watch face complications, which are like mini-watch faces within a larger watch face design. These usually show things such as heart rate (beats), steps taken, altitude (floor or story height), battery power used, day of week or month, date, seconds, temperature, humidity, or other chronometer-like indicators you wish to add to your watch face design.

Chapter 11 covers the smartwatch gyroscope sensor, as well as the Gyro Effects section of the Galaxy Watch Designer Properties pane. Almost all of the watch face design properties panes feature the Gyro Effect section, and we look at how to dissect sample watch face designs that come with the Galaxy Watch Designer in order to learn more about the features.

Chapter 12 covers how to add weather features to the watch face design using the Open Weather API. This chapter covers how to sign up for the Open Weather API, how to get a key, how much the different plans cost, what are the weather watch face limitations, and how to build a weather-capable watch face.

Chapter 13 covers Tag Expressions, which allow developers to add algorithms to their watch face design. This chapter covers which sensors feature Tag Expression keywords and the syntax that is used to develop Tag Expressions which can be used in watch face design.

Chapter 14 finally ends the book covering how to publish your watch face designs in the Samsung Galaxy Watch Store as a Seller, as well as covering Samsung Theme Development which is closely tied to Galaxy Watch Face Design.

This Samsung Galaxy *Smartwatch Design Fundamentals* book is chock-full of tips, tricks, tools, topics, terminology, techniques, and work processes. This watch face design fundamentals book can help you to transition from Tizen smartwatch designer amatuer to a knowledgable professional where your smartwatch design compositing pipeline is concerned, so that you will understand how to incorporate other valuable open-source software packages (Inkscape, GIMP, Blender, Audacity, Fusion, Resolve, etc.) with the Samsung Galaxy Watch Designer software package covered within this book.

CHAPTER 1

Smartwatch Design History, Concepts, Terms, and Installation

In this first chapter of the *Smartwatch Design Fundamentals* book, let's look at the history of some of the popular smartwatches of the past decade, some of the concepts involved with smartwatches, as well as popular terminology used for watch face design components.

First we'll cover some of the popular smartwatches released under the Android (Google) and Tizen (Samsung) operating systems. As part of this, we will cover smartwatch development platforms such as Android WEAR, WEAR2, and Tizen as well as popular terminology. This book covers Samsung's Tizen development platform for Galaxy or Gear, while my previous *Pro Android Wearables* book covered Android WEAR and WEAR2 smartwatch watch face design technologies.

Finally, we'll finish up this first chapter by making sure that you have the design and development software package used for the book properly downloaded and installed on your Windows 10 (or a MacOS) system.

© Wallace Jackson 2019
W. Jackson, *SmartWatch Design Fundamentals*,
https://doi.org/10.1007/978-1-4842-4369-5_1

Since most readers are using the popular Windows Operating System, as hardware systems running that are available at stores such as Walmart and are quite affordable, often costing less than $500 per computer tower. We are using Windows for the screenshots used in the figures utilized throughout this book. The MacOS screens are identical.

The History of the Smartwatch

The first thing we're going to do is look at some of the major smartwatches released nearly a decade ago, starting in 2012. Some watches released before then were electronic, but did not utilize an advanced OS platform like Android or Tizen, so I'm not terming these "smartwatches," but instead "digital watches," and therefore not including watches prior to Sony's Smartwatch in this history section. We'll look at how display resolution and 3G/4G connection capability have evolved over time, as color depth, resolution, and sensors define what the watch face application developer can do using a given smartwatch device.

Sony Smartwatch (2012)

Going back almost a decade, the first popular smartwatch was the Sony Smartwatch, released in 2012, running the Android WEAR API on a 1.3" OLED (Organic Light-Emitting Diode) display. The Sony Smartwatch (V1) has been succeeded by the Sony Smartwatch 2 in 2013 and the Sony Smartwatch 3 released in 2017, which runs the Android WEAR2 API. The Sony Smartwatch 4 is slated for release sometime during 2019. The Sony Smartwatch 4 will finally feature 4G connectivity, so it can be used without "tethering" it to a smartphone using Bluetooth, which the previous three Sony Smartwatches required.

Pebble Smartwatch (2013)

By 2013, in response to the Sony Smartwatch, a start-up company named Pebble had developed a smartwatch in 2012 and released an affordable smartwatch by January of 2013. Pebble smartwatches could be connected to Android or iOS phones and were able to show notifications and messages which came into the smartphone on the smartwatch. Support for Pebble smartwatches stopped in June of 2018.

Samsung Galaxy Gear Smartwatch (2013)

Thanks to Sony and Pebble, 2013 turned out to be a huge year for smartwatches. In September of 2013, another major industry player, Samsung Electronics, released the Galaxy Gear Smartwatch. There was a Galaxy Gear running Android WEAR and another version which ran an open source **Tizen OS** from **the Linux Foundation**. A recent version was recently rebranded as the Samsung Galaxy Watch and is one of the smartwatches we will be developing for throughout this book.

Neptune Pine Smartwatch (2013)

In 2013 Neptune announced the Neptune Pine Smartwatch. The Neptune Pine became available to users in 2014 and ran the full Android OS. I covered the development of the Android WatchFace API in my *Pro Android Wearables* book for Neptune Pine because it did not need to be "tethered" to a smartphone, which is far more common these days. The Pine is still under development in 2018 for the Android OS.

Samsung Gear Fit Smartwatch (2014)

In April of 2014, Samsung released the Gear Fit Smartwatch, which had a slim, curved OLED screen and fitness tracking sensors, which are a popular smartwatch feature for users who like to track their fitness. Features include a Heart Rate sensor, Pedometer, Exercise Modes for Running and Walking, Companion Modes for Cycling and Hiking, and Sleep sensor. Samsung Gear Fit features a slim 1.84" curved Super AMOLED touch display with 432 x 128 pixel resolution. A 210 mAh battery gives users 3–5 days of usage before recharging. The watch body measures 23.4 mm x 57.4 mm x 11.95 mm (0.92 in x 2.26 in x 0.47 in), has replaceable watch bands, and weighs only 27 g (less than 1 ounce).

LG "G" and "R" Smartwatches (2014)

The LG G Watch (model W100, also code named Dory) is an Android WEAR-based smartwatch announced and released by LG and Google on June 25, 2014. It is compatible with smartphones running Android 4.3 or later that support Bluetooth LE. The G Watch "R" version features a round face using an OLED. These smartwatches used a Qualcomm Snapdragon 400 quad-core 1.2 GHz CPU and 512 MB of system memory with 4 GB of solid-state (Flash memory) storage. The display was a 1.65 in (42 mm) LCD with a RGB matrix using a lower screen resolution of 280 by 280 pixels. The smartphone connectivity was accomplished using Bluetooth LE, and the battery power was 400 mAh.

Samsung Gear S Smartwatch (2014)

Samsung released the Gear S in August of 2014, this smartwatch is untethered from the smartphone using 3G connectivity and has increased display quality using a 2 inch curved Super AMOLED display, with a 360 by 480 resolution. The Gear S is powered by a dual-core Snapdragon 400 processor from Qualcomm and has half a gigabyte of system memory (512 MB) and 4 GB of SSD (Solid-State Data) storage (equivalent to a high-speed hard disk drive, or HDD). The display is a large 2-inch (51 mm, for those who prefer larger, 46–56 mm, watches) curved Super AMOLED with RGB matrix technology using 172,800 pixels (360 x 480 pixels at a 3:4 aspect ratio). Display input is accomplished via a capacitive multitouch screen, and features include an Accelerometer, a Gyroscope, a Compass, a Heart Rate Monitor (HRM), an Ambient Light sensor, a UV sensor (the Gear S is the only smartwatch which features one of these), and a Barometer. This smartwatch is a pretty amazing value for a couple hundred bucks, being the only smartwatch with a UV sensor on the market, and it is also still available half a decade later, in 2019! For these reasons, this is one of the smartwatches supported by the GWD software that we will be covering in this book.

Samsung Gear S2 Smartwatch (2015)

Samsung released the Gear S2 in 2015, which can be untethered from the smartphone using optional 3G connectivity and has increased display quality using a 1.2" 302 PPI (Pixels Per Inch) Super AMOLED circular display with a 360 by 360 resolution. The display features capacitive touchscreen input, dual microphones, and sensors for a Pedometer (9-axis sensor), PPG heart rate monitor, and ambient light sensor. The non-3G model can connect with Wi-Fi (802.11 b/g/n) or Bluetooth LE. The Gear S2 also has a Speaker (available on the 3G version only). This watch features a rotating bezel user interface (UI) and an IP68 rating for water resistance up to 1.5 meters deep for up to 30 minutes. It is compatible with 20-mm-width watch straps for Men who like larger-sized watches. The processor on the non-3G model is an Exynos 1 GHz dual-core ARM Cortex-A7 CPU, and the processor on the 3G model is a Qualcomm Snapdragon 400 1.2 GHz dual-core ARM Cortex-A7 CPU.

Apple iWatch (2015)

In April of 2015, Apple unveiled the iWatch, with significantly lesser resolution than the 360 x 480 Samsung Gear S, at 340 x 272 pixel and 390 x 312 pixel versions. Apple smartwatches use the WatchOS 2 API to tether to the iPhone, much like early Android WEAR smartwatches tethered to Android smartphones. A second generation was released in 2016, a third generation in 2017, and a fourth generation in 2018. The iWatch uses a 32-bit ARM CPU and system memory ranges from 512 MB for iWatch V1 up to 768 MB in later versions. Since this book focuses on open-source Tizen (Linux Foundation) smartwatch development for Samsung smartwatch models, which sport the most features at the lowest price points, I will focus primarily on those models and specifications throughout this chapter, as we will be developing for them in the rest of this book.

Huawei Watch (2015)

On September of 2015, Huawei released its Android Smartwatch. The Huawei Watch form factor is based on the circular design of traditional watches, like many of Samsung's smartwatches. Huawei Watch supports a 42 mm (1.4 inch) AMOLED display. The screen's resolution is one of the highest (best) at 400 x 400 pixels at more than 285 PPI, although LG now has a model which features 480 by 480 pixels. This first Huawei Watch used a powerful 1.2 GHz Qualcomm Snapdragon 400 processor. All versions of the original Huawei Watch had 512 MB of RAM and 4 GB of internal data storage, along with a gyroscope, accelerometer, vibration motor, and heart rate sensor. It supports Wi-Fi and Bluetooth 4.1 LE, but does not support GPS location. The watch uses a magnetic charging cradle, with a day and a half of battery life at 300 mAh.

The watch face case is impressive, comprised of stainless steel, covered with a sapphire crystal glass on the watch face front, and is available in six custom finishes: Black Leather, Steel Link Bracelet, Stainless Steel Mesh, Black-plated Link Bracelet, Alligator-pressed Brown Leather, and Rose Gold-plated Link Bracelet.

Samsung Gear Fit 2 Smartwatch (2016)

The successor to the Gear Fit came out in June of 2016 and was aptly named the Gear Fit 2. Compared to the Gear Fit of 2014, the Fit 2 has a new wristband and has an updated design, a built-in GPS, and an ability to automatically recognize different fitness activities. The Gear Fit 2 features a Barometer and a Heart Rate Monitor. It is compatible with Android phones running OS 4.4 or later. It uses the Tizen operating system and featured a 1 GHz CPU with a 4 GB SSD. The display is a slim curved AMOLED, at 38 mm (1.5 in) of diagonal size, with 216 x 432 pixel resolution at a 1:2 aspect ratio. It is powered by a 200 mAh lithium-ion battery.

Samsung Gear S3 Smartwatch (2016)

On November 18 of 2016, Samsung unveiled the Gear S3 Smartwatch, with 360 by 360 resolution at 278 PPI (Pixels Per Inch, a pixel density measurement) in a 1.3 inch Super AMOLED (round) screen. Samsung Gear 3 Smartwatches use the Tizen 3.0 OS and feature sensors for an Accelerometer, Gyro, Barometer, Heart Rate Monitor, Ambient light, and Speedometer. The Gear S3 has two models: the Classic and Frontier. The Classic has a silver watch case and black leather band; the Frontier has a black watch case and rubber band. Both are water resistant, rated IP68, and have GPS. One notable feature is that the bezel ring rotates as part of a user interface, although users can also navigate by swiping the screen or using the two buttons on the side. The Gear S3 features advanced 380 mAh wireless charging, using a WPC inductive charger.

Huawei Watch 2 (2017)

By April of 2017, Huawei had released its Android WEAR2 Smartwatch.
The Huawei Watch 2 form factor is also based on the circular design of
traditional watches, like many of Samsung's smartwatches. Huawei Watch
supports a 45 mm (1.2 inch) AMOLED display. The screen's resolution
is slightly lower at 390 x 390 pixels at more than 325 PPI. This watch uses
a powerful 1.1 GHz Qualcomm Snapdragon 2100 WEAR processor. The
Huawei Watch 2 has 768 MB of RAM and 4 GB of internal data storage,
along with a gyroscope, accelerometer, vibration motor, and heart rate
sensor. It supports Wi-Fi and Bluetooth 4.1 LE, but does not support GPS
location. The watch uses a magnetic charging cradle, with a day and a half
of battery life at 420 mAh. The Huawei Watch case is impressive, and looks
like a conventional analog watch, comprised of stainless steel with Corning
Gorilla Glass 3 on the watch face front. It is available in six custom finishes:
Black Leather, Steel Link Bracelet, Stainless Steel Mesh, Black-plated Link
Bracelet, Alligator-Imprinted Brown Leather, and Rose Gold-plated Link
Bracelet.

Samsung Gear Sport Smartwatch (2017)

In 2017 Samsung unveiled the Gear Sport Smartwatch, with 360 by 360
resolution at 302 PPI (Pixels Per Inch) in a 1.2 inch Super AMOLED
(round) screen. Samsung Gear Sport Smartwatches feature a simpler and
more durable exterior bezel and strap design, which is more optimized
for use in sporting scenarios, but use advanced technologies such as the
Tizen 3.0 OS and advanced sensors for Accelerometer, Gyro, Barometer,
Heart Rate Monitor, and Ambient Light. The Gear Sport also features water
resistance to five atmospheres (5 ATM) and weighs only 67 g. It uses the
latest Gorilla Glass 3 standard and Bluetooth 4.2, NFC, GPS, and Wi-Fi
connectivity. It features 768 MB (3/4 GB) system RAM and sports a 300
mAh battery.

Samsung Galaxy Smartwatch (2018)

The Samsung Galaxy Smartwatch was released on August 9 of 2018. There is a 46 mm Galaxy Watch in Silver and a 42 mm Galaxy Watch in Rose Gold or Midnight Black. The 63g (gram) 46mm model has a 1.3" (33 mm) display, and the 49g 42mm model has a 1.2" (30 mm) display, both with 360 by 360 pixel (round) screen resolution, featuring the latest Corning Gorilla Glass DX+ quality and durability. The Galaxy Watch features the latest Tizen 4.0 OS running on top of an Exynos 9110 1.15 GHz dual-core CPU. Memory is doubled at a whopping 1.5 GB, with the standard 4 GB of SSD Flash Memory for storage (the Bluetooth-only version has 768 MB and 4 GB). All versions can connect with 802.11N Wi-Fi, Bluetooth 4.2, and NFC, and one of the versions also supports 3G LTE. Sensors include advanced A-GPS, GLONASS, MEMS Accelerometer, MEMS Gyroscope, MEMS Barometer, an Electro-optical HRM sensor (for heart rate monitoring), and a Photodetector (for ambient light level sensing). The only thing I would want added to this in the future is another 120 (480x480) to 280 (640x640) pixels of screen resolution for the screen, taking it up to the 480x480 or 640x640 pixel resolution.

Smartwatch Concepts and Terms

The smartwatch has a significant number of concepts and terms which must be understood by the watch face designers so that they may do their jobs effectively, so it's best that I cover these areas in the first chapter so that readers are not surprised when they come across them in the following chapters of the book. We'll take a look at concepts and terms such as Power Consumption (Always-On), Complications, Components, Conditions, Sensors such as the Gyroscope, Tag Expressions, Layers, Resources, Notifications, Widgets, Apps, and Quick Panel.

Power Consumption (Always-On)

Smartwatches only feature a 200–500 mAh battery capacity, as you have seen in the previous section, and this is a specification you should be aware of and consider when purchasing a smartwatch. For this reason, smartwatches are very particular about the amount of resources, such as colors, pixels, animation, features, and the like, that are used and, more importantly, when they are used. For this reason there is an "Always-On" design that is required that only uses 15% or less of these resources. This design will be used as a default when the user is not looking at their watch face, which is why it is termed the Always-On version of the watch face. A more colorful, animated version of the watch face will be used when the watch detects (via gyro sensor) that the user is looking at the watch face and will give them your "sexy" more colorful (High Color or True Color) animated watch face design.

Complications

Complications are non-time features on a watch face that don't show hours and minutes. They allow a watch to do more than tell time. The Galaxy Watch Designer (GWD) allows you to enhance watch face designs by adding a variety of information regarding date, health, weather, fitness, sensors, steps taken, and the like. These custom watch face components are called complications and can be made into UI elements and tapped like buttons to launch other apps, such as a timer.

Components

Watch face design is comprised of building the watch face using various components that tell the user about the date and time, battery level, the weather, fitness activity, health monitoring, and similar features offered by the smartwatch sensors. If you design a custom complication, that, for instance, would be a component of your watch face design. Watch face components have a Preview section as well as a Properties section in the GWD software to control how they look.

Conditions

Using the Timeline area at the bottom of the Galaxy Watch Designer software, which we will install and take a look at briefly in the next section of this chapter, watch faces can be designed to change their appearance based on certain conditions, such as the time, step count, gyro data, or the date, using various "conditional lines" in the Timeline pane. This is an extremely powerful feature that allows watch face designers to differentiate their watch faces based upon what the smartwatch user is doing or upon what is happening around them or both. This includes time of day or time of year as well as watch orientation, steps taken (for the fitness models), or even the weather.

Expressions (Tag Expressions)

To add the element of programming code to your watch face design, you can develop (code) "expressions" that contain "tags" that reference watch face design elements as part of the expression. These are aptly named "Tag Expressions" in the Galaxy Watch Designer (GWD) software and add an advanced capability to watch face design similar to what you can achieve by coding in complicated environments like Android WEAR2. Note that tag expressions are only supported in GWD versions after 1.6.0 (GWD was just upgraded to 1.6.1 while I was writing this chapter).

Resources and Layers

Your watch face design can use "Resources" (I like to call these watch face design assets) developed outside of the GWD software using open-source new media content (asset) development software, which I am going to be making you aware of in the final sections of this chapter. Different design elements can be placed onto different "Layers" using the area at the left side of the Timeline pane (shown in the next section of this chapter, on installing and exploring the Galaxy Watch Designer, or GWD, software). Resources supported by the GWD include PNG (Portable Network Graphics), JPEG (Joint Photographic Experts Group), and GIF (CompuServe Graphics Information Format) file formats, such as you would create in GIMP 2.10, and vector font formats for SVG spline data, such as you would create using Inkscape.

We will be taking a look at how you can get these resources for free using the **Creative Commons Zero (CC0)** licensing model, in the next chapter of this book, so that we have some really cool watch face assets to use throughout this Internet of Things (IoT) development book. At the same time, we'll discuss the basics of each new media asset type when we look at assets of that type, including digital imagery (rasters, pixels, resolution, aspect ratio, color depth, alpha channel, etc.), vector splines (vectors, lines, vertices, splines, curves, fills, patterns, etc.), and digital audio.

Sensors

Different smartwatch models feature different sensor hardware, which is passed through to the Tizen software used to run your watch face design. This is why I covered sensor hardware in the history section of this chapter on a model-by-model basis. There are many different types of sensor hardware, all of which provide really cool feedback on things such as Watch Rotation (Gyroscope), Acceleration (Accelerometer), Altitude (Altimeter), Cardio Health (Heart Rate Monitor or HRM), Fitness (Steps), Sun Exposure (UV Monitor), Ambient Light (Photodetector), Barometric Pressure (Barometer), Geolocation (GPS), Pedometer, and Speedometer. It is amazing how these hardware components can turn the physics reflecting the world around us into usable data for the watch face designer to use to create amazing watch face user experiences.

Gyroscope

The gyroscope is one of the most integrated sensors in the GWD software, as you can design watch faces whose characteristics are tied to the X and Y movement data which comes out of the gyroscope sensor in real time based on the user's wrist/arm movement. This means that you can simulate 3D and perform other cool visual effects (VFX) that are based on how the user is rotating his or her smartwatch device.

Weather

Although the sensor for weather worldwide is not actually in the smartwatch device hardware itself, Galaxy Watch Designer provided this data from an open-source weather satellite system API called **OpenWeatherMap**. If you are interested in displaying weather features on your watch face design, you will want to visit the OpenWeatherMap. org website. This data can be used in apps and websites as well, as you will see once you visit this site or any of the related 2500+ OpenWeatherMap weather API repositories currently hosted on GitHub.

Smartwatch Home Structure

All models of Samsung Smartwatches have a home structure which can be accessed in the same fashion outside of the watch face. This allows users to access other non-watch-face features, such as installed apps, notifications, pop-up alerts, widgets, and smartwatch settings, using the "Quick Panel." Even though you are a watch face designer who uses the Galaxy Watch Designer software to design watch faces, you must understand smartwatch design principles and make sure that your watch face designs integrate properly with other smartwatch apps and follow smartwatch design conventions, such as properly displaying alert and notification information from other apps running on the smartwatch on your watch face designs.

Quick Panel

The quick panel contains smartwatch settings, such as airplane mode, volume, and brightness, as well as device hardware status information such as network connections and battery levels. Users can access this quick panel from a watch face app by swiping down from the top of the watch. Users can edit Quick settings buttons in the center of the screen.

Notifications

Notifications deliver meaningful information to the watch face from another application and should connect users to the next required action as part of the notification design. You should make your notifications understandable at a quick glance, that is, a notification should deliver a clear message to the user using only a quick glance. In this way, users will be able to check and understand the notification subject matter effortlessly, even while the user is doing something else. Your notification should connect the user to their next logical step smoothly, for example, provide a link to the notification calling app menu to allow the user to provide input in response to the notification.

Pop-Up Alerts

There are two types of alerts, full-screen pop-ups, which fill the watch face screen entirely, and partial-screen pop-ups, which allow part of your watch face design to remain on the watch face while still notifying the user of an impending incoming information alert. It is important that your watch face implement these optimally to alert your users of things such as incoming calls and messages.

Full-Screen Pop-Ups

Full-screen pop-ups appear when a notification arrives when the smartwatch is turned off. Full-screen pop-ups lead to corresponding notification cards, depending upon the user's settings, that is, if Auto Show Details has been activated by using **Galaxy Wearable ➤ Notifications ➤ Auto Show Details** by the smartwatch user.

Partial-Screen Pop-Ups

Users can view details or perform a task on the notification card. Partial-screen pop-ups will appear at the top or sides of the screen when the watch face has been activated. These partial-screen pop-ups minimize interruptions to the user's usage of the watch face and should take them to corresponding notification card containing the message when the partial-screen pop-up area has been tapped by the user to deal with the incoming information accordingly.

Widgets

Widgets are like single-screen "mini-apps" and provide users compact access to often used tasks and content. These are usually used when a user is engaged in another endeavor. Users can also access "full-blown app" key features without launching the app by using a widget version of that app.

It is important that you understand as a watch face designer how the different types of widgets work and which widget design paradigms are well suited for your watch face design undertaking.

Widget Design Basics

The Design Basics include a number of important concepts, most of which also apply to Watch Face Design as well. First, you should design widgets to fit on one watch face screen. Widgets, like Watch Faces, occupy the entire smartwatch screen. Design both watch faces and widgets to occupy on single page without having to scroll. Design watch faces and widgets to only take a single tap to use effectively. Tapping is the primary gesture (see next section) that widgets and watch faces use to perform tasks or open apps. It is important to note that one app can have multiple widgets for different implementations if that is so desired. Like watch faces, widgets are refreshed automatically, by the Tizen OS.

Widget Permissions

User permission might be required to display information in a widget. Users can modify permissions using **Settings ➤Apps ➤ Permissions**. If a user doesn't agree to grant permission, you will provide an additional notification screen stating permission is required in order to view widget. This needs to provide app or widget name and a link to the Permission.

App Management

An app screen shows the icons and titles of all apps installed. Note that you can design your own app icons. For app management, users download apps for Galaxy Wearables on the user's mobile phone or from Galaxy Apps via the watch itself. Use the edit mode to rearrange or uninstall the apps. You can enable edit mode by touching and holding an app icon or icon title. Users can hide applications from the Apps screen by going to **Galaxy Wearable ➤ Apps ➤ Hide**. When an app icon is hidden, related widget, watch face complications, or app configurations are still available.

Smartwatch Interactions

Smartwatches offer a number of ways to interact with watch faces, widgets, applications, and websites. These include taps, pinches, vibrations, voice recognition, and (unlike smartphones) bezel rotation!

Touchscreen

Many of the Gear and Galaxy smartwatch models feature a capacitive touch screen display, which can accept input directly on top of the watch face UI that you have designed. Be sure your watch face components have sufficient touchable area and that space between components is large enough so touch areas don't overlap. You can tap, double-tap, touch-and-hold, and swipe your screen in different directions.

Gestures

Gesture interaction takes the user's gestures as input. Users can make a hand movement or change the position of their arm, and the watch's accelerometer and gyro sensor provide sensitive and quick responses. We will cover a few of the most important built-in gestures here for Gear and Galaxy smartwatch face design and development.

Smart Relay Gesture

The smart relay feature opens watch notifications on the user's phone if the phone is within a certain distance from the watch and the user lifts the phone at a certain angle. When the paired watch and phone are within a certain range, users can open information from the watch on the phone.

Wrist-Up and Wrist-Down Gestures

If a user raises their arm to view the watch, a wrist-up gesture activates the screen. The opposite downward movement deactivates the screen.

Press Home Key and Swipe Screen Gestures

To take a screenshot, press the Home key and swipe the screen from left to right. The captured screen moves upward to indicate that you have successfully taken the screenshot. The screenshot is saved to the Gallery.

Palm Touch Gesture

Touching your watch's display with the palm of your hand deactivates the screen. It can be activated again by pressing the Home or Back keys. When a call comes in, a palm touch mutes the sound and deactivates the screen. It also snoozes and deactivates alerts.

The screen deactivates when users place their palm on it.

Bezel Rotation

Bezel rotation interaction refers to rotating a bezel to explore the watch. Users interact by bezel rotation (both clockwise and counterclockwise). Bezel rotation can adjust values, answer/reject calls, and check alerts.

Voice Control and Speech Recognition

The Tizen OS supports speech recognition, allowing users to use their voice to control interaction with a given user interface (UI) design. Voice interactions can utilize the user's voice for input. Speech-to-text converts that voice into text, and then voice commands can perform tasks. This helps a user control a watch when they're busy performing another task.

Haptic, Audio, and Visual (Imagery) Feedback

The smartwatch device can offer visual (imagery or animation assets), auditory (audio assets), and haptic (length of vibration) feedback. Haptic feedback involves using the watch to generate vibrations to alert users.

Installing Galaxy Watch Designer

Galaxy Watch Designer has IDE (Integrated Development Environment) software versions for both Windows 10 and Macintosh OS. To find them online, you can use Google or another search engine using the keyword string "Samsung Galaxy Watch Designer Software" or even just "Samsung Galaxy Watch Designer" as seen at the very top of Figure 1-1. You will see a search result about halfway down the first page that references the **Galaxy Watch Designer | Samsung Developers** website using the `https://developer.samsung.com/galaxy-watch/design/watch-designer` link, as is shown in purple and green at the very bottom of Figure 1-1.

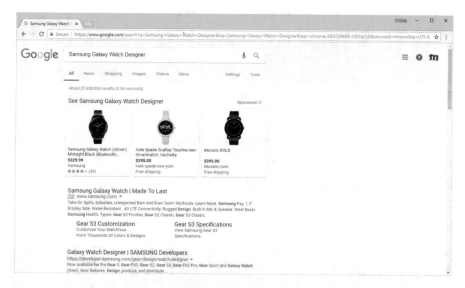

Figure 1-1. *Search on Google for the Samsung Galaxy Watch Designer software*

Click the `https://developer.samsung.com/galaxy-watch/design/watch-designer` link to open the Galaxy Watch Designer website, which is shown in Figure 1-2. Click the latest version (1.60 at the time of taking this screenshot and upgraded to 1.61 while I was writing this chapter content) for your OS, which would be either MacOS or Windows 7, 8.1, or 10. The Tizen 2.5 SDK and IDE are also available for Ubuntu.

Figure 1-2. *Locate and download the Samsung Galaxy Watch Designer software*

Test your software installation by launching the software, which should show you the GWD start-up screen, which is shown in Figure 1-3. I am developing this book using the beta version, as the final version of GWD should be released at about the same time as this book publishes in the first part of 2019.

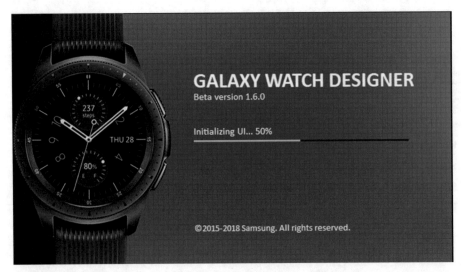

Figure 1-3. *Launch your Galaxy Watch Designer to test the software installation*

After the GWD software loads, the first dialog that is presented to the developer is the **New Project** dialog, which is shown in Figure 1-4. This has three icons at the top, which allow developers to load sample watch faces and recent watch face designs or to create an empty (New) watch face design. I have selected New as we want to look at the empty IDE.

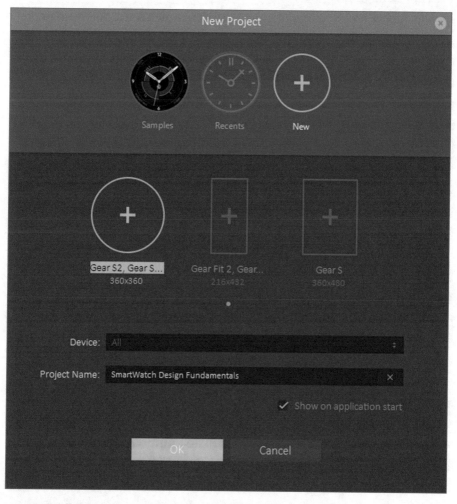

Figure 1-4. *New Project dialog appears after the Galaxy Watch Designer launch*

In the middle of the New Project dialog, developers can select the specifications for the smartwatch they are designing for, including the pixel resolution, aspect ratio, and watch model they will be designing for. We will be using this 1:1 (square) aspect ratio for the round Galaxy Watch product for this book, at the highest screen resolution possible.

We will be making sure that you know all about new media concepts such as Raster and Vector, pixels, resolution, aspect ratio, color depth, alpha channels and masking, waveforms, and the like in the next chapter where we will cover these concepts along with where you can go on the Internet to get free CC0 (Creative Commons Zero) vector, raster, and waveform assets to use for images, illustrations, audio sound effects, and the like.

The third section of the New Project dialog has a spinner UI element which contains all for all the devices which you have attached to your development workstation for testing, so you would use that to choose the smartwatch you will be developing watch face designs for in the current development session.

The final section is a Project Name field that allows you to name the project. I have put the book title in this field as the project name, just for now for this screenshot. You need to name your watch face designs using a version and Tizen version (3 or 4) as well, which we will discuss in the chapter covering how to publish and distribute your Watch Face Designs in the Samsung Online Store.

I like to show this dialog whenever I start GWD, so I leave the "Show on application start" checkbox checked. To start the software package, which is shown in its empty state in Figure 1-5, click the "OK" button at the bottom of the dialog, which will open an empty GWD user interface if you selected the New option at the top-right corner of the dialog. If you selected Samples or Recents, the software panels will be populated with the chosen sample or previous watch face designs you were working on. We'll learn more about all these areas in the rest of the book as I get deep into using the software IDE for development.

Different chapters will focus on how to use the different panel areas in the GWD software, but to summarize here with Figure 1-5, the top left pane shows the watch face design preview on a medium-gray background, and the left pane of icons allows you to select watch face design components to add to your design. This pane can be shown (opened) or hidden (closed) using the up/down arrow next to the title of the Component pane, giving you more room for the watch face preview.

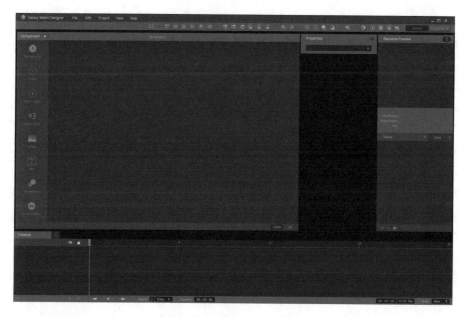

Figure 1-5. *Galaxy Watch Designer software and its five separate design panels*

There is also a Properties pane on the right side of the preview which will outline the selected (active) component properties so you can adjust that part of the watch face design.

The far-right panel is for Resource Preview of external resources (images, animation, etc.) that you have added to the watch face design. There is a preview and technical specifications area at the top of this panel as well as Name and Type spinners at the bottom that allow you to select different external image assets which you've created for your watch face design.

At the bottom of the GWD software design package is the Timeline pane, which controls watch face components in the fourth dimension, with a selector on the left and time (playback) controls along the bottom of the panels. There are two parts of the Timeline pane, a left selector (small) portion of the panel and a wide timeline portion of the panel on the right. Each of these UI panels will be covered in at least one chapter of this book, which applies to each of these panel areas.

Installing Asset Creation Software

Smartwatch design involves much more than just using the GWD software package, as watch face designers can import a number of what I call "assets" or new media elements which add imagery, audio, illustration, animation, effects, and so forth to enhance and differentiate their watch face design. In this section and the next, I will tell you how to download and install the leading open-source software packages, which all work across Windows 7, 8.1, and 10, MacOS, and all Linux distributions (Ubuntu, Fedora, Mint, SUSE, Red Hat, etc.), for digital imaging, digital audio editing, digital illustration, 3D animation, VR, Non-Linear Editing (NLE), and visual special effects (VFX), all at zero cost to the watch face developer. In this way, you will have a complete watch face development workstation for only the cost of computer hardware.

Digital Imaging and Compositing

The premiere digital imaging and compositing software in the open-source community is called GIMP 2.10.10 and can be found on GIMP. ORG and downloaded for free by clicking the red download button shown in Figure 1-6. On Windows 10, you would download the 64-bit Windows version and install it by right-clicking the downloaded installation file and selecting "Run as Administrator." If you want to learn more about GIMP,

I wrote a book for Apress called *Digital Image Compositing Fundamentals* which covers the many concepts involved in digital image editing and compositing as well as many of the core features in GIMP, so that might be a good companion book for this one, if you wanted to dive into more advanced smartwatch image composition, animation, effects, and editing. Once you install the GIMP 2.10.10 software, be sure to add a Launch Icon shortcut to your Taskbar so that you can easily start the software during the watch face development work process.

Launch the software to make sure you have the correct version installed and to make sure that it will load and execute. The start-up screen should indicate GIMP 2.10, as is shown in Figure 1-6.

Figure 1-6. *The GIMP.ORG website and the red Download 2.10 button*

Figure 1-7. *A GIMP 2.10.6 start-up screen launches the digital imaging software*

Once the software loads, you should see a screen which looks quite similar to the Adobe Photoshop paid software package, only it is GIMP 2.10.6 (or later, if available) which can be seen in Figure 1-8.

Figure 1-8. *Make sure that GIMP is installed by launching the software package*

Next let's add digital audio editing software since many smartwatches have microphones and speakers in them, so you can add audio assets to your watch face app design, to enhance the overall user experience.

Digital Audio Editing

The leading digital audio editing software package, which I cover in detail in my *Digital Audio Editing Fundamentals* book from Apress, is called Audacity 2.2.2, and it has many of the same features as Pro Tools but as an open-source software package is free for commercial use. To find the AudacityTeam.org website, you can go directly to the site in your browser address bar or you can Google "Audacity" and click the homepage link, which will take you to the page shown in Figure 1-9. Once you get there, click the blue Download Audacity button at the bottom left to download the software. Install it and create a shortcut icon, and launch the software to make sure it is working. I will forgo a screenshot of Audacity since it is shown prominently in Figure 1-9 on the right-hand side, which saves me some space in this chapter. As you can see, I am setting you up with some very professional software here!

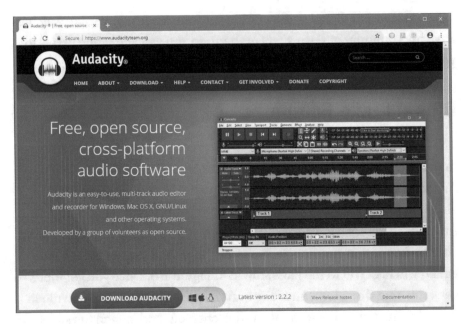

Figure 1-9. Go to AudacityTeam.org and click a blue Download Audacity button

Next, let's set you up with some "vector" editing tools so that you can create digital illustration watch face designs as well. As you might have imagined, an open source equivalent to the popular Adobe Illustrator software has been created over the decades called "Inkscape." Let's take a look at that next.

Digital Illustration

The leading digital illustration software package in the open-source realm, which I cover in detail in my *Digital Illustration Fundamentals* book from Apress, can be found at Inkscape.org. You can go to this website directly using your browser address bar or simply Google "Inkscape" and click a link to the homepage. You will see a green Download button on the right side of the page, as shown in Figure 1-10, which will download the proper version of the software for your operating system. Like GIMP and Audacity, there are versions for Windows and MacOS and all versions of Linux, including Ubuntu, Mint, and Fedora.

Figure 1-10. *Go to Inkscape.org website and click the green Download button*

Install Inkscape and create your shortcut icon on the Taskbar, and then launch the software to make sure it is working properly. The empty (fresh launch) digital illustration software is shown in Figure 1-11. Inkscape is different from GIMP (raster imaging software) in that it is a "vector" software for creating vector (spline-based) assets in the SVG, EPS, or AI formats. We will cover the differences between raster and vector as well as audio and animation concepts that provide the foundation for the watch face assets we will be creating in this book.

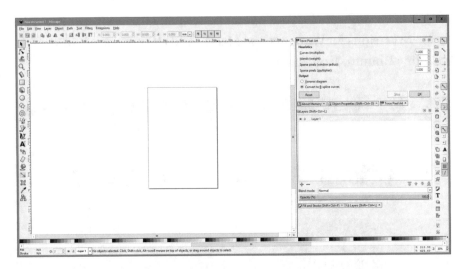

Figure 1-11. *Launch your Inkscape software to make sure it is working*

Although we will not install them here in this chapter, or utilize them in this book, I will cover the other four major genre software packages which, amazingly, are free for commercial use and which I utilize in my own advanced watch face design production pipeline, in case you wish to mimic the past three sections and also install these on your burgeoning smartwatch face design and production workstation. These include 3D, NLE, DVE (digital video editing), and VFX software packages which would normally cost several thousand dollars each to purchase, if they were not now offered as open-source software packages for Mac, Windows, and Ubuntu, Mint, Fedora, SUSE, and Red Hat (among others) in Linux.

Visual Effects (VFX), NLE (DVE), and 3D

There are other more advanced open-source software packages which you can use in watch face design, so I could go on for quite some time here, expanding this chapter even further. I will mention these briefly here, in case you wanted to add them to your primary imaging, audio, and illustration packages that form the core of watch face asset design.

Visual Effects Design and Virtual Reality (3D)

Blackmagic Design Fusion 9.02 used to be known as EyeOn Fusion and cost thousands of dollars, until Blackmagic Design purchased the software, ported it to Linux, and made it free for commercial use (other than the advanced "Studio" version which costs an affordable $299). The Fusion 9.02 VR (and VFX) software, which I cover in great detail in my Apress *VFX Fundamentals* (2016) book, can be found at https://www. blackmagicdesign.com/products/fusion/ if you scroll down to the bottom and click the Free or Studio version download buttons. I highly recommend the Studio version, although the Free version has 90% or more of the features in it already, so it's one of the best values in open-source software today, along with GIMP 3, DaVinci Resolve 15, Daz Studio Pro 4.10, and Blender 2.8.

Non-Linear Editing (NLE) for Digital Video Editing (DVE), Color Correction, and Grading

DaVinci Resolve 15 was also purchased by Blackmagic Design (thank you BMD from all watch face designers internationally), ported to Linux, and split into Free and Studio (again, $299, down from thousands) DV software versions. Resolve also supports all Windows, MacOS, and Linux versions and can be used for watch face animation and special effects. Resolve is primarily a Non-Linear Editing (NLE) software package for Digital Video Editing (DVE) and Special Effects (SFX), and it seamlessly integrates/ connects with/to Fusion 9.02 as well. It can be used for Color Correction, also known as Color Calibration and Color Grading, as its use for this in the film industry is quite popular.

3D Modeling, Rendering, Animation, and VFX

The most popular professional 3D modeling, rendering, animation, and special effects software in the open-source continuum is Blender 2.8. It can be downloaded from the Blender.org website and is scheduled for final release in early 2019. A number of feature films have actually been created with Blender, and 3D games can be created using Blender, as well as 2D (Cel Shader) content. This bodes well for all of us watch face designers, as it's just a matter of time before the coolest watch face designs are being created using Blender and its 2D Illustration, Cycles, and EEVEE 3D Ray-Tracing Rendering Engines. And yes, it's FREE!

Character Design, Animation, and Posing

The most popular open-source character design, posing, and animation software is Daz Studio Pro 4, which can be found at Daz3D.com and is currently at version 4.10 (soon to be 4.11). The public is eagerly awaiting Daz Studio Pro 5 as you will see if you Google it. Daz Studio Pro is also completely compatible with Blender 2.8 in the production pipeline for 3D content creation, texturing, posing, rendering, and animation.

Summary

In this chapter, we set up our smartwatch development system and learned a bit more about the smartwatch. We downloaded and installed the Galaxy Watch Designer 1.6 software as well as a lot of asset creation software available as open source, including a couple of packages we will be using in this book. All of the software we have garnered in this chapter is free for commercial use, so you are well set up to produce new media content for smartwatches and any other platform as well for that matter.

CHAPTER 2

Smartwatch Design Assets: Acquisition, Concepts, and Terms

In this second chapter of the *Smartwatch Design Fundamentals* book, let's look at how you can acquire free for commercial use smartwatch face design resources (I call them assets) online for digital images and digital illustration resources for use in watch face components. We will also be discussing the terms and concepts used for working with these assets, as we will be transforming them for our own watch face designs using the software which you downloaded and installed in Chapter 1.

First, we will cover Digital Imaging (raster assets), as these are used in the Galaxy Watch Designer "background" placeholder for your watch face design, as well as for animations and watch face decoration components. You will learn the terms and concepts involved with raster image compositing and how to use the GIMP 2.10.10 software package.

After that we'll cover Digital Illustration (vector assets), as these are used for nonphotographic design, for fonts, 3D, and components, if you decide to incorporate these into watch face design and development. We will also learn to use the Inkscape 0.92 Digital Illustration software.

© Wallace Jackson 2019
W. Jackson, *SmartWatch Design Fundamentals*,
https://doi.org/10.1007/978-1-4842-4369-5_2

Finally, we'll cover data footprint optimization and how to convert vector and raster assets via rendering, so you can take a 4 MB resource, and turn it into a 62 KB resource, almost one thousand times smaller!

Creating Watch Face Image Assets

The first thing we're going to do is to use a search engine to find free for commercial use image assets, then we'll learn how to use the free design and editing software packages that we installed in Chapter 1.

Digital Image Acquisition

Use the keyword search term "royalty free images for commercial use" in one of the search engines, such as Google, as seen in Figure 2-1. At the bottom of the search results page, you will see my two favorite digital images for commercial use websites, Pexels and Pixabay. I'm going to use Pexels in this chapter, to show you how I turn the free image data into a smartwatch face background image using the GIMP 2.10.6 open-source digital image editing and compositing software package, which we downloaded and installed in the final part of Chapter 1.

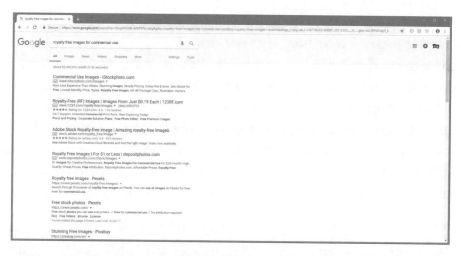

Figure 2-1. *Google "royalty free images for commercial use" and find pexels.com*

Click the `http://www.pexels.com` link at the end of the search results, which will take you to the Pexels homepage. When I arrived there, one of the images was perfect for the **Gear S** watch face design. This 360 by 480 (Gear S watch resolution) digital image (purple field of stars seen at the right side of the homepage) can be seen in Figure 2-2.

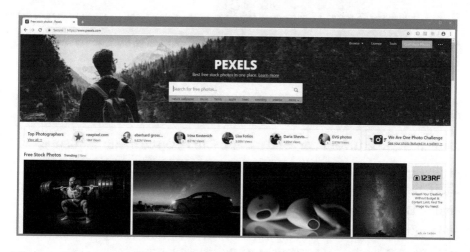

Figure 2-2. *Click the Pexels.com link to visit the PEXELS image website*

Click on the star field image from Johannes Rapprich on the far right (it is also in the book repository, if it's not on the home page anymore), which will take you to its Pexels page, which can be seen in Figure 2-3. Click the down arrow, and Pexels will give you a choice of a UHD (4K), HD (1920), Blu-Ray, web, or custom image size option. Since we are going to learn GIMP, I decided to use the Blu-Ray (1280 pixels) version, which we will resize from 1280 to 360 pixels for watch face usage. Save the file to an assets folder on your hard disk drive, where you will know where to find it in the next section of the chapter where we will learn digital imaging concepts.

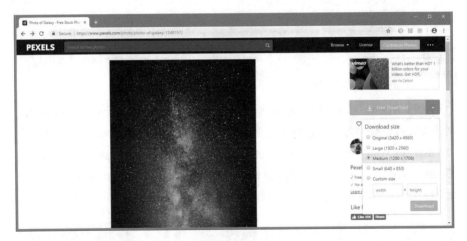

Figure 2-3. *Click the stars image, on the right, to develop as a Gear S backdrop*

Digital Image Asset Creation Workflow

Launch GIMP 2.10 (or later) and use the **File ➤ Open** menu sequence, as shown in Figure 2-4, to open the image in GIMP for pixel processing. GIMP has an image preview area on the left, compositing layers and color channels on the top middle, brushes and patterns in the bottom middle, and tools and tool settings on the far right. You can arrange these panels in any way that is optimal for your work with digital images.

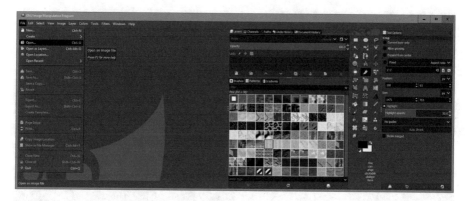

Figure 2-4. *Launch GIMP; use a File ➤ Open menu sequence to load image data*

The **File ➤ Open** menu opens the **Open Image** dialog shown on the left side in Figure 2-5. Find the Pexels file you downloaded, and use the **Open** button to invoke the **Convert to RGB Working Space** dialog, shown on the right side of Figure 2-5.

The top of this dialog tells you what color profile is used in the Pexels image, which is the manufacturer IEC (Hewlett-Packard) profile number IEC61966-2.1 which most likely comes from an imaging device (camera utilized) with its own custom raw color data profile, which GIMP will convert to a standard RGB three 8-bit color channel paradigm used by GIMP for its internal processing. I am converting color using the default **relative colorimetric** algorithm, as you can see in Figure 2-5.

I'll leave the default **Black Point Conversion** option selected as well and click the **Convert** button to convert the color space to a version which can be utilized in GIMP. This then imports this data into GIMP.

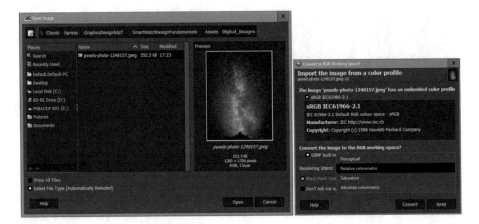

Figure 2-5. *Find the image; allow GIMP to convert it to RGB color space*

Figure 2-6 shows the image within the GIMP user interface, in its own layer in the layer stack (named from the imported file name, which is pexels-photo-1248175.jpeg), and is scaled down to **33%** (see bottom left of screenshot), to fit the preview area based on how you've sized GIMP on your own display (my display is a Samsung 43" HD iTV Set, utilized as a PC monitor, running at 1920 by 1080 HD iTV resolution).

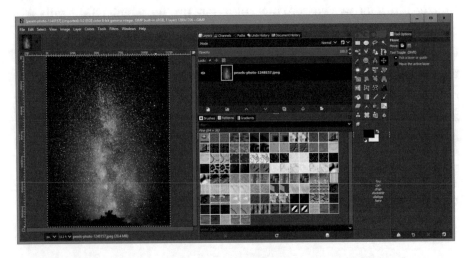

Figure 2-6. *GIMP loads the image at 33% zoom, so it fits in the preview area*

The next thing that we have to do is to scale this image down, to fit the Samsung **Gear S** smartwatch face, which uses a 360 by 480 pixel background resolution. To do this we'll use the **Scale Image** algorithm.

The Scale Image dialog is found on the Image Menu under the Scale Image sub-menu. The dialog can be seen in Figure 2-7 over the "actual pixels," or 100% image view (scale) setting, in the middle of the figure. As you can see when you enter 360 to replace the 1280 width value in the first data field, the second turns to 480, which tells us that this portrait version of the image on Pexels is an exact fit for the Gear S background resolution of 360 by 480 and 3:4 aspect ratio, which we will be learning about soon. Click on the **Scale** button to scale this image.

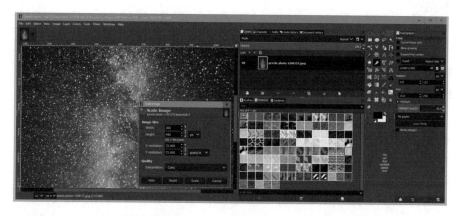

Figure 2-7. *Use an Image* ➤ *Scale Image menu to open the Scale Image dialog*

Since there are very few colors used in the image, let's do some data footprint optimization and reduce the number of colors used to 256 by converting the image to **indexed 8-bit color**, as shown in Figure 2-8.

Figure 2-8. *Use Image ➤ Mode ➤ Indexed to open Color Conversion dialog*

Use the **Image ➤ Mode ➤ Indexed** menu sequence to open the **Indexed Color Conversion** dialog, and select the **Generate Optimum Palette** with the maximum **256** color value. This will take the 16,777,216 colors in a 24-bit RGB image, and remove over 99% of this color, while the image will look much the same as it did before! You'll see just how much data (file size) you saved in Figure 2-9, which shows the file size using 16,777,216 colors (PNG24 file is 337 kilobytes, seen on the left) and the PNG8 and GIF files on the right using 300% less data. In the next section of the chapter, we'll go over some imaging concepts which will explain why this happens, so you have the foundational knowledge regarding what you'll be doing in digital imaging throughout this book.

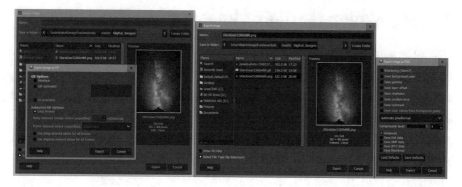

Figure 2-9. *Save PNG8 and GIF 8-bit color assets using File ➤ Export As dialog*

As you can see on the left, I saved the 24-bit RGB 360 x 480 version as StarsGearS360x480 as a PNG24, using RGB 24-bit, so that I could see the file size for a 24-bit true color 360 x 480 image prior to data footprint optimization (by using 8-bit indexed color space), which you've seen does not affect the visual quality of the image at all, especially on a smartwatch face, which uses 300 PPI (extra small) pixels. We export the image as an 8-bit GIF as shown on the left using the **Export Image as GIF** dialog, using the default settings. Notice that GIF files can be animated, in which case they are known as **aGIF** files. We will look at this a bit later on in the book, when we deal with animation. Next, let's take a look at some of the foundational digital imaging concepts, so you have a comprehensive overview of how everything fits together.

Digital Image Concepts and Terminology

In this section of the chapter, I'm going to give you some of the concepts and terminology used in digital image editing, so that you'll understand what I'm talking about in the last dozen chapters of this book.

The Foundation for Digital Imagery: The Pixel

Digital Images are made up of two-dimensional, or 2D, arrays (or grids) containing something called "pixels." This industry term pixel is a conjugation of two words: pictures (which are commonly called "pix") and elements (shortened, to be just els). These elements dictate everything about a digital image, including its file size, dimension, color, translucency, shape, format, and many other characteristics. There is also digital illustration and 3D rendering; these aren't made up of pixels.

Raster vs. Vector: Imaging vs. Illustration

Besides the term pixel, let's get into some other terminology related to pixels, just so we cover everything thoroughly in this second chapter of the book on watch face assets (also known as watch face resources). Pixel-based digital imagery is also called "raster imagery." This is because this array of pixels can be said to be "rasterized" by the devices which are used to display these pixels. Devices can include everything from iTV Sets to tablets to smartphones to smartwatches. There is another type of digital image that is called a "vector" image, which is defined using mathematics, rather than pixels. A vector image uses points, called "vertices," and lines or curves between these points, to "draw out" your digital illustration. Digital Illustration is what this vector imagery is commonly referred to as in the multimedia industry today.

Vector imagery has its own genre of 2D software which is called: digital illustration software. You may be familiar with Inkscape, an open-source digital illustration package that you downloaded and installed in Chapter 1, or paid software such as Illustrator, Freehand, or Corel Draw.

Rendering: Convert Vector into Raster Images

Vector imagery can be converted into raster imagery with a process called "rendering." A rendered image is inherently a raster image, and both 2D vector artwork and 3D vector artwork can be rendered into raster imagery, which as you now know is pixel-based (rasterized). At this point, all of the concepts which are outlined in this section of the chapter can be applied, or inherently do apply, to this pixel-based raster imagery. Remember to keep a back-up of your vector artwork, so that you can enhance it further, and then render it again, at any point in time. The primary advantage of vector illustration over raster imagery is that, since it's defined using math, it can be scaled up or down to any size. Scaling raster imagery will cause "pixilation" or enlarged blocks of color.

Resolution: The Number of Image Pixels

The number of pixels contained in your digital image assets should be expressed using a term called **resolution**. This is the number of pixels contained in your image. Images have a width, which is usually denoted using a W, or, alternatively, by using an X, which stands for your x-axis, as well as a height, which is usually denoted using an H, or using a Y, for the y-axis. The resolution gives you a digital image's 2D dimensions. The resolution of an image asset in Galaxy Watch Designer and Tizen needs to be expressed by using two integer numbers, a Width or an X value and a Height or a Y value. Image resolution is generally expressed using two integer numbers with an x in the middle. For instance, a Gear S watch face resolution is expressed by specifying 360 x 480. Alternately, you can also use the word "by" as in 360 by 480.

Let's take a look at the basic mathematics of resolution, so that you can see how to calculate how many pixels are in your watch face background image. This total number of pixels has a lot to do with the amount of data, and therefore the smartwatch memory, the image uses. Smartwatches use a lower resolution and do not need a lot of system memory, which you saw in the 512 MB to 1.5 GB models in Chapter 1.

Doing the Math: Calculate Total Image Pixels

To find the total number of pixels that are contained in any 2D digital image, you will want to multiply width pixels by height pixels or in mathematical terms: Resolution = Width * Height, if you're coding. Hopefully, you remember that area of a rectangle equation from school. Here it is again, in a professional watch face design digital imaging context. I didn't realize that there were fun, professional applications for what was being taught while I was in grade school, so I didn't really listen, and therefore I had to go back and relearn my math and physics. For an example, a Gear S resolution 360 x 480 image would contain 172,800 pixels if you multiplied the width and height together. If you're into digital photography, you'll be familiar with the term two megapixels, which is referring to 2.0 million pixels. This is essentially what HD iTV Set resolution is giving you (because 1920 * 1080 = 2,073,600 pixels).

The more pixels that are contained in the digital image, the higher its resolution will be said to be. Higher-resolution images will give the viewer more detail or image subject matter definition. This is why HDTV is called High Definition, and why the new 4K resolution UHD iTV Sets are called Ultra High Definition, and why I want more watch face pixels!

Matching Image Resolutions to Tizen Devices

One objective in developing optimized digital image assets for use in Galaxy Watch Designer or Tizen Studio is matching the number of pixels in a digital image to the target hardware device the asset is going to be viewed on. There used to be dozens of different resolution devices on the market. Recently the number of different resolutions found on devices has been decreasing, which is great for us developers. The reason for this is more and more displays, especially smartphones, e-readers, and tablets, have been conforming to three iTV Set resolutions.

This has become possible since the display screen's **pixel pitch** (dot size) has been getting smaller, thanks to display technologies, like super Active Matrix OLED (AMOLED) displays, found in smartwatches.

These flexible screens allow laser-printer-like resolutions on display screens and allow things such as Gear S smartwatches which curve around your wrist, since an AMOLED display can be bent/curved.

There is one other category of consumer electronic devices, called smartwatches, which has resolutions of 360 by 360 and 480 by 480 (LG). Look for higher pixel densities (pixel pitches) by 2019 in the smartwatch space, affording 480 by 480 pixel screens, and hopefully, 560 by 560, 640 by 640, or 800 by 800 pixel screens, by early 2020.

Aspect Ratios: The 2D Ratio of W:H Pixels

Closely related to the number of pixels in your digital image is the ratio of X to Y in the digital image. This is called the "aspect ratio." The concept of aspect ratio is more complicated than the image resolution, because it is the ratio of width to height, or W:H, within your image resolution dimensions. This aspect ratio defines the **shape** of your image and also applies to the shape of a watch face display screen. For instance, a Galaxy Watch will have a square aspect (1:1) for a round face, and a Gear S uses a 3:4 aspect for a curved portrait face. It is important to note that it is this ratio between these two numbers which defines the shape of the image or display screen, not the numbers themselves, and that's why it is called an aspect ratio, although it's often called aspect for short. A 2:1 aspect ratio would create the widescreen aspect ratio commonly used on another popular iTV Set device out now.

Screen Shape: Display Device Aspect Ratios

Many HDTV resolution display screens use the 16:9 HDTV widescreen aspect ratio. Some iTV displays use a taller 16:10 (or 8:5, if you prefer the lowest common denominator or LCD) aspect ratio. Even wider screens will also appear on the market soon, so look for 16:8 (or 2:1, if you prefer) ultra-widescreens, which will feature a 2160 x 1080 screen resolution. The three different aspect ratios supported in GWD span the Galaxy (1:1), Gear S (3:4), and the Gear Fit and Fit 2 (1:2) watch faces.

Early television screens were almost square; they used a 3:2 aspect ratio. Early computer screens featured the 4:3 aspect ratio, such as Macintosh's 512 by 384, or the PC 640 by 480 VGA screen resolution, which would be great for watch faces. Once you learn how to calculate aspect ratio in the next section, you can check the aspect math yourself.

Doing the Math: How to Arrive at Aspect Ratio

An image aspect ratio is generally expressed using the smallest set or pair of numbers that can be achieved (reduced) on either side of the aspect ratio colon. I would do this mathematical matriculation by continuing to divide each side by two. Let's take a fairly weird 1280 x 1024 (termed SXGA) resolution as an example. Half of 1280:1024 is 640:512, and half of 640:512 would then be 320:256. Half of that is 160:128, and half of that is 80:64. Half of that is 40:32, and half of that is 20:16. Half of that is 10:8, and half of that is 5:4. Therefore, an SXGA resolution uses a 5:4 aspect ratio. Interestingly, all the above ratios were all the same aspect ratio, and thus all were valid aspect ratios. Thus, if you want to take the really easy way out, replace that "x" in your image resolution, with a colon, and you have one aspect ratio for that image. The industry standard involves distilling the aspect ratio down to its lowest format, as we've done here, as that is a far more useful ratio.

Color Theory: Using Pixel Color Channels

Within the image array of pixels that makes up your resolution and its aspect ratio, each of your pixels will be holding color values using three **color channels**, which is called an RGB color space. Color channels were originally used in digital image compositing programs like GIMP for compositing digital imagery for use on display screens, or to be printed using inks on printers, which use a different color space called **CMYK**. In GIMP the color channels have their own **Channels** palette, seen in Figure 2-6 at the top middle, allowing us to work on just that color channel, which can be quite useful for a number of special effects.

An opposite of additive color (RGB) is subtractive color (CMYK) which is used in printing and involves using inks. Inks subtract color from each other, rather than adding color, which is what happens when you combine colors by using light. Let's use the Red and Green colors as an example. Using additive color, Red + Green = Yellow. Using subtractive color, Red + Green = Purple, so, as you can see, additive gives you brighter more vibrant color (adds light) great for watch faces, while subtractive color gives you darker color (i.e., it subtracts light).

To create millions of different color values using these RGB color channels, what you will need to do is to vary the levels, or intensities, for each of the individual RGB color values.

Mathematics of RGB: Multiplying Intensities

The amount, or numbers, of red, green, and blue values or levels of intensity of light which you have available to mix together will determine the total number of colors that you will be able to reproduce. For RGB devices today, pixels can produce 256 levels of light intensity for each Red, Green, and Blue (RGB) color. Color needs to be generated for each image pixel; thus, every pixel in an image will have 256 levels of color intensity for each of these RGB (red, green, and blue) color values.

Each of these RGB channels would use 1 byte (8 bits) of color intensity data. Eight bits of data will hold 256 different values, so you have 256 levels of brightness for each pixel's RGB color channel.

The color intensity (brightness) data inside each of the digital image pixels is represented with a brightness level for each color. This can range between 0 (brightness turned off) and 255 (brightness fully on) and controls the amount of color contributed by each pixel for each of these red, green, and blue colors in your digital image.

To calculate a total amount of available colors is easy, as it is simple multiplication. If you multiply 256 times 256 times 256, you get 16,777,216 colors. This represents unique color combinations of Red, Green, and Blue, which you can obtain using these 256 levels of color that you have to work with across these three color channels.

In this next section of the chapter, we will look at how these bit depths apply to different digital image file formats, such as an 8-bit GIF, or a 24-bit JPEG, or a 32-bit PNG digital image asset.

Color Depth: Bit Levels That Define Color

The amount of color available to each pixel in a digital image is referred to in the industry as the **color depth** for that image. Common color depths used in digital image assets include 8-bit, 16-bit, 24-bit, 32-bit, 48-bit, and 64-bit. Galaxy Watch Designer supports three of these color depths: 8-bit using GIF and PNG8, 24-bit using JPEG and PNG24, and 32-bit using PNG32. A true color depth image will feature the 24-bit color depth and can contain a maximum of 16,777,216 colors. File formats supporting 24-bit color depth include JPEG (or JPG), PNG, BMP, XCF, PSD, TGA, TIFF, and WebP. Galaxy Watch Designer supports three of these, JPG, PNG24 (24-bit), and PNG32 (32-bit). Using 24-bit color depth will give you the highest quality level. This is why I'm recommending the use of PNG or JPEG for your watch faces. Next, let's take a look at how we can optimize the image size by using less colors!

Indexed Color: Using Palettes to Hold Colors

The lowest color depth exists in 8-bit indexed color images. These feature a maximum of 256 color values, which is why they are 8-bit images, and use an indexed "palette" of colors, which is why they are called indexed color images. Popular image file formats for indexed color include GIF, PNG, TIFF, BMP, or Targa. The indexed color palette is created by the indexed color codec when you "export" your file from an imaging software package, such as GIMP. Codec stands for COde-DECode and is an algorithm that can optimize a file size to be smaller using compression. Galaxy Watch Designer supports two indexed color image formats, GIF and PNG. To convert true color image data into indexed color image data using GIMP 2.10.6, you will use the **Image ➤ Mode ➤ Indexed** menu sequence, as you saw used in Figure 2-8.

This menu sequence will call up the **Indexed Color Conversion** dialog. I used the GIMP **Floyd-Steinberg** diffusion dithering algorithm, which reduces color bleeding, keeping image edges clean and sharp. Next, let's take a look at the other formats which are recommended for use in Gear Watch Designer, 24-bit true color JPEG, or 32-bit PNG32.

True Color: Using 24-Bit Color Imagery

One of the most widely used digital image file formats in the world is the JPEG file format, and it only comes in one flavor: 24-bit color. Other file formats which support 24 bits of color data include Windows BMP, TIFF, Targa (TGA), Photoshop (PSD), GIMP (XCF), and PNG24. Since PNG also supports 8-bit (PNG8) or 32-bit (PNG32) color, I call a 24-bit PNG format PNG24, to be precise. Galaxy Watch Designer supports two of these popular formats, JPEG and PNG24. The primary difference in these true color formats supported in watch face design comes down to one, primary differentiating factor: lossy vs. lossless compression.

Lossy compression means that an algorithm, which is also called a codec (COde-DECode), is throwing away some of the data to achieve a smaller data footprint. For this reason, save your original uncompressed file format using a lossless data format, prior to applying any lossy compression, in this case, JPEG.

Lossless compression, used by the PNG, BMP, TGA, and TIFF formats, doesn't throw away any original image data; it applies an algorithm that finds patterns that result in less data used and that can 100% reconstruct all of the original pixel values.

Using more than one image in your Galaxy Watch Design application (or in any application, such as GIMP for instance) is called **image compositing**. Compositing involves using more than one image layer. The background or image uses 24-bit image data. All the other layers in the compositing stack above a background plate need to support transparency and, therefore, will need 32 bits of data, which is also known as ARGB or RGBA.

This transparency is provided by a fourth channel, known as the **alpha channel**. I'm going to introduce you to this in the next section of the chapter, as it's a key compositing concept.

True Color Plus Alpha: Using 32-Bit Imagery

Besides 8-bit, 16-bit, and 24-bit digital images, there are also 32-bit digital images. Formats which support 32-bit color data include PNG, TIFF, Targa (TGA), Bitmap (BMP), GIMP, and Photoshop. I like to use PNG32 as it is supported in Galaxy Watch Designer, Tizen, HTML5, JavaFX 9, CSS4, JavaScript, and Android. These 32 bits of image data include 24 bits of RGB color data, plus 8 bits of "alpha" or transparency value data, held in what is commonly referred to as an "alpha channel." Since you now know that 8 bits holds 256 values, it will make sense to you that an alpha channel will hold 256 different levels of transparency data values, for each pixel in a digital image. This is important for digital image **compositing**, because it allows **layers** that hold this 32-bit image data to allow some portion (from 0 to 255, or all of that pixel's color) of the color data to bleed through to (or to blend with) layers below. Next, let's take a closer look at what alpha channels can do.

Alpha Channels: Defining Transparency

Let's take a look at how alpha channels define digital image pixel transparency values and how they can be used to composite digital imagery in Galaxy Watch Designer. Alpha channels provide transparency inside of digital image compositing software packages such as GIMP 2.10.6, which I would term "static" use, but can also be used via PNG32 image assets to composite digital imagery in real time using open platforms such as Galaxy Watch Designer, Tizen Studio 2.5, Android Studio 3, HTML5, CSS, or JavaFX. I would term this "dynamic" use, as code allows you to access these pixel transparency values in different moments of time, so you can animate the data in any way that you like, for example, in games, watch faces, websites, apps, or eBooks.

For example, hour, minute, and second hands on a watch face use alpha channels, to allow them to be overlayed on the background.

Digital image compositing involves a seamless blending together of more than one layer of digital imagery. As you might imagine, this per pixel transparency is an important concept. Digital image compositing is used in graphic design, film, game design, print design, or watch faces.

Digital image compositing needs to be used when you want to create an image on your display that appears as though it is one single image (or an animation) but is actually the seamless collection of more than one composited image layers. One of the principal reasons you would want to set up image, or animation, composition is to allow you more control, over various elements in an image composite, by having components on different layers. You'll see this in Galaxy Watch Design.

To accomplish multi-layer compositing, you always need to have an alpha channel transparency value, which you can utilize to precisely control the blending of the pixel's color with the pixels in the same X,Y image location on layers below it. Like RGB color channels, the alpha channel will have 256 levels of transparency, from 100% transparent (0) to 100% opaque (255). Each pixel will have alpha transparency data, just like each pixel will have different RGB color data.

Porter Duff: Algorithmic Blending Modes

There is another powerful aspect of image compositing called **blending modes**. Any of you who are Photoshop or GIMP 2.10 users have seen that each layer in a digital image compositing software package will be able to be set to use a different blending mode. Blending modes are algorithms which specify how the pixels for a layer are blended (mathematically) with the previous layers (underneath that layer). These pixel blending algorithms will take into account a pixel transparency level, so, between the two image compositing controls, you can achieve virtually any compositing result that you are trying to achieve. Some of the powerful Porter Duff blending modes include XOR, SCREEN, OVERLAY, DARKEN, LIGHTEN, MULTIPLY, and ADD.

Smoothing Edges: Antialiasing

Antialiasing is an important imaging technique for watch face design which is also implemented by using an algorithm. What the algorithm does is to find where two adjacent colors meet along an edge and blend those pixels around that jagged edge. Antialiasing will add averaged colors along the edge between two colored areas to visually smooth those two colors together along that (formerly) jagged edge. This will make the jagged edge appear to be smooth, especially when the image is zoomed out and the pixels aren't individually visible. What antialiasing does is trick your eyes into seeing smoother edges, to eliminate what is commonly called "the jaggies." Antialiasing provides impressive results, using few (usually fewer than eight) intermediary averaged color values, for those pixels which lie along the edges within the image which need to be made to look smoother.

I first created a seemingly smooth red circle seen in Figure 2-10, against a yellow background. I zoomed into the edge of that circle, and then I grabbed this screenshot showing the orange intermediary values.

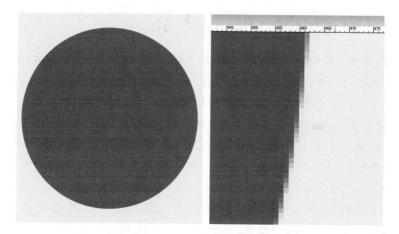

Figure 2-10. *A zoomed-in view (right) showing the antialiasing algorithm effect*

I placed this alongside of the zoomed-out circle to show the antialiasing (orange) pixel values, for colors between red and yellow. Color values bordering each other along an edge of the circle are now orange. Always-on watch faces do not use antialiasing due to the drain of the algorithm on a watch battery. Next, let's look at digital illustration assets.

Creating Digital Illustration Assets

Again what we are looking for in this section is "royalty-free illustration for commercial use"; however, with digital illustration assets, you need to make sure they are Creative Commons Zero (CC0) to ensure they are legal to use. For this reason I am going to direct you to a digital illustration for commercial use website I have vetted, which is called PublicDomainVectors.org that hosts CC0 artwork. I'm going to use this site in this section of the chapter to show you how I can turn free illustration data into a smartwatch face background image using the GIMP 2.10.6 open-source digital image editing and compositing software, which we downloaded and installed at the end of Chapter 1.

53

Digital Illustration Acquisition

What we are looking for with vector or digital illustration is vector assets created under the CC0 (Creative Commons Zero) license that would be great to use as watch faces and in a "native" **vector file format**, such as **SVG** (Scalable Vector Graphics), **AI** (Adobe Illustrator), or **EPS** (Encapsulated PostScript). I prefer SVG, as it's WebKit compatible with major browsers and will easily open and edit in Inkscape. As digital illustration CC0 assets are not as abundant as digital image assets are, I decided to provide you with the www.PublicDomainVectors.org/ website directly, as many of the free vector websites play games, and ultimately require you to become a member, or advertise their site for them (Attribution Requirement), as you will see if you search for "free for commercial use vector artwork," for instance. Figure 2-11 shows the site.

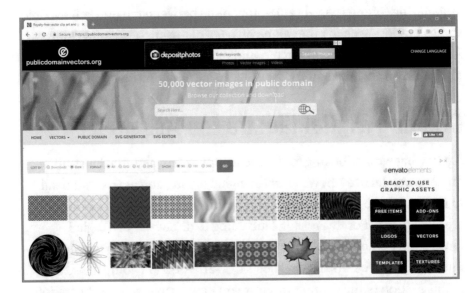

Figure 2-11.   *Visit the PublicDomainVectors.org website to find CC0 vector asset*

Click on the round illustration on the bottom-left corner of the site; if it is not there anymore, search for an "Abstract vortex with colorful details" item, which looks like it would work well within a Galaxy Watch Design project, and go to its vector download and information page seen in Figure 2-12. This page will tell you information about this vector asset, such as tags, size, source, and similar specifications. Click the **DOWNLOAD** button to download it into your /**Assets** folder (and /Digital_ Illustration subfolder).

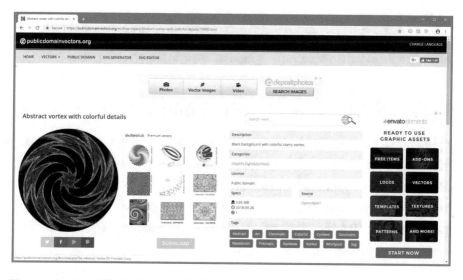

Figure 2-12. *Click the watch face optimized vector asset at the bottom-left corner*

Once this **Abstract-Vortex-53-Prismatic-2.svg** file is in your Assets folder, which can be seen in Figure 2-13 on my workstation, in a **SmartWatchDesignFundamentals/Assets/Digital_Illustration** folder, you can right-click on the file to get a context-sensitive menu, and select the **Open with ➤ Inkscape** menu sequence to open the file in Inkscape.

Figure 2-13. *Right-click the downloaded SVG file; select Open With ➤ Inkscape*

Next, before we go any further with vector assets and their data optimization for watch face design and development, let's learn about vector graphics principles, concepts, and terminology a bit first.

Digital Illustration Concepts and Terms

Digital illustration vector images are composed of points using coordinates in 2D space and lines or curves that connect those points together. We will be looking at concepts and terminology for these points and lines in this section. If you create a "closed" shape, that is, one where there are no openings, for a fill (color, pattern, or gradient) to escape, you can also fill a vector shape, so that a shape looks solid.

The Vertex: The Foundation for 2D Shapes

The foundation for any 2D or 3D vector asset is called a **vertex**. Multiple vertices are required to create a line or arc, which require two vertices, or a closed shape, which requires at least three vertices. Vertices are used in both 2D vector (SVG) data processing and 3D vector (OpenGL 4) data processing, both of which can be used in watch faces.

Vertex data is outlined in SVG (Inkscape) using X,Y coordinates, as you might have guessed, which tell the processor where a vertex is located in 2D space, similar to what is done with pixels. Without these vertex coordinates, lines and curves can't be drawn, as they must have an origin, as well as a destination vertex coordinate, as part of the line drawing operation. A line or arc would be an example of an open shape.

When we get into creating and looking at SVG assets, you will see that lots of vertex X,Y locations comprise the majority of SVG data, which means improperly optimized vector assets can grow to be larger than raster assets. We'll be looking at how to solve this problem in a bit, if you want to still use that cool vector asset in your watch face designs.

An X,Y coordinate all by its lonesome is what can be termed **one dimensional** or 1D. It takes two vertex coordinates to be considered **two dimensional**, or 2D, so a line or a curve is an **open shape**. **Closed shapes**, which take three vertex coordinates, can also be 2D.

The Path: Connect Vertices to Create Shapes

A path is defined in SVG using a "path" data element. Both an open shape and a closed shape are technically a path according to the SVG specification. An SVG Path represents the outline of an open or a closed shape that can be filled, stroked, and used as a clipping path (which is the vector equivalent of an alpha channel). A **fill** deals with the interior of the path, a **stroke** deals with the line or curve thickness that makes up the path, and the **clipping path** is used for Boolean (cut out) operations.

In SVG data an SVG Path object represents 2D "geometry," used to outline a Path object. SVG path data can be defined in terms of SVG commands, which are actually what is inside an SVG file, which is why it can grow so large in file size. Some of these include a **moveto** command, which sets your current point; a **lineto** command, which draws straight lines; a **curveto** command that draws cubic Bézier curves; an elliptical **arc** command, which draws an elliptical arc; and a **closepath** command, which closes a current shape, drawing a line to its starting point. These are all covered in Apress's *Digital Illustration Fundamentals* (2015) book.

Compound paths are also possible in SVG; these allow you to create complex, Boolean shape special effects. For instance, you could use a compound path to create a hole in your shape, like you would in a raster composition by using an alpha channel.

Lines: The Simplest of the Path Components

The simplest way to connect point coordinates along a path is to use **straight lines**. Different shapes like triangles, squares, pentagons, and hexagons can be created using SVG's lineto command. There are three lineto commands, a lineto, a horizontal lineto, and a vertical lineto.

To code an octagon shape using SVG, you would use a moveto (M) command, from a point (vertex) at 60,0, and then draw seven lines, using the lineto (L) command. This will look like the following SVG XML:

```
M 60 0 L 120 0 L 180 60 L 180 120 L 120 180 L 60 180 L 0 120 L 0 60
```

The Cubic Bézier Curve

If you have ever used the Pen tool in Photoshop or GIMP, or used Inkscape as we will in this chapter, or any of the 3D modeling tools out there, then you are probably familiar with Bézier curves. I am not going to delve into all of the math behind how the curves are constructed, as this is a fundamentals book and not an advanced book, but we will be looking at how to use open-source tools to generate the digital illustration vector assets you will need for your Galaxy Watch applications. In a nutshell, you would draw cubic Bézier curves using SVG commands by defining your start and end points, as well as two **control points**, one control point for the start point and one control point for the end point. These control points control the curvature of a curve, also called a spline in the industry, going away from the first point and coming into the second point. The cubic Bézier curve command will therefore utilize this format inside of an SVG XML data file format:

```
M x,y C (or c) x1,y1 x2,y2 x,y
```

The starting point is defined by moveto M x,y, and the C (or c) defines an absolute or relative cubic Bézier curve type. The x1,y1 is your control point for beginning of the curve, and the x2,y2 is your control point for end of curve. Finally, your x,y coordinate at the end of the command string is an end point for the cubic Bézier curve.

The Quadratic Bézier Curve

Your inclination will be to assume that quadratic Bézier curves are more complicated, given that quad means four, and therefore that there are even more control points for this type of curve. However, the exact opposite of this is actually the case, because a quadratic Bézier curve actually has only **one control point** that connects to both the start and end points of the curve segment, and moving this control point controls how the curve is shaped between these two points. Thus, if you are looking for coordinate data reduction of 100% as far as control point specification goes, then use quadratic Bézier curves. An SVG command specification for a quadratic Bézier curve will thus look like the following:

```
M x,y Q (or q) x1,y1 x,y
```

Therefore, a quadratic Bézier command requires only one single control point, which is then used as the control point for both the start and the end points. So, it's like the two control points in a cubic Bézier curve are connected together as one control point, which moves the curvature from the start point and into the end point at the same time. There are numerous SVG curve generators on the Internet; if you want to experiment with the parameters, search for Bézier Curve Generator.

Next, let's take a look at your CC0 vector asset in Inkscape, and take a look at how to optimize vector for use in watch face development. As you have seen (on the far right side of Figure 2-13), the vector asset we found on PublicDomainVectors.org is fairly huge in its data footprint, at a whopping 3.8 megabytes of SVG XML data. Let's see if we can use what we have learned in this chapter to reduce the asset's data footprint (in both watch face download size and memory used) significantly next.

Vector Assets: Optimizing Rendering Workflow

Once Inkscape has loaded into memory, after you use a right-click and Open with Inkscape work process on the SVG asset itself (shown in Figure 2-13), you will see what is shown in Figure 2-14. Use the **Zoom** (Magnifying Glass Icon at the top left, selected in blue, about four icons down) tool, and click several times the vector artwork to zoom it up to fill the screen, so that we can look at the splines (Bézier curves) which are used to create this design. There are two reasons that this vector artwork is 3.8 megabytes in size. First, there are a lot of curves utilized to create the designs, and second, each curve uses a lot of vertices to create the curve, rather than using the spline curve control handles to create the curvation. This design could be optimized to less than 1 MB.

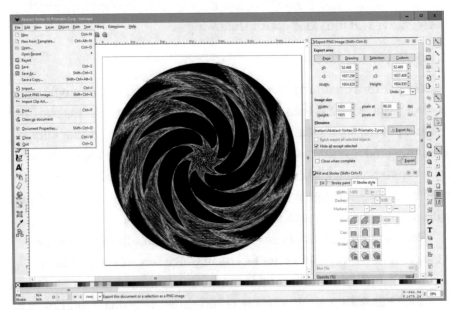

Figure 2-14. *Zoom into the vector artwork to see why it is over 3 megabytes data*

Since 1 megabyte is still too large for a watch face asset, and spline optimization is beyond the scope of this chapter (it is discussed in the *Digital Illustration Fundamentals* book, however), there's another way to optimize a vector asset for use as a watch face background element!

The way to optimize this asset considerably is to "render" it from vectors (spline curves) into rasters (pixels) using the **File ➤ Export PNG** image, which I also included in Figure 2-14 (on the left) to save a figure!

After we render a PNG24, which you learned about earlier in the chapter, we'll optimize it to be a 360 pixel 1:1 square indexed color data format, and make it into a PNG8 (or a GIF), so you can see the file size difference (both formats are supported in the Galaxy Watch Designer).

To render the file, use the **Export** button, also included in Figure 2-14 on the middle right with a green check on the button, to export the PNG24 file. This will show you a progress dialog, shown in Figure 2-15. You will notice that this rendering algorithm is compute-intensive, it will take a minute or two to complete, as it is turning thousands of vertices into a few hundred thousand pixels (360 x 360 = 129,600 pixels). You learned how to perform this calculation in the first part of this chapter.

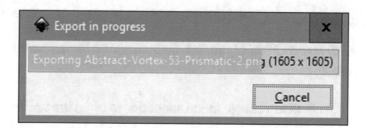

Figure 2-15. *Click on green Export arrow button to start SVG to PNG rendering*

As you will see, the PNG24 comes out as a 2.5-megabyte file, saving 1.3 MB of data footprint. This image is 1605 by 1605, so we can further reduce the data footprint by taking this resolution down to 360 pixels square, as well as using indexed color, to reduce the color depth.

Raster Asset Optimizing Data Footprint

So now that we have optimized a nearly 4 MB vector (SVG) asset down to a 2.5 MB raster (PNG24 at 1605 x 1605 resolution) asset, let's go back into GIMP, and perform the same type of data optimizations that we did in the first section of this chapter covering raster image assets. Open the exported true color PNG24 file in GIMP, as is shown in Figure 2-16.

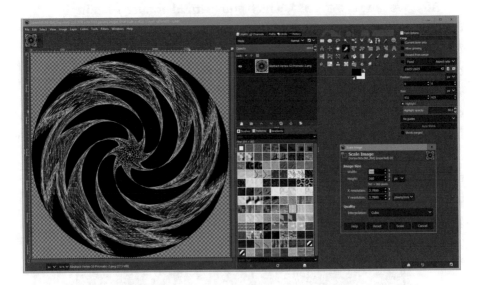

Figure 2-16. *Open PNG24 file in GIMP, to see vector as raster on transparency*

Use **Image ➤ Scale Image** menu sequence to open the **Scale Image** dialog shown in Figure 2-16 and reduce the 1605 pixels down to 360 pixels in both the X and Y dimensions. Next use the **Image ➤ Mode ➤ Indexed** menu sequence to open an **Indexed Color Conversion** dialog seen in Figure 2-17 to color map the true colors to a 256 indexed color palette.

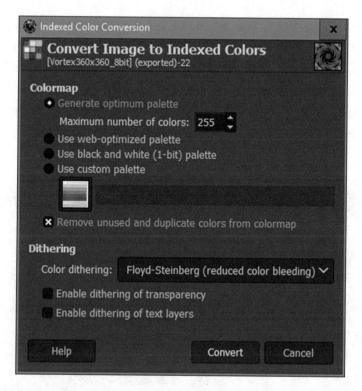

Figure 2-17. *Indexed Color Conversion dialog*

A 3.8-megabyte SVG file to a 2.5-megabyte PNG24 file is a 66% (a 33% or 1/3 reduction in data) optimization, so now let's optimize the resolution for Galaxy Watch and the color depth from 16,777,216 colors used down to 256 colors used (true color optimized down to indexed color depth). It is important to notice that some 24-bit to 8-bit data footprint optimizations, such as the ones we are doing inside of this chapter, do not result in any loss of color fidelity or image quality, and in these cases, I will change my recommendation of using PNG24 to using PNG8 instead as it can save three times (in this particular case, it is saving 1000 times the data, as you will see) data footprint, which is simply amazing, which is why I am showing you how to do it here!

As you see in Figure 2-18, when you use the **File ➤ Export As** menu sequence to open the **Export Image** dialog, your PNG8 file is now 62 kilobytes, which is 99.997528% (61.8K / 2.5 MB = 0.00002472) smaller! If you calculate 61.8 KB / 3.8 MB, you'll get 0.00001626315, so the data optimization that you have just performed is saving 1000 times the watch face memory, not to mention zero watch face CPU rendering!

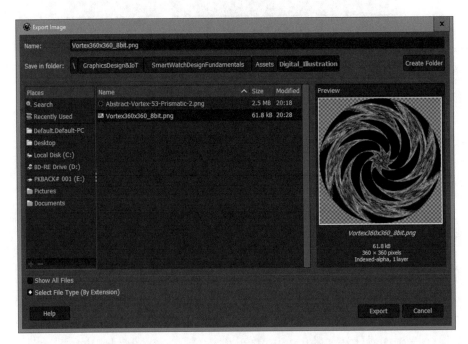

Figure 2-18. *Use Export Image dialog to save the 61 KB PNG8 file*

You are now a watch face vector and raster asset optimization master. This will become critical in the watch face design power saving!

Summary

In this chapter, we took a look at how to obtain digital illustration assets from the vector (SVG, or Scalable Vector Graphics) open-source (CC0, or Creative Commons Zero) website called publicdomainvectors.org. We looked at how to open these SVG vector illustration assets using open-source software called Inkscape and how to "render" these from vector (spline-based) format into raster (pixel-based) format.

We then used the open-source GIMP 2.10 package to "optimize" this watch face design asset, from nearly 4 GB of data down to less than 82 KB of data (thousands of times less data), so we can use this vortex pinwheel in future watch face designs, in the course of this book.

It is important to learn Inkscape and GIMP 2.10 for watch face design, which is why I cover this in the book, because Samsung's watch face market is extremely competitive, and most of the stunning watch faces that are available in Samsung's Watch Face Store were primarily created using Raster Imaging and Vector Illustration software, such as GIMP and Inkscape, in combination with the "core" Samsung Galaxy Watch Designer software package. For this reason, I am going to cover all the software (open source) which can be acquired for free and used to create watch face designs in this book. This will make the book more complex than it would be if it just covered the Galaxy Watch Designer software package, as many features which will set your watch faces apart from the others will be created outside of Galaxy Watch Designer using other software packages such as Inkscape and GIMP 2.10.

CHAPTER 3

Smartwatch Design Considerations: Watch Face Types

In this third chapter of the *Smartwatch Design Fundamentals* book, let's look at the most important considerations you will be making regarding the attractiveness of your watch face design, which will greatly affect the sales volume of the watch face. By attractiveness, I am talking about the watch face's visual design, which we are obviously going to learn how to maximize over the course of this book, and about the display of its sensor features. We'll be using Analog Watch Face and Digital Watch Face features with sensors indicating how much power the watch face uses, steps taken, date, weather, and heart rate.

We'll also look at stepping outside of the Analog vs. Digital watch face design box, as Galaxy Watch Designer allows us to come up with our own new and innovative designs, which I will term "Hybrid" watch face designs in this chapter. I will show you how to create one of my favorite hybrid watch face designs, the "Analog with Digital Time display in watch background" made popular by Sector Watches in Italy. This will show you how to use Galaxy Watch Designer software to create an entire range of watch face designs in this chapter so you can get familiar with the major feature and design areas (Preview, Component, Timeline, and Properties panels) of the software package.

© Wallace Jackson 2019
W. Jackson, *SmartWatch Design Fundamentals*,
https://doi.org/10.1007/978-1-4842-4369-5_3

Types of Watch Face Designs

The first thing we're going to do is to go over the different types of watch face designs you can create, as this is one of the primary decisions you have to make before you get started working in Galaxy Watch Designer. Different watch models display different design types more optimally; for instance, the Galaxy Watch square 1:1 aspect ratio 360 x 360 screen will be perfectly suited for a round, analog watch face design, although digital and hybrid watch face designs can also be created with careful spacing of the watch face components. The Gear S 360 by 480 square screen might be better suited for both analog and digital watch face designs on the same screen, with 360 by 360 pixels used for the analog watch face component and 360 by 120 pixels (top or bottom of the screen) used for the digital watch face component. I would call this a "hybrid" watch face design. The Gear Fit or Gear Fit 2 would be better situated for a sideways digital watch face (to use a much larger font size for readability), as it has a 1:2 aspect ratio, 216 by 432 pixel screen.

Digital Watch Faces

The simplest watch faces to create are digital watch faces, which feature numeric readouts with **HH : MM : SS for** hours, minutes, and seconds along with a date and possibly a stopwatch or timer readout. These digital readouts use a digital font in most instances and must be placed on the screen in an attractive location (usually centered) and may show some other watch features, such as steps, heart rate, weather, battery power, day of week, date in month, and so forth. These watch faces are easier to create, due to the lack of radial elements and calculations which pivot from the center of the screen and array themselves around the round watch face, such as is found on the 360 by 360 resolution Galaxy Watch, Gear S2, S3, and Sport models. Arraying analog elements around rectangular watch faces (Gear S or Gear Fit 2) is difficult, as the design becomes somewhat asymmetrical, due to the top and the corners being farther away than the sides.

Launch Galaxy Watch Designer and you will be presented with the New Project dialog. If you are not (i.e., if you have un-checked "Show on application start"), then use the **File➤ New** menu sequence to open this dialog, which can be seen in Figure 3-1. Select the **New** Project (top-right icon), the **Gear S2, Gear S3, Gear Sport, and Galaxy Watch** 360 x 360 option (middle-left icon), and then name the project CH3_Digital_Watch_ Face (or My_Digital_Watch_Face if you prefer), and click the **OK** button to create an empty project and open Galaxy Watch Designer on your Windows 10 or MacOS workstation.

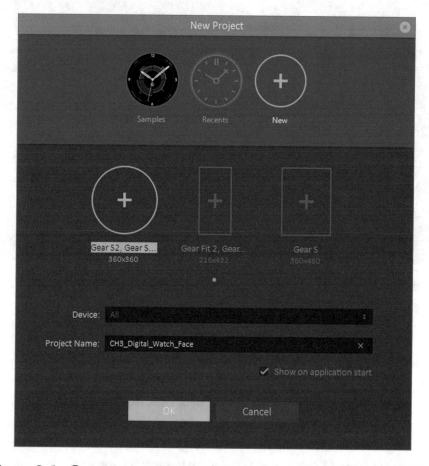

Figure 3-1. *Create a new 360 pixel watch face named CH3_Digital_ Watch_Face*

Click the **Digital Clock** icon in the **Component** panel on the left-hand side of the Galaxy Watch Designer software. This can be seen encircled in red in Figure 3-2. A Digital Clock display will be displayed in the center of your watch face in the **Preview** area, with properties in the **Properties** panel on the right of the preview which you can adjust to get the result that you desire for your new digital watch face design.

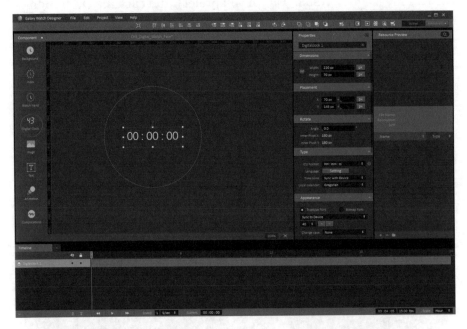

Figure 3-2. *Click the Digital Clock Icon on the middle left to insert Digital Watch Face Readout*

Some of the panels in the Galaxy Watch Designer can contain quite a bit of information and settings, so let's learn how to scroll these panel properties so you can be sure to access everything during your watch face development process. Put your mouse in or over the pane, and use the middle mouse button scroll wheel to move the panel info up and down. You may need to click (but not on a setting) to show where you want the scrolling to occur. Try it out, you'll get the hang of it soon enough! As you

70

can see in Figure 3-3, I have exposed the other half of the properties for the Digital Clock Component, and as you'll see, there are some very advanced features available, which we will be covering a bit later on in this book, as we become more advanced designers!

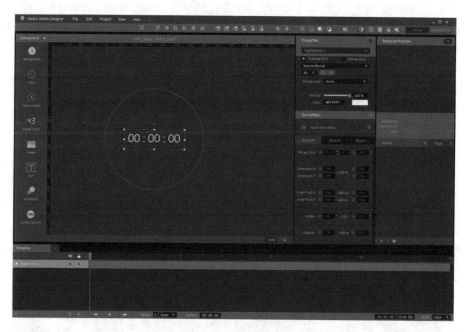

Figure 3-3. *Use Center Mouse Scroll button to scroll the Properties panel down*

Next, let's take a look at how we would design an Analog Watch Face using your Galaxy Watch Designer software, which will take more steps as Analog Watch Faces have considerably more components to add to the watch face design than digital watch faces have.

Analog Watch Faces

Let's design an Analog watch face and see exactly what is involved and learn more about GWD. Launch Galaxy Watch Designer and you will be presented with the New Project dialog. If you are not (i.e., if you have unchecked "Show on application start"), then use the File ➤New menu sequence to open this dialog, which can be seen in Figure 3-1. Select the New Project (top-right icon), the Gear S2, Gear S3, Gear Sport, and Galaxy Watch 360 x 360 option (middle-left icon), and then name the project CH3_Analog_Watch_Face (or My_Analog_Watch_Face if you prefer), and click the OK button to create an empty project and open Galaxy Watch Designer on your Windows 10 or MacOS workstation.

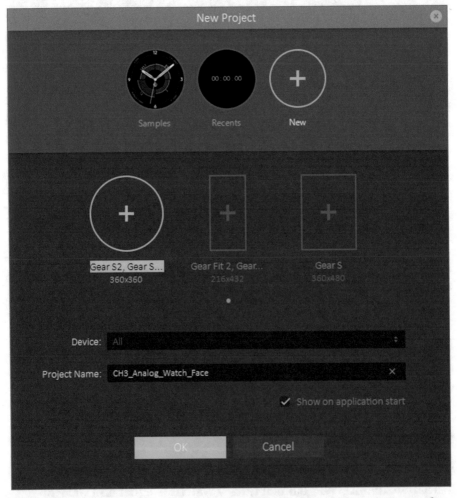

Figure 3-4. *Create new CH3_Analog_Watch_Face 360 x 360 watch face project*

Click the **Background** icon in the **Component** panel on the left-hand side of the Galaxy Watch Designer software. This can be seen encircled in red in Figure 3-5. An Analog Clock background menu will be displayed on the left side of the watch face in the Preview area, with properties next to the Component panel on the left side of the preview. As you select Background assets provided with Galaxy Watch Designer, you will see a preview of the asset pop-up on the right of the menu item. I selected blue ch_bg_a_01, as I wanted to use white watch face design elements (other than a red second hand), and I wanted to have enough **contrast** (the difference between dark and light), for better readability.

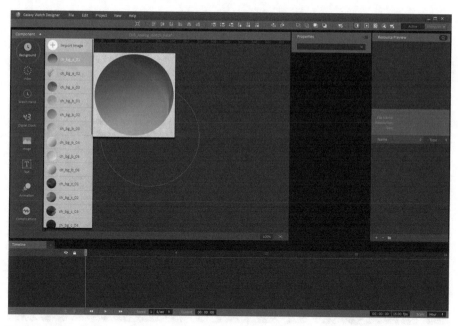

Figure 3-5. *Add an attractive background asset of your choice from the menu*

Click the **Index** icon, in the **Component** panel, on the left-hand side of the Galaxy Watch Designer software. This can be seen encircled in red in Figure 3-6. An Analog Clock indices menu will be displayed on the left side of your watch face in the Preview area, with properties next to the Component panel on the left side of the preview. As you select **Index** assets provided with the Galaxy Watch Designer, you will see the preview of each index asset pop-up on the right of each menu item. I selected 360_modern, as I wanted to use a modern watch face design, and this option has large readable numbers and large lines ("ticks") as well around the perimeter.

Once you select the Index to use, the Galaxy Watch Designer will place it over the Background you selected, which can be better in the next screenshot in the series (Figure 3-7) if you wanted to look ahead. We will start to add Watch Hand Components next, which is what will be shown in that screenshot, which shows what the index will look like over the blue background color, and ultimately, it looks fairly readable from what I can ascertain.

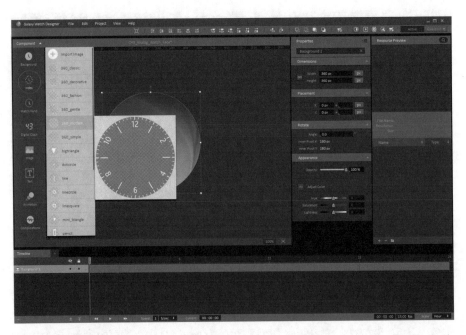

Figure 3-6. *Use the Index Icon to add a watch face index with ticks and numbers*

Once you select an index to use, you will see the Properties (or Options) for that design component populate the Properties panel, and at the same time, the index you selected will be overlaid on top of the background you selected in the Preview area.

In this Analog Watch Face design section, this will be shown in the next screenshot (Figure 3-7) for this series of screens.

The next step, shown in Figure 3-7, is to click the **Watch Hand** icon, seen encircled in red in the **Component** panel, and select the **classic_sec** (classic second hand) watch hand design element from the drop-down menu, which will contain (you guessed it) different types of Watch Hands! This includes Hour, Minute, and Second Hands, which are key components of Analog Watch Face design.

As you can see in Figure 3-7, the classic second hand is red and slim and, as we will learn later on, saves power and screen burn-in due to its sparing use of pixels and bright colors.

Also, as you add watch face design elements (Components), notice that they are added to the Timeline panel as layers in your watch face design compositing pipeline that Galaxy Watch Design processes.

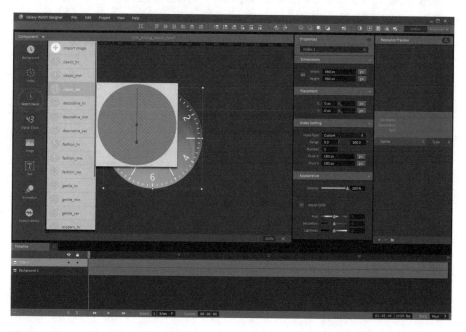

Figure 3-7. *Use the Watch Hand icon to select watch face second hand element*

Once you select a second hand to use, you'll see the Properties (or Options) for that design component populate the Properties panel, and at the same time, the second hand you selected will be overlaid on top of the background and index that you selected in the Preview area.

In this Analog Watch Face design section, this will be shown in the next screenshot (Figure 3-8) for this series of screens.

The next step, shown in Figure 3-8, is to again click the **Watch Hand** icon, seen encircled in red in the **Component** panel, and select **gentle_ min** (a gentle minute hand, not a gentleman) watch hand design element from the Watch Hands drop-down menu. Now we have our (not Hour) Minute and Second Hands, which are key components of Analog Watch Face design. We only have to add our Hour Hand, and we'll be ready to add a day of the month display.

As you can see in Figure 3-8, the gentle minute hand is white and hollow and, as we will learn later on, saves power and screen burn-in due to its sparing use of pixels. Notice that we now have three layers of watch face design components in the Timeline pane on the lower left of the Galaxy Watch Designer software user interface.

Figure 3-8. *Use the Watch Hand icon to select watch face minute hand element*

Once you select a minute hand to use, you'll see the Properties (or Options) for that design component populate the Properties panel, and at the same time the minute hand you selected will be overlaid on top of the background, index, and second hand you selected.

In this Analog Watch Face design section, this will be shown in the next screenshot (Figure 3-9) for this series of screens.

The next step, shown in Figure 3-9, is to again click the **Watch Hand** icon, seen encircled in red in the **Component** panel, and select the **gentle_ hr** (a gentle hour hand) watch hand design element from the Watch Hand drop-down menu. Now we have Hour, Minute, and Second Hands, which are key components of Analog Watch Face design. Now we only have to add our day of the month display.

As you can see in Figure 3-9, the gentle hour hand is white and hollow and, as we will learn later on, saves power and screen burn-in due to its sparing use of pixels. Notice that we now have four layers of watch face design components in the Timeline pane on the lower left of the Galaxy Watch Designer software user interface.

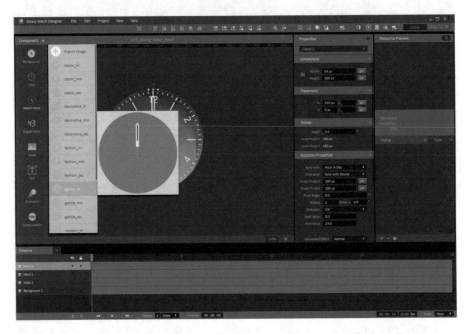

Figure 3-9. *Use the Watch Hand icon to select a watch face hour hand element*

Once you select an hour hand to use, you'll see the Properties (or Options) for that design component populate the Properties panel, and at the same time, the hour hand you selected will be overlaid on top of the background, index, and minute and second hands you selected.

In this Analog Watch Face design section, this will be seen in the next screenshot (Figure 3-10) for this series of screens.

The next step, shown in Figure 3-10, is to click the **Complications** icon, seen encircled in red in the **Component** panel, and select the **Date_Digital_A** (Digital Date Box) watch face design element from the Complications drop-down menu. Now we have a Date Box as well as

Hour, Minute, and Second Hands, which are key components of Analog Watch Face design. Now we will only have to position this Date Box on the display, next to the 3, on the right side.

As you can see in Figure 3-10, the Date Box is Black, and as we will learn later on, this saves power and screen burn-in due to its sparing use of bright pixels (only a few white pixels for the number). Notice we now have five layers of watch face design components in the Timeline pane on the lower left in the Galaxy Watch Designer software.

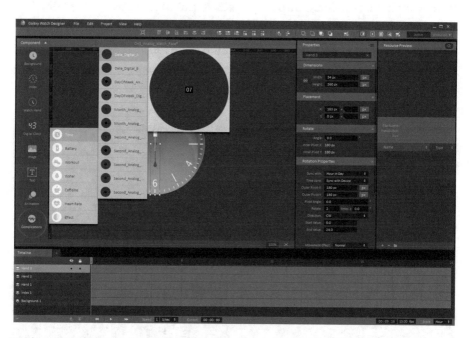

Figure 3-10. *Use the Complications icon to select a watch face date readout*

Figure 3-11 shows that we can drag and drop any watch face component (watch face design element) around the Preview area to position it within our design – in this case, an Analog Watch Face design. The Galaxy Watch Designer software has automatic "snap-to-grid" features and also adds magenta guidelines in both the X and Y dimensions to show designers what their design components are going to line up with. This is a pretty cool and useful feature and makes your design process more fun, as well as more precise.

Also notice that since we are not adding watch face design components to the preview area, we have a clear view of our design at this point as well. It is important to notice at this point in time the "Z-order" of the watch face design components. Z-order is the position above and below each other, which is determined by the layer order in the Timeline pane, which serves as the watch face design compositing stack, much like you saw in GIMP (and will see much more later). After we add some cool elements to the watch face design to create a Hybrid Watch Face design (the next section of the chapter), you will "optimize" this watch face design, so you can put the second hand on the surface.

Figure 3-11. *Drag to position date readout using magenta positioning guidelines*

This Z-order is quite important in watch face design if you think about it. The hour hand should overlay on top of the minute hand, and the second hand should overlay both of those. All watch face hands should overlay the date window, which means that as we become more optimized watch face designers, we'll add components such as the day of the month and cool complications such as heart rate and battery power first, so that they are behind the watch hands when the hands pass over them!

I'm going to do this optimization phase/section of the chapter last, to make it stand out more in the process and so that I can continue to add the digital time readout and heart rate monitor to this watch face to turn it into a Hybrid watch face design and continue with this design workflow and feature learning workflow before we look at the Z-order optimization and layer compositing and similar more advanced features. I am thus attempting to stratify this book so that later chapters build upon earlier materials, to make the learning process as smooth, fast, and seamless as possible for the readers.

Hybrid Watch Faces

Let's continue building up this watch face design and add a digital time readout to the bottom of the watch face, making it both an analog and a digital watch face. I like to call this a "Hybrid" watch face design, that is, one that is beyond or different than a traditional analog or digital watch face design. In this case the design has both analog and digital features and is thus a Hybrid Watch Face. We'll also add a heart rate monitor in the area next to the 9 (on the left) to balance out the areas of the watch face. It is important to have a balanced use of the watch face so that the watch face components and compliments do not overcrowd each other.

The first thing we want to do, which we did in the "Digital Watch Faces" section of this chapter (without the repositioning we will be doing here), is to click the Digital Clock icon on the middle left and then drag this Digital Clock readout to the bottom of the hybrid watch face design, between the 8 (on the left) and 4 (on the right). This should yield a very balanced placement of a digital time readout, as you see in Figure 3-12.

Figure 3-12. *Add a Digital Clock, and drag the digital readout to the very bottom*

As you can see in Figure 3-12, the digital time readout is a bit large and needs to fit better between the 8 and the 4, so let's edit some of the Properties for this Digital Clock readout so it fits perfectly at the bottom of the watch with even spacing and is still readable. I reduced the font size from 40 to 28 by clicking on the downward facing arrow on the font size UI, so that the digital time readout numbers were similar in size to the numbers around the Analog Watch Face perimeter, as you can see in Figure 3-13. Next, let's add a heart rate monitor readout across from the day of the month readout to balance out this design.

Figure 3-13. *Edit the Digital Clock readout font size from 40 to 28 for a better fit*

To add a Heart Rate Monitor readout, which is kept under the watch face complication (shown encircled in red) in Figure 3-14, click the Complications icon at the bottom of the Component pane, which will bring up the menu of different types of complications. Each of these menu items has its own sub-menu, as you can see in Figure 3-14. There are menu items for Time, Battery, Workout, Water, Caffeine, Heart Rate, and Effects. Click Heart Rate and Heart_03 to insert the heart icon and bpm readout previewed at the bottom of Figure 3-14.

Figure 3-14. *Add a watch face complication for a heart rate readout on the left side*

Drag the Heart Rate Complication to the left side of the watch face, opposite the day of the month readout on the right. As you can see in Figure 3-15, as you drag this Heart Rate Complication, the snap and alignment lines will kick into play, and you can align your heart rate readout to be perfectly centered on the 3 and 9, using similar spacing that you used to center the digital readout (between the 8 and 4), but this time between the 8 and 10 vertically, rather than horizontally.

Also notice that in the Timeline panel, five new layers have been added for the various components of the Heart Rate Complication, including the numeric readout, the white (Heart Off) and red (Heart On) off-screen, and the bpm text portion beneath the readout. Later in this chapter, we'll learn how to use the layer select and layer visibility icons to ascertain what every layer added to the Timeline panel contains and what it references in the Preview area.

For the moment let's continue learning the features of the Galaxy Watch Designer software, including how to use **File ➤ Save As** to save the new Hybrid Watch Face design that we created using your Analog Watch Face design, using a **Save As** dialog to assign a new file name.

Figure 3-15. *Position heart rate indicator evenly with 3 and 9 opposite the date display*

Use the File ➤ Save As menu sequence to open the Save As dialog, shown in Figure 3-16, and name the CH3_Hybrid_Watch_Face to differentiate the new hybrid watch face design from the analog and digital watch face designs you created earlier using the File ➤ New dialog that comes up when you start Galaxy Watch Designer. Notice the file location in **Wallace Jackson ➤ GearWatchDesigner ➤ workspace**.

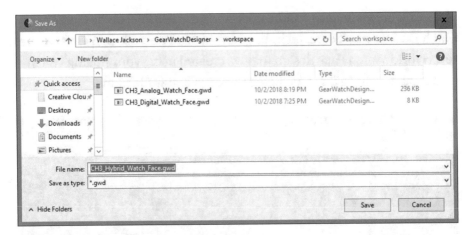

Figure 3-16. *Use File ➤ Save As and save design as CH3_Hybrid_*
Watch_Face

The software package was recently renamed Galaxy Watch
Designer, and this part of the code still needs to be updated to create a
GalaxyWatchDesigner folder on developer's workstations rather than a
GearWatchDesigner folder. This may have been done by the time you get
this book and download the latest version of the Watch Designer.

Tweaking Watch Face Designs

Next, there are a few things we need to adjust, regarding **Z-order**, as we
need the second hand at the very top of the design, and the hour hand
needs to be visible above the minute hand as well, as it is shorter and
is usually visible in this way in Analog (non-smartwatch) Watches. We
also need to make sure that the three Watch Hands are all above the day
of month readout, the Digital Clock readout, and the heart rate monitor
readout. To do this, we can select and drag Timeline layers to reorder
them. The layers are at the top of a watch face design. If you drag a layer up
and drop it on the topmost layer, it will land above it.

Figure 3-17. *Select the second hand (Hand 1) to drag it upward to higher Z-order*

Figure 3-18 shows your second hand layer moved to the top of your Timeline layer stack compositing pipeline. As you'll see, in Figure 3-18, the Preview reflects this compositing change, by rendering the second hand on top of the hybrid watch face. Let's fix the other Z-order issues.

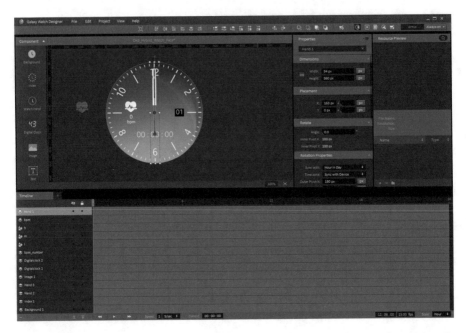

Figure 3-18. *Resize the Timeline panel so there's room to drag Hand 1 to the top*

Let's do the same exact work process with the hour and minute hands, as these also need to "render" in front of all the other watch face design elements, such as heart rate and date indicators and the digital time readout. Since I've resized the Timeline pane to be half the screen, placing the cursor between the two panes, so it becomes the up-down pane resize cursor, I can now drag the other two hand elements to the top of the stack. This is seen in Figure 3-19, moving the Hand 3 Z-order.

As you can see, Galaxy Watch Designer shows you the layer you are moving in blue and where you wish to drop it (move it above), using a blue tint and outline effect, so you can see exactly what you are doing. Since the watch face hands need to move over all the other face design elements, we will need to do this for all of the Hand (1, 2, and 3) elements in the Timeline compositing stack area, so let's do this next!

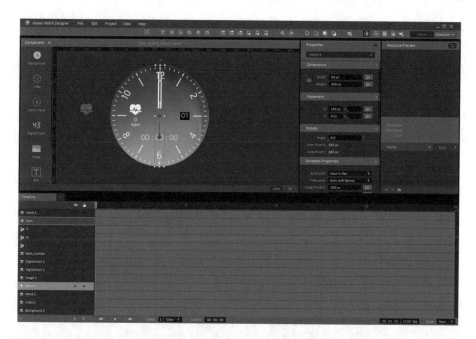

Figure 3-19. *Use File ➤ Save As and save design as CH3_Hybrid_ Watch_Face*

Next, let's grab the Hand 2 element and drag it up so it will also be moved on top of the bpm layer and to the top of the layer compositing stack, along with your other three watch hand design elements, as shown in Figure 3-20. Let's look at how to rename these layers next.

As a user of other software packages, such as GIMP 2.10.6 and Inkscape, you can make some assumptions about the way that things are being represented in similar software user interfaces. For instance, in GIMP 2.10 (and most other new media production software), layer or component names can be changed by clicking (or double-clicking) on the name that you wish to change in the user interface. If the clicked-on name becomes selected, it can usually be changed (replaced), using the name of your choice. In this case, Hands 1, 2, and 3 should become Seconds, Hours, and Minutes, so that your layer stack in the Timeline window will become clearer to you when you open the file later or to other watch face developers who open your GWD (Galaxy Watch Designer) files. This is important if you have a team working on watch face design, allowing you to clarify the Watch Designer user interface.

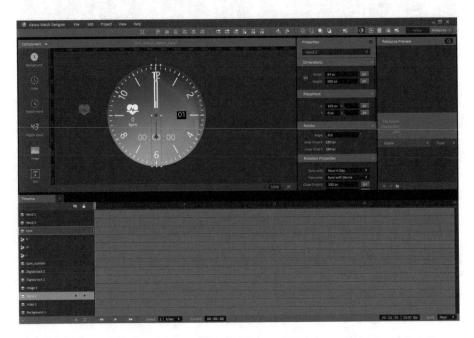

Figure 3-20. *Use File ➤ Save As and save design as CH3_Hybrid_ Watch_Face*

We should rename these layers so we can be clear what design element we are working with, since element names when they are added to the design use a generic name and the order number which indicates the order they were added to the design. Once you have some experience designing watch faces, you will probably add components and complications in the back to front Z-order they should render in to avoid having to change your layer Z-order to correct rendering issues, but it's good to learn about the various features of the Galaxy Watch Designer as we progress along the way so you become an expert!

As you can see in Figure 3-21, I have selected the text in the top three layers and typed in new descriptions. The way that you find out what layer is attached to what design element you are working with in the preview is by either selecting the layer (selecting the design element in the preview) or using the "visibility" on/off dot (becomes a white x once selected) in the first column on the right side of the layer pane (the second is a Lock Design Element Into Place dot/option). Using this we can make sure that watch face layer options progress from Seconds to Hours to Minutes, so the hour hand overlays the minute hand correctly.

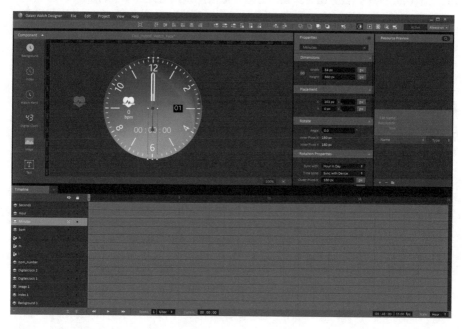

Figure 3-21. *Double-click layer name to rename it; rename hour, minute, second*

Uncheck the Visibility for the Minutes layer so that you can see the minute hand in the watch face design again, and let's get to tweaking the background color. Our objective here is to increase the watch face contrast, which is the difference between the dark and light colors, so that things like the watch face ticks (time and in-between markings around the perimeter of the watch face), hands, digital time readout, heart rate monitor readout, and so forth are more apparent to the user.

The easiest way to select the Background watch face design component is to click the Background layer to select it, as shown in Figure 3-22. This will also select the Background in the Preview pane and place the Background properties into the Properties pane where you can edit them. In this case, it is the Hue, Saturation, and Lightness of the color of the Background that you wish to edit, so scroll the Properties pane to the bottom with your middle mouse button scroll wheel until you see the **Adjust Color** section of the panel and its three slider indicators. Grab the arrow indicator in the middle of the Hue slider, and drag it to the right to rotate the Hue 45 degrees, so that watch face background goes from light purple to blue, as is shown in Figure 3-22.

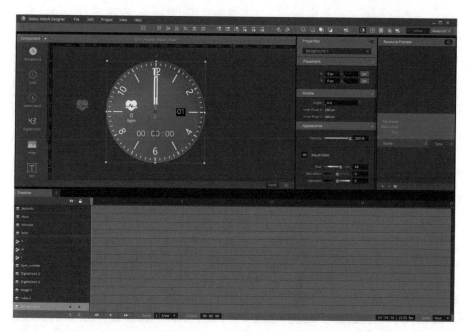

Figure 3-22. *Select the Background Layer in the Timeline, and shift Hue by 45°*

The next thing that we want to "tweak" is the Luminance, or lightness to darkness, of the watch face background. In order to make the white elements, and the second hand, which we will shift later on to a gold color to stand out in the design better, we need the Background component to be a dark purple to dark blue spectrum, as is shown in Figure 3-23.

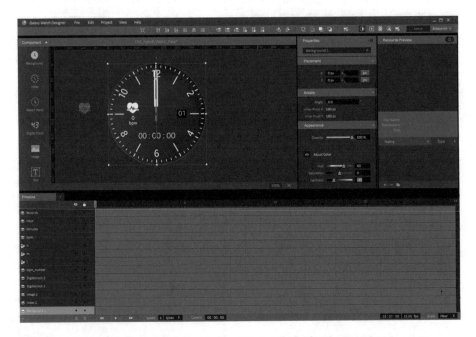

Figure 3-23. *Reduce Lightness by 45, and shift Hue to 60° to get a better purple*

Finally, let's select the Seconds layer which contains the second hand and color-shift the red hue by 45 degrees to be a gold color, which looks better against the purple and dark blue portions of the watch face background. When I tried to do this, the Eye (Visibility or Editability) icon in the Adjust Color Properties area was toggled off, so I had to click it to enable this color value. This means that you can use this feature to "lock" certain design properties, just like you can lock an entire watch face design component layer, using the Lock icon in the Timeline layer stack. As you can see in Figure 3-24, the Gold Second Hand looks great with the Hybrid Watch Face design we are working on, and the watch face we have created during this chapter looks professional enough to host in the Samsung Galaxy Smartwatch store for sale.

In case you are wondering what the red heart that is off-screen on the left is, keeping an alternate state of a graphic outside the edge of the screen is a popular technique in game design; if you have read my *Pro Java 9 Games Development* book, you may be familiar with this game design technique. Tizen uses this off-screen representation to toggle the Heart Rate Icon to be red when the HRM data is being actively read.

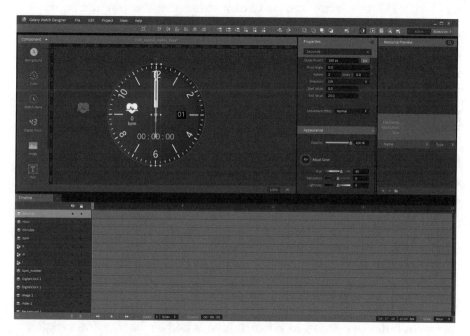

Figure 3-24. Select the Seconds layer; toggle the Eye icon in Properties to set color

You can select this red heart design element and adjust its color properties (for instance, turn it pink like a real-world heart is) using these same selection, visibility, and adjustment techniques outlined within this chapter. Try tweaking some of the other watch face design elements to get some practice.

For instance, change the digital time readout to a bright yellow color against the dark blue, or change the day of the month readout to a more readable green color, to get some practice with the work process which is needed to master the Galaxy Watch Designer.

Congratulations, as you have learned how to use the Galaxy Watch Designer software at its most rudimentary level to create Analog, Digital, and Hybrid Watch Faces, and we're only three chapters into the book! This is going to get more and more exciting, as what watch faces can do is limited only by the sensor hardware and Tizen APIs available to Tizen smartwatch developers.

Summary

In this chapter we looked at how to use the Galaxy Watch Designer software to design Digital watch faces, Analog watch faces, and Hybrid watch faces (Analog + Digital Features) as well as how to "tweak" or adjust the settings for these watch faces to achieve your desired end result.

This gave our readers a good introduction regarding how to start creating watch faces using the Galaxy Watch Designer software, and it showed what the major watch face design components on the left-hand side of the GWD software do, as well as how to add them to your watch face design in order to create a new watch face, whether that may be a digital watch face, analog watch face, or hybrid watch face.

Finally, we covered more design quadrants, or "panes," of the Galaxy Watch Designer software when we looked at how to "tweak" the analog, digital, and hybrid designs we had created in the first part of the chapter, so that readers could learn more about how to use the Galaxy Watch Designer to create their watch face designs.

In the next chapter, we will learn even more about how to create advanced watch face designs that include all of the modes and features that watch face consumers desire.

CHAPTER 4

Smartwatch Design Considerations: Watch Face States

In this fourth chapter of the *Smartwatch Design Fundamentals* book, let's look at the second most important consideration you will be making regarding (other than the attractiveness covered in Chapter 3) your watch face design: optimizing power (battery) usage. At the end of the day, this will also greatly affect the sales volume of the watch face, even if it's by word of mouth between smartwatch users. By optimizing power, I am referencing the design's ratio of off (Black) pixels to fully on (White) and partially on (red, green, blue, cyan, magenta, yellow) pixels. This ratio will determine how much battery power your watch face design will use. This in turn determines how fast your watch face design drains the smartwatch battery and how well it passes the watch face store design inspection process (i.e., does it closely follow their **Always-On Rules**). This is why I included milliamp-hours (mAh) in the first part of Chapter 1.

The watch face power states (**Active** and **Always-On** State) will be where you spend most of your watch face design time and energy, because you actually have to spend twice the amount of time (possibly even more

© Wallace Jackson 2019
W. Jackson, *SmartWatch Design Fundamentals*,
https://doi.org/10.1007/978-1-4842-4369-5_4

than twice, due to low color or high color Always-On modes), creating two to three different watch face designs. This gives you a chance to expand further on the imaging concepts you mastered in Chapter 2.

Optimize Power: Watch Face States

Smartwatch hardware is designed to optimize battery power, as smartwatches are small in size, meaning their batteries are also small, in order to fit inside of the smartwatch case. For this reason, smartwatches tend to utilize different states (also called "modes") that activate when your users turn their wrist to view the watch face (invoking what is called an "Active" state) and which otherwise use a low-power state (called an "Always-On" state) when the watch face is perceived to be unused (or not being looked at). The Always-On mode (I may use the words "state" and "mode" interchangeably in this chapter) uses a lot of Black (or "off") pixels, which do not use any power to generate their 256 different levels or intensities of RGB color, which you learned about in Chapter 2, covering digital imaging fundamentals.

Active States: High Battery Power Usage

In the previous chapter, we designed Active State Analog and Digital and Hybrid watch faces, using a full array of color Background components and as many white, gold, red, and true color spectrum pixels as we wanted, to create the watch face design that your end users will see when they turn their wrist to look at their smartwatch face.

In this chapter we will look at the many important considerations in the design of your Low color (think: Low-power) watch face design. Think of this watch face design as your watch face "screensaver," as it will both prevent screen burn-in and save the user's battery life.

The Always-On design should mirror (mimic in component and pixel positioning) your Active design, so the true color design can simply replace the pixels of the 3-bit color design. However, it is important to note here that the two watch face designs can be completely different if you so desire, although I am going to show you how to "sync" these two designs in this chapter, as this is what is usually done (see Figure 4-2) in the watch face market currently. But feel free to be unique if you wish!

Always-On: Minimize Battery Power Use

Smartwatches use an Always-On "state" and watch face design for that state. This state is used when the watch face is not being actively viewed, which is called the "Active" state, which is not Always-On but instead is "Temporarily On" when the user rotates their wrist to view the full color watch face design or show it off to their friends. Designing Always-On watch faces is not as easy as just adding black (pixel off) values to your watch face full color version in order to "dim" it, as the color values are still used, and **dimming** them by adding black color value **won't save any power,** because the colored pixels are still (barely) turned on. In other words, on at all, with any intensity, from 1 (almost off) to 255 (fully on) is the same as 255 (fully on), so you'll want to design Always-On watch faces using fully on pixel colors, so your users will have the maximum watch face readability. Only Black value Zero (zero means power off) pixels use no power! These fully off Black pixels also provide the best contrast for the rest of your Always-On watch face design, which should always utilize fully on white (256 Red, 256 Green, 256 Blue) or RGB or CMY colored pixels.

Default Always-On: Lower Battery Power Use

The lowest battery power usage Always-On State (or Mode) uses what would be called the Smartwatch built-in or "default" Always-On watch face design. This is built into (part of the OS codebase) each smartwatch model and would always be utilized if you do not provide an alternate, customized, Always-On watch face design for the Low-Bit Color Mode Always-On State or the High Color Mode Always-On State; we'll be covering how to create these in this chapter. Shown in Figure 4-1 (also available on the Samsung Developer website) are Always-On Low-bit color mode for Samsung's Gear S2 smartwatch and Always-On High color mode for Samsung's Gear S3 smartwatch. As you can see, very minimal components, compliments, and colors are utilized so that the amount of power taken from the battery is minimized.

Figure 4-1. *Default Always-On states for the Samsung Gear S2 and Gear S3*

If any smartwatch model does not support a High Color Mode Always-On State, then your Low-Bit Color Mode Always-On State will be utilized over the default Always-On State (Mode) that comes with the smartwatch model, so include both modes with your watch face design. We will be focusing on Low-bit color mode design in this chapter, as only the Gear S3 and Galaxy Watch models currently support the High color mode of the Always-On smartwatch state.

Low-Bit Color Mode: Low Battery Power Use

The Low-Bit Color Always-On State (or Mode) uses what would be called 3-bit (or 8) color, or Low-bit color mode, to build on what we learned regarding color depth back in Chapter 2. I shared that it took 8 bits (contained in 1 byte) to hold a palette of 256 colors and showed you that fairly impressive imagery can be created using the relatively few colors found in an 8-bit image. This is far more difficult to do with a 3-bit color palette, as you might imagine, so I hope you're up for a real challenge. The eight colors in this Low-bit color Always-On palette include black and white; Cyan, Magenta, and Yellow (the CMYK subtractive colors used in printing); and Red, Green, and Blue (the RGB additive colors used in computer displays and iTV Sets). An example which you can also see on the Samsung Developer website is shown in Figure 4-2. It's important to look at the "bright" side (no pun intended) of Always-On watch face design: at least you have the foundational color for additive color imaging (RGB) and subtractive color (print) imaging (CMYK) to use, along with White, for your designs!

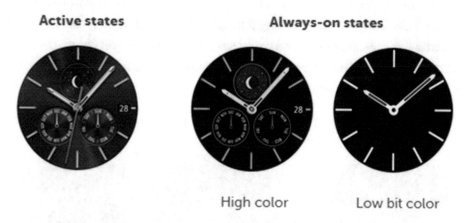

Figure 4-2. *Examples of Active States and High and Low color Always-On States*

To make sure your watch face designs can sell across the many Gear and Galaxy Watch models, be sure to include Low-bit color mode designs with all of your watch faces. In essence, what only having eight colors available to create a watch face design with does is it forces you to really showcase your design chops by using low color image assets, so you can't just fall back on using true color image compositing chops for your watch face designs. It is possible to have both Low color and True color watch faces in your design that will stun your users, whether or not you turn over your wrist and show the Active state watch design. This is the ultimate goal of the watch face designer: to provide a watch face with great Low color and True color designs.

High Color Mode: Medium Battery Power Use

The Gear S3 and Galaxy Watch (and later) support a High color mode that can be used instead of Low color mode (which means always create a Low color Mode Always-On watch face design, unless you are selling Gear S3 and later watch faces). For all of you digital imaging aficionados out there, this is not referencing 16-bit color, commonly termed High-Color in digital image TGA (Targa) or TIFF (Tagged Image File Format) data types. In a smartwatch, 16-bit color space won't save power over 24-bit color space, so use 24-bit color for Active (also called Ambient) Mode and 3-bit color for Always-On, as shown in Figure 4-3.

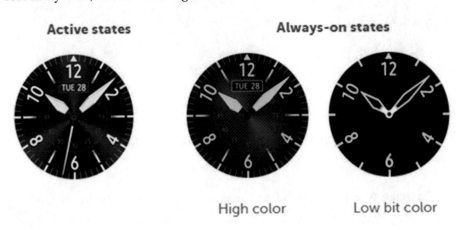

Figure 4-3. *More examples of Active States and High and Low color Always-On States*

Next let's look at how Samsung measures optimization using an "OPR."

OPR: Optimizing Per-Pixel Power Usage

The OPR, or **On Pixel Ratio**, is limited for Samsung Smartwatches to a total of **15% OPR** (maximum, or your watch face will not be approved for publishing) for an Always-On watch face design. This means that 15% of your total displayed pixels can be white. So using the calculations we learned in Chapter 2, on a Gear S this means that 360 x 480 x 0.15 pixels can be white, or 25,920 pixels. Since white uses an RGB value that is three times (one red, one green, and one blue pixel) more than a Red, Green, or Blue color pixel used alone, this means that you can use 25,920 x 3 = 77,760 colored pixels, if you use Red, Green, and Blue (RGB) pixel colors. If you use two pixel colors (remember Yellow = one Red pixel on plus one Green pixel on), as in Cyan, Magenta, or Yellow (CMY) pixels, you would cut this color pixels' number in half (77,760 / 2 = 38,880). Thus, RGB pixels use 33% of one white pixel, and CMY pixels use 66% of one white pixel, and black (the K value in the CMYK color space) use 0% of one white pixel, which is why Always-On watch face designs tend to use the black background color and sparing use of the other seven 3-bit indexed color palette color values. This is important information for designing an Always-On watch face design, as is the information in the next section on burn-in!

Minimizing the AMOLED Screen Burn-In

When a smartwatch uses its Always-On state (yes, all smartwatches feature this), many times the watch face OS will shift watch face pixels around the screen slightly to prevent what the industry terms a "burn-in effect" from occurring on the Active Matrix (AM) OLED display. Screen burn-in originated on Cathode Ray Tubes (CRT displays) when the CRT electron gun would shoot out a stream of electrons which would burn a prolonged image into the luminance material which coated the back of the glass screen. This would cause a ghost of any prolonged image to be visible after the CRT was turned off. It is important to note that design elements near the very edge of your watch face design can be pushed off of the visible display (especially on round or analog watch face designs) when this OS controlled pixel-shifting effect happens.

Just like Always-On optimization, screen burn-in optimization involves replacing high RGB value colors with black for the background, especially at the center (pivot) of the screen for your Analog watch face designs. You may want to avoid designing with high-brightness (white), and even high-chroma (CMY) pixels, in any larger areas of pixels.

For analog watch faces, since pixel on/off varies less the closer you are to the center (pivot) of the watch face (hour, minute, and second hands), you should strongly consider leaving the center pixels using the Black (pixel turned off) color value, or possibly use the Red color value.

Those of you with an Analog Photography ("old school" cameras using film, not digital cameras) background will have experience using a Red light in the "darkroom," as this wavelength of light won't even burn in hypersensitive film stocks, so, it's a safe assumption that using Red pixel color on fixed components will minimize the burn-in effect by using only 33% power, as far as Always-On watch face design is concerned. The wavelength for Red is long/wide, so it carries less (burning) energy within the wavelength to affect either film or organic light-emitting diode screen composition materials. In the next section, where we create the Always-On state for the Hybrid watch face design that we created in the previous chapter, I will use Red for the fixed (Index) part of the design.

Creating an Always-On Watch Face

Since the Always-On watch face design needs to be a part of the Active watch face design, we will need to open the CH3_Hybrid_Watch_Face design we created in the previous chapter and add an Always-On watch face design to that project file. There are two ways to do this, the first is to click "Recents" in the New Project dialog and then to select the Hybrid project, which is not showing up for selection as you can see in Figure 4-4.

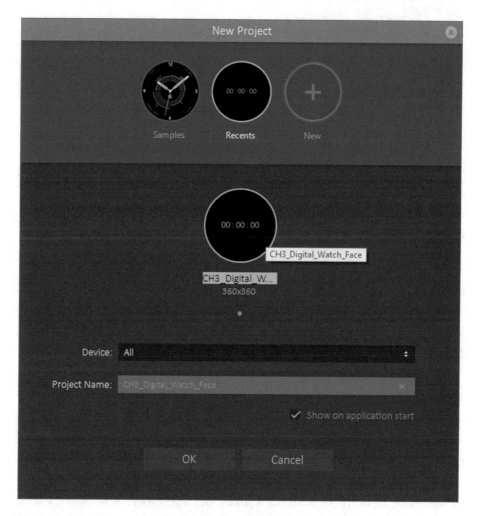

Figure 4-4. *Try to locate the Hybrid_Watch_Face project in New Project dialog*

If for some reason the New Project dialog is not finding all of your recent projects and listing them, use the Cancel or New options and open up an empty version of the Galaxy Watch Designer software and then use the **File ➤ Open** menu sequence to access the **Open** dialog, which is shown in Figure 4-5.

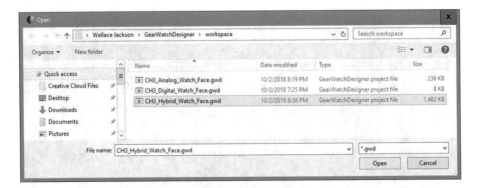

Figure 4-5. *Use the File ➤ Open menu sequence to access the File Open dialog*

Select the **CH3_Hybrid_Watch_Face** project file, and click the **Open** button to open it in the Galaxy Watch Designer software package.

This will open up the project in Galaxy Watch Designer as seen in Figure 4-6. Look in the upper-right corner of the Galaxy Watch Designer user interface, and you will see buttons labeled Active, which will be depressed (selected) currently, and another next to it labeled Always-On. If you click the Generate Always-On button next to the Run button to enable High color and low color profiles, then you can click the Always-On button, and a menu will drop down with choices to put the GWD software package into two different design modes, the Low-bit color mode and the High color mode, which will reset the GWD software to what looks like the empty watch face design state, so that you can design your (two, if you wish) Always-On watch face designs from scratch for each of these modes. In this way, one GWD project file can be loaded with up to three different watch face designs to be used for Active, Always-On Low (3-bit color), and Always-On High (True Color) compositions (as dictated by the Timeline pane).

You can toggle (switch between) your designs in GWD simply by clicking these buttons (and sub-menu) any time you wish, as you are working in the Galaxy Watch Designer software. Pretty cool modal operation for watch design software, if you ask me. Kudos to Samsung!

Figure 4-6. *The Always-On State Toggle is in the upper-right corner of the GWD*

As you can see encircled in red in Figure 4-6, I selected a Low-bit color mode, which then put me into an entirely new design, which now features the Black background color, as shown in Figure 4-7. The OPR (On Pixel Ratio) for an All-Black design is 0.0% as you can see at the bottom of the Preview pane, which means we can see how the OPR will grow, from 0.0% to the maximum 15.0%, as we create your Always-On Low-bit color watch face design.

Since we are going to learn from what we did in Chapter 3, and do not need to add a background component (as you can see GWD has added a Black solid color Background component for us), let's add the Index over the background so that we add things in the proper Z-order.

This will make your Always-On design match your Active design pixel for pixel, so components won't move; then the user turns their wrist over to view the Active watch face design. We will be configuring this Index to use the low-vibrating-red wavelength however to minimize the AMOLED screen burn-in in the next step in the process, to build upon what we have learned previously about low-power watch face design in the first half of this chapter.

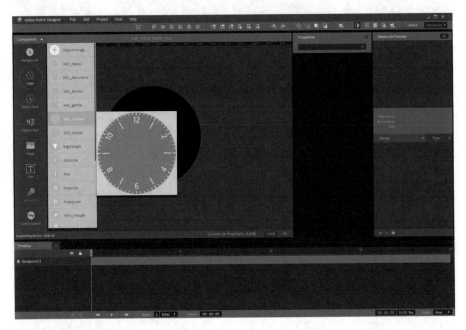

Figure 4-7. *Add the same Index Component that you did for your Active design*

To configure the Properties of the Always-On Low-bit color watch face Index component, select the component's layer in the Timeline pane, so that it turns blue and selects the component in the Preview pane in Figure 4-8, and then use your center mouse button scroll wheel to scroll the Properties pane to the bottom so that we can set the color value from White to Red.

As you can see, the Galaxy Watch Designer software is paying close attention to what we are doing and has changed the Appearance section of the Properties pane to utilize the 3-bit color palette selection user interface, rather than a True color 24-bit color Hue, Saturation, and Luminance selection user interface widget collection as it did for our Active watch face design workflow. Now you are seeing how the Galaxy Watch Designer software is helping out to make salient Always-On watch face design decisions, which is also pretty cool, if you ask me.

Click the Red color swatch in the 3-bit color palette and you will see the watch face Index component turn from White to Red, and thereby save on your OPR as well as the dreaded screen burn-in. In fact, you can see that with a Red Index, your OPR is now at only 1.3%.

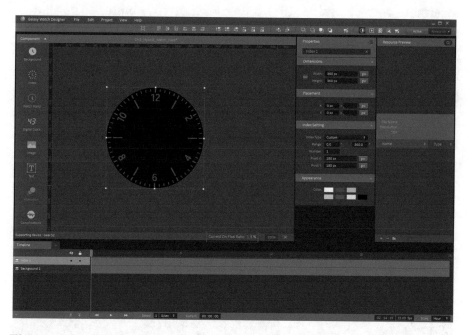

Figure 4-8. *See the Current On Pixel Ratio readout at the bottom of the preview*

Since we are adding watch face design elements (components) from back to front, let's make the Always-On design a Hybrid design and add a Digital Clock component at the bottom of the watch face. Make it 28 pixels in font size, and Green, so that it stands out, by using one of the RGB color values, which only uses 33% of what a White readout would use, as far as OPR is concerned. As you will see, this will take our OPR to 1.7%, or about one-tenth of the maximum allowable value.

I tried to change the readout of the Digital Clock component to match the **HH : mm : ss** used in the Active watch face design, but GWD does not allow seconds on Always-On watch states, which means that I will have to manually position (center) the digital readout over the 6, and at the same Y pixel height value as we are using in your Active design.

To accomplish this, use snap and grid line positioning in GWD to ascertain a correct X value (103), then click the Active button to be able to read the Y (height) positioning value of 225 from your Active design. Next, enter a Y of 225 manually in the Always-On design after switching back into that design mode, by again clicking the Always-On Low-bit color button and sub-menu selection. This correctly aligns your readout.

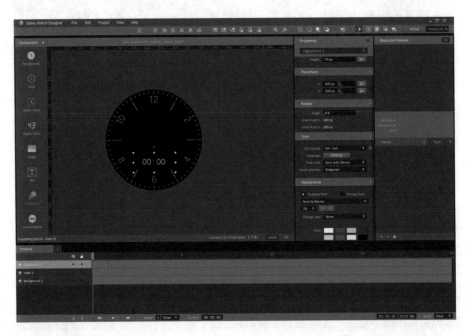

Figure 4-9. *Add a digital clock and set it to 28 (font), green, and a 225 Y location*

Next, let's add your Minute Hand, again using something other than White, to save on OPR. This is done by clicking the Watch Hand icon in the Component pane, and we want to click the Minute, then the Hour, then the Second so they are added in the proper Z-order.

The Cyan color looks good with the red and green, and stands out well in the watch face design, so I chose that color for the Hour and Minute hands.

Scroll down the Properties panel and find the 3-bit color palette swatches in the Appearance section, and click on the Cyan color to set the Minute Hand to this color value.

You will notice that the OPR has now risen to a value of 2.9% which is less than a fifth of our allowed 15% OPR value, and we are already starting to look like a real watch face design!

Next, we are going to add the Hour Hand, and make the same color selection, and then a Second Hand which we will make Yellow in order to differentiate it from the Hour and Minute hands.

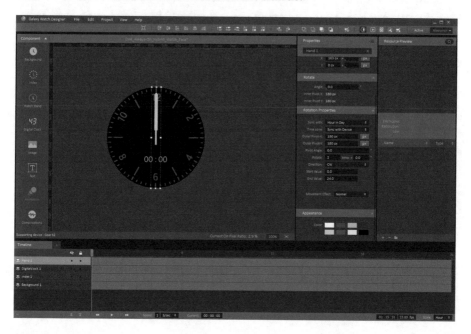

Figure 4-10. *Add a Minute Hand to the Always-On design and set it to cyan color*

Next, let's add an Hour Hand, so it is on top of the Minute Hand. This is done by clicking the Watch Hand icon in the Component pane, and we want to click the Hour Hand, and then add your **Watch Hand ➤ Seconds Hand**, so both of these are added in the proper layer Z-order.

Let's also rename the three layers in the Timeline to Seconds, Minutes, and Hour Hand, like we did in the Active version of the watch face, so that we can identify what we are doing in the software later on. Again we will want to use something other than White, to save on OPR.

Scroll down the Properties panel and find the 3-bit color palette swatches in the Appearance section, and click the **Cyan** color, to set the Hour Hand to this color value. A Cyan color looks good with red and green and stands out well in a watch face design, so I chose that color for the Hour and Minute hands. You will notice the OPR has now risen to a value of 3.2%, more than a fifth of our allowed 15% OPR value.

The Yellow color makes the second hand stand out also, but be aware that the second hand may not always work reliably in Always-On mode and that you may want to leave the second hand out of your design when creating Always-On Mode watch face designs.

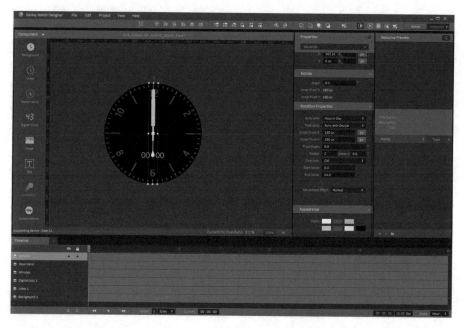

Figure 4-11. *Add an Hour Hand and Yellow Second Hand to Always-On design*

I am including the Second Hand here just to be complete from a watch face design perspective, since that is the primary subject of the book. Let's add the compliments near the center of the watch face (by the 3 on the right-hand side) next.

Since an Always-On Low-bit color watch face can't monitor your heart rate, we'll just add the day of the month compliment to get the day displayed, and come close to replicating our Active Hybrid watch face design. Since the Background is already Black, we also will not need the small black square (layer) that puts a black background behind the White number to improve its contrast.

After we add the **Data_Digital_A** compliment, as seen in Figure 4-12, we'll fix its Z-order, visibility, and alignment in the next section of the chapter.

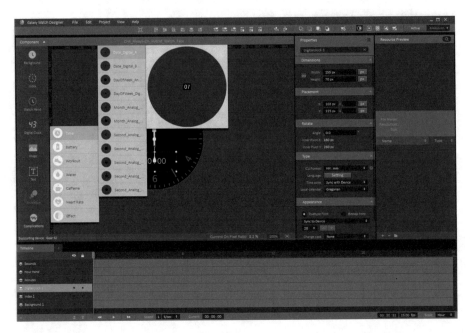

Figure 4-12. Add a Minute Hand to the Always-On design and set it to cyan color

Notice that I selected the Digital Clock Layer in the Timeline pane before I added the Day of the Month compliment. What I was doing was to see if this software was smart enough (as yet, it will be, someday) to add the selected compliment in the Layer order that I was specifying using this selection (much like the drag to move layer works).

Since GWD added the day of the month compliment to the top of the layer stack, I will drag the numeric readout portion down on top of the Digital Clock readout, as seen in Figure 4-13 in the Timeline pane Layer section.

I can delete the Image 1 (black square box outlined with white) that serves as a background for the day of month (date) on the watch face design. I want to make sure that the month day number matches pixel for pixel with the Active design and that it stands out, so I am keeping it white in color.

I was thinking of adding the Heart Rate Monitor as a Magenta element (since it's pink like a real heart), but when I tried to add it, the software gave me an error message, which tells me that the heart rate sensor does not work when the watch is in a low-power mode.

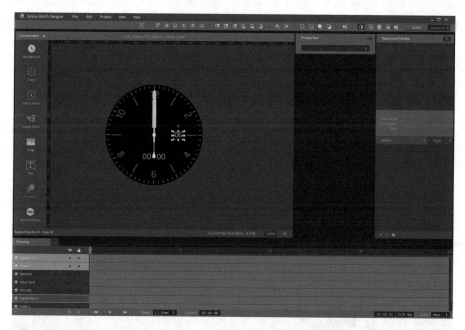

Figure 4-13. *Drag Digitalclock 2 layer on top of Digitalclock 1, to move it down*

To delete the Image 1 background image layer, select it so that it's blue, and right-click the selected layer to open a context-sensitive menu. All software can (and should) have context-sensitive menus for all of the major features, as it allows professional users to navigate the features of the software more rapidly during the development process.

Notice that things you can do to a layer using this shortcut include Cut, Copy, Paste, Delete, Rename, Swap Image, and Group and Ungroup. You may have noticed grouping being used in the past when we added Heart Rate and

Date compliments to the watch face design, as these were multi-layer groups that were designed to stay, and be used, together in the watch face design.

Let's right-click and select Delete from the menu to remove the background Image 1 from the watch face design, as it is redundant, as the background of the watch face is already black, and we can reduce the OPR using this "move."

This reduced our OPR to 3.3%, which is fairly low as far as OPR goes for watch face designs. I notice the pixel positioning is slightly off for the date display, so let's learn how to micro-adjust components next.

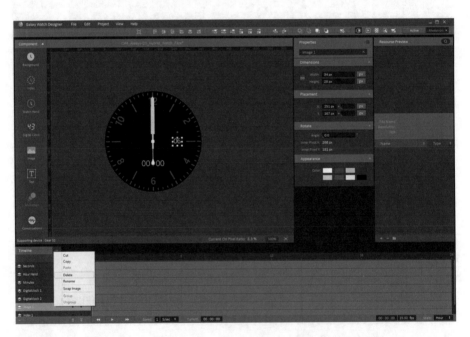

Figure 4-14. *Right-click the Image 1 layer; select Delete from a context menu*

To micro-position watch face design components (elements), you can select the layer holding the component or compliment, so that it will turn blue. At that point in time, you'll use the **Up – Down – Left – Right** arrow keys on your keyboard to move (and adjust) the positioning of the element by one pixel at a time.

As you can see in Figure 4-15, we were a few pixels too high for the day to be centered on the line that emanates from the 3 at the right side of the watch face design, so we move the 164 Y position down to 166 pixels in the Y dimension, so this component is better positioned.

We need to remember to also do this in the Active Hybrid watch face design, which, as you will see in Figure 4-16, better centers your day of the month readout inside of the Image 1 black box background area behind the date readout in the Active watch face design as well.

After we finish this design process, our OPR is at 3.3%, which is quite low, which means that users with this watch design will not run out of battery power due to the watch face design, which will serve to make it more popular in the watch face marketplace.

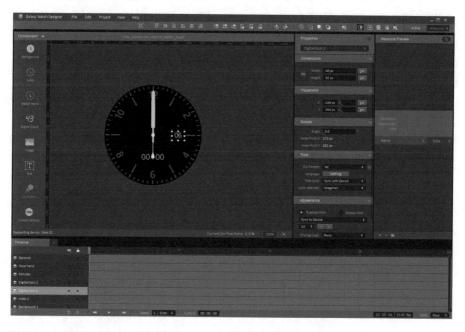

Figure 4-15. *Select Digitalclock 2 layer and use down arrow key to center it on 3*

Let's see how to change the day number position in Active watch face design to match Always-On design. Note the **X, Y** position of this component in Figure 4-15 by noting the **249, 166** coordinate used for the **Placement** section of the **Properties** pane for the selected layer named **Digitalclock 2** in the **Timeline** pane.

Next, click the Active button at the top right of the Galaxy Watch Designer software to switch back into Active watch face design mode, and go to this same for the **Placement** section of the **Properties** pane for the selected layer named **Digitalclock 2** in the **Timeline** pane by selecting that layer in the Active design to make that date component active for editing, and its positioning data available for updating to the new X, Y coordinate you tweaked the Always-On watch face design version to utilize. Making the Active and Always-On Low-bit color states (or modes) use the same positioning data for all of these components means that you will only get certain portions of the watch face design that change when the user rotates their wrist, which can be a fairly cool effect. In this case, the background turns black (off), the Index turns red, and the time indicators become green, cyan, and yellow (colored).

Figure 4-16. *Switch to Active design mode and set Day X,Y to the 249.166 value*

Seconds and Second Hand usage is not always available on smartwatches earlier than the S3 and Galaxy Watch. Watches that come out later than the Galaxy Watch are likely to have better battery life, faster processing, and better screens and will be more likely to do things such as High color Always-On watch face designs that would accurately advance the second hand and display seconds on your digital clock, if you so desire. After all, most users do not use the second hand unless they are using a stop watch application, so for telling time this is not a huge functional loss for your Always-On watch face design attributes.

Notice in Figure 4-17 that your OPD is down to 3.1% using the current design. Let's see if we can get this down by another percentage point, to around 2%, so that our user's battery life will be significantly extended. The first step toward doing this is to delete the unneeded Yellow second hand

119

entirely and then to change the White and Cyan watch face components to be one of the low-power RGB color values.

Click the Seconds layer in the Timeline pane, as shown in Figure 4-17, and then select the **Delete** context menu option. This will remove that layer and component from the watch face design.

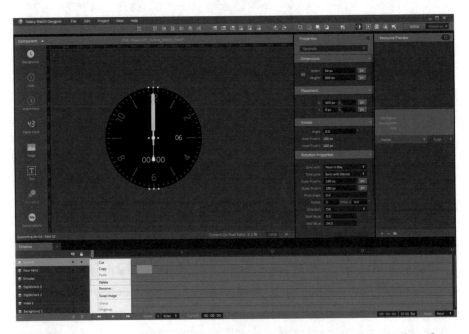

Figure 4-17. *Select Seconds layer; right-click it and select Delete from the menu*

Next, select the Digitalclock 2 layer and the day of the month numeric component of the watch face design, and scroll down into the Appearance section of the Properties pane, and click the green color swatch in the 3-bit color palette options at the bottom.

This will reduce the white pixels used by 67% to green pixels, which will reduce the OPD even further. We can reduce the hands by 33% as well by using a Blue color rather than Cyan, which will reduce the OPD even further toward the target 2% on pixels displayed usage.

To do this, select the Hour Hand layerh then go to the Properties pane, and scroll down to Appearance and select the Blue color for the Hour Hand. Do the same thing with the Minutes layer, and you will see that the OPD goes down to 2.3% or 2.2%. On my system, I dragged the Timeline time marker indicator to the right and noticed that the OPD is modulating between 2.2% and 2.3%, which means that your OPD can change based upon what time it is on the user's smartwatch!

Keep this in mind when you design for Always-On as you might want to target 14% rather than 15% when working in the Galaxy Watch Designer software.

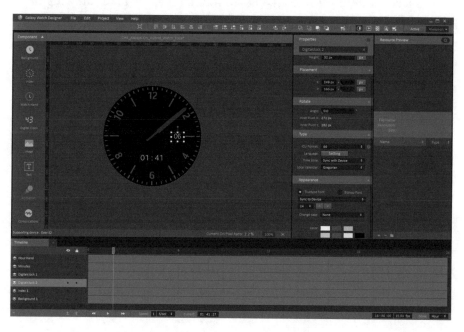

Figure 4-18. *Optimize colors used to RGB to reduce OPR to 2.2% and animate*

Now you have a complete watch face design with an Always-On mode using the Low color (3-bit color palette) mode that works in all of the Samsung smartwatches out there. If you want to practice using the Galaxy Watch Designer a bit more before we dive into the fourth dimension of animation in the next chapter, you can click the Always-On button in the upper-right corner and select High color mode and create a third watch face design (more similar to the first one you did in Chapter 3 in true color, only without the compliments/sensors and possibly without a second hand and seconds) to get some practice using the Components, Timeline, Properties, and Preview panes in the Galaxy Watch Designer.

We'll cover even more concepts in Chapter 5 as we take static digital imaging concepts from Chapters 2 through 4 and learn how 2D and 3D assets can move over time to become animation. After that, we will learn how to attach code to these 2D and 3D assets so that they can become i2D and i3D interactive assets, so we can take your watch face designs even further into the stratosphere! This is getting exciting!

CHAPTER 5

Smartwatch Design Motion Assets: Watch Face Animation

In this fifth chapter of the *Smartwatch Design Fundamentals* book, let's look at making your watch face design animated, using motion assets. These are usually implemented as a series of numbered PNG graphic elements, so we will be able to continue to build upon your knowledge of digital imaging concepts, covered in Chapters 2 through 4, when we add in the fourth dimension of time to create motion using a series of images which will be played over time much like an old-school "flip-book." This will involve using a specialized area of the Galaxy Watch Designer software called the **Animation Component**, which is located right above the Complications Component.

The first part of the chapter will go over some of the basic topics involved with animation including concepts, terminology, formats, and the like. After that, we'll look at how to take an **animated GIF** file format and extract the animation frames as **PNG8 image assets** that we can utilize inside the Galaxy Watch Designer Animation Component.

© Wallace Jackson 2019
W. Jackson, *SmartWatch Design Fundamentals*,
https://doi.org/10.1007/978-1-4842-4369-5_5

We will take you through how you can utilize watch face design animation components, in conjunction with the animation assets that we have extracted from the animated GIF file format, using the open-source software called **GIMP 2.10**, which you installed in Chapter 1.

Animation: Using the Fourth Dimension

Now that you have an understanding of the fundamental concepts, terms, and principles of digital imaging assets and how to use these as a Background in Galaxy Watch Designer, it is time to get into motion-capable new media assets such as animation and digital video. Digital Video and Animation are essentially the same, and after the first part of this chapter, you will be able to take digital video assets and turn them into animated images (which is what they are, actually) and use them in your watch face designs. Animation and Digital Video assets introduce the fourth dimension (known as time) to make static (still) images move.

We'll look at how animation as well as digital video is created by displaying image "frames" at rapid rates of speed and look at animation and digital video concepts, such as frame rate and resolution, which we also covered in Chapter 2, regarding "static" (motionless) image assets.

Animation Concepts and Terminology

Both Animation and Digital Video are comprised of digital imagery, and digital video adds digital audio into the asset as well, which is how digital video differs from animation. Digital video can be converted into animation assets for use in Galaxy Watch Designer as long as you do not need the digital audio portion of the data. Animation can be very effectively used in a smart watch design background or even in watch face components or compliments. We'll look at animated assets and their core concepts in this chapter, so that you know how to include the animated assets you create outside of Galaxy Watch Designer, using tools such as GIMP 2.10 or Photoshop, into the Galaxy Watch Designer using the Animation Component, which we will learn how to utilize in this chapter. There are also other ways to animate watch face design elements in Galaxy Watch Designer by attaching them to code, so that a watch face can use seconds, minutes, dates, weather, sensors, and so on to animate watch face design components and compliments.

Animation Data: Pixels, Colors, and Frames

Both animation and digital video extend digital imagery into 4D, the fourth dimension of time. This is done using something called **frames** in the animation, digital video, and film industries. A frame is simply a digital image, one that is contained within a collection of slightly different digital images, making it into an animation or a digital video asset.

Both animation and digital video assets are therefore comprised of an ordered sequence of frames which are displayed rapidly over time and create the intended illusion of motion imagery.

The primary concept regarding frames holds true in animation or 2D animation and 3D animation and in digital video assets. It builds upon the primary concepts for 2D digital imaging and 3D animation rendered into a 2D animation, which we learned about in Chapters 2 through 4.

Frames also contain pixels, for each image frame, which means that the animation asset also has a resolution, as well as an aspect ratio, and a color depth as well. All of the frames in any 2D animation asset usually use the exact same resolution, aspect ratio, and color depth, though it's possible to mix different file formats and color depths.

Animation File Formats: PNG8 and PNG24

Supported formats in Galaxy Watch Designer include PNG8 or PNG24. Most animation assets will use the 24-bit color depth PNG, unless the animation is extracted from an aGIF or animated GIF file, which we will do in this chapter so that you can see how it is done. The aGIF file format is also popular, so you may have to use this aGIF to PNG8 work process at some point in time in your watch face development.

Just like what pixels do in digital imagery, animation frames multiply your data footprint, with each frame used, as you'll see in the mathematics section. In animation, not only does the frame resolution greatly impact your resulting file size, but so does the number of frames per second. As you know, more data to compress equals larger file sizes, even if the compression algorithm is reducing that data.

Animation Speed: Frame Rate or FPS

The speed of an animation is determined by a number of frames played over 1 second and is commonly referred to as FPS (Frames Per Second) and is also commonly referred to as the "frame rate" in the 2D and 3D animation, digital video, and film production industries. The common frame rates include 60 FPS for i3D Console Games, 30 FPS for Digital Video, 24 FPS for Feature Film, and **20 FPS** for 2D Animation.

As you will see later on in this chapter, there is a capability in the Galaxy Watch Designer to support even **lower frame rates**, such as 15 FPS or even 10 FPS. The lower the frame rate, the lesser work your processor (or multicore if you have dual-core or quad-core smartwatch) is doing, which means that it is using less power for slower animation.

Thus, as you might imagine, the more complex and feature-filled watch face design is going to cost you as far as a user's battery use is concerned. This will hold true for adding pixels, colors, frames, sensor data, components, compliments, seconds, audio, weather data (network access), and similar features which would require power to get them to the surface of the watch face screen.

Animation Speed Mathematics: Division

To find out how long each frame is displayed, based on a Frames Per Second (FPS) value, divide the 1 second display length of the animation by the FPS value to get the fraction of a second to use to set each frame's display rate. So, 20 FPS frames are displayed for .05 of a second, 30 FPS frames display for .033 of a second, 24 FPS frames display for .04167 of a second, and 60 FPS frames display for .0167 of a second.

Next, let's look at the mathematics to calculate raw animation data to be used, or how much system memory will be needed. Again, more system memory usage means a greater draw on battery power, as each byte of memory requires power to maintain its values or states.

Animation Data Mathematics: Multiplication

In Chapter 2, you learned that if you multiply the number of pixels in your image by the number of color channels, you will get the raw data footprint for that image. With 2D animation, you will now multiply that number again, against the number of frames per second which the digital video is set to play back at, to get the data footprint per second. To get the total data footprint, you would multiply that number again by the number of seconds that represent the duration of the animation.

So with Galaxy Watch or Gear S2 or S3 animation, 360 by 360 resolution with a 24-bit color depth, you'll have [(360x360)x3]=388,800 for one frame of animation. At 10 FPS this is 388,800 x 10 = 3,888,000 bytes of data. Note that a 10 FPS animation will play 6 times in every 60 seconds (1 minute) and 360 times in 1 hour.

Animation Data Footprint Optimization

If you use Indexed color PNG8 files, you will not get any data footprint optimization, as far as system memory is concerned; only the app download size will be smaller as PNG8 assets held in the app file will be three times smaller (on average). However, system memory does not use (understand or have a way to represent) color palettes for pixels, so the 256 colors will be represented using the 24-bit color space, which means that you might as well use PNG24 (or JPEG) images for your animation frames as far as memory optimization is concerned.

You can convert other formats such as GIF and JPEG into PNG8 or PNG24 files; however, due to color reduction (GIF, PNG8) and artifacts (JPEG), it is better to start with the original (pristine) true color imagery and use PNG24 or PNG32. If you can get PNG8 images to look like they are true color (which we will show you how to do in this chapter), that is also a great approach, as it keeps your watch face app download size small. However, since it still uses 24-bit color per pixel in memory, it's still important to pay attention to optimizing (conserving) pixels (resolution) and frames (frames, or pixels displayed over time).

Obtain Animation Asset: Using GIMP

The next thing I need to show you how to do is to take an animated GIF (or aGIF) file and process it to extract the GIF animation sequence, as well as make sure the resolution fits the (in this case) 360 by 360 Gear S2, S3, Sport, or Galaxy Watch resolution. This can also be done with digital video asset frames and 3D animation; the same concepts, terms, and techniques covered in this chapter apply to both asset types. We will also make sure to optimize the PNG files into a PNG8 (Indexed) smaller data format, as animated GIF format uses an Indexed color (up to 256 colors) data format, so doing this step is a "no brainer" as well, to save on the watch face download size (especially if the animation uses a lot of frames). This animation uses only **15 frames** (0 through 14), so it will play four times per minute, if it cycles continuously. I will show you how to make it play once a minute, as we learn all of the ins and outs of the Galaxy Watch Designer Animation Component in this chapter. Start by opening the GIF file that's part of the book's code download (Figure 5-1).

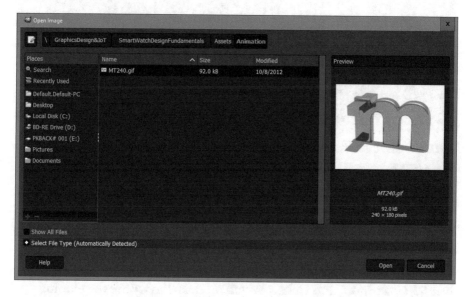

Figure 5-1. *In GIMP, use File ➤ Open to find the MT240.gif in Open Image dialog*

Figure 5-2 shows 15 frames in GIMP's **Layer** pane. You can show each frame of the animation in the **Preview** area by using the layer **Eye Icon**.

Figure 5-2. *Use the Eye (visibility) Icon to show each animation state on its layer*

Turn off your layer **Eye Icon** for each of your animation frame's layers from 2 through 14 so that you are only looking at the Background (Frame 1) layer, which is shown in Figure 5-2. Since this animation isn't using the correct size (360 by 360 pixels) or aspect ratio (1:1) to use for the Gear S2, Gear S3, Gear Sport, and Galaxy Watch models that we are developing this watch face design for, we need to use the **Image ➤ Canvas Size** menu sequence to access the **Set Image Canvas Size** dialog, shown in Figure 5-3.

Since we want to continue to use the White background color, set the Fill with: drop-down selector to **White** and Resize Layers: drop-down selector to **All Layers** at the bottom of the dialog, to determine how your Canvas Size will be propagated across all the layers in the GIMP document, as Canvas Size is a "Global" document operation and not a "local" per layer operation (so we only have to do this once!).

Set the expanded Canvas Size **Width** and **Height** to 360 by 360, and then use the **Y** (spacing) Up/Down Arrow UI in the **Offset** section of the dialog to set the MT animated subject matter in the center of the new 360 by 360 animation size. Do not use the Center button as the MT is not quite centered in the original animation sequence, as you can see in Figures 5-2 and 5-3. To complete the operation, click the **Scale** button.

Figure 5-3. *Use Set Canvas Size dialog to scale the animation to fit watch faces*

Once you scale the canvas, you scale the entire animation asset and all of its layers, which will push many of your Layer previews off the screen, as the Layers themselves become thicker (taller) and the 14 frame layers will no longer fit in the Layer pane so that you can see them all. To fix this, click the left-facing arrow at the top-right corner of the Layer pane (shown encircled in Red, in Figure 5-4) and drop down the Layer pane configuration menu, which allows Layer pane customization.

Select the **Preview Size** menu option to drop down the **Preview Size Sub-Menu,** and reduce the Layer Preview Icon Size to the **Medium** value, at which point all 14 of the layers will again fit into the Layer pane because the smaller preview icon will allow each layer to again become thinner (less tall). This will allow more of the project layers to be viewed.

The reason you may want to do this is because in the next step, we will go through and select each layer frame and then use the **File ➤ Export As** menu sequence, to export (convert) each frame of this animated GIF file that we imported to PNG8 Indexed Color. This turns a GIF into a PNG8 animation frame asset, which we will later import into the Galaxy Watch Design software and use to create your animated watch face design. Before we do that, let's check the color depth of this project to see if we need to convert to Indexed color depth.

Figure 5-4. *Use the Layer pane configuration drop-down and select Medium Preview*

Drop down the **Image ➤ Color ➤ Mode** menu you learned about in Chapter 2, and see if your GIMP project is using a color depth of RGB (true color) or Indexed Color (8-bit color). Since you imported animated GIF frames, GIMP correctly set your GIMP project mode to **Indexed**, as that is what a GIF file uses by default (always).

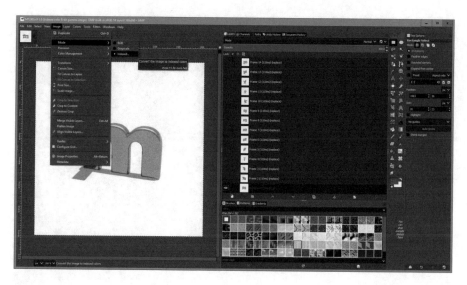

Figure 5-5. *Check Image* ➤ *Mode* ➤ *Color Depth to set to Indexed or RGB 24-bit*

Note that if the color mode had been RGB, we would have at this point set it to be Indexed, to optimize the animation data. This animation asset is perfect for optimization as it only uses White, Gray, and Gold, so spreading these across 256 different color values (especially for the gold M element) is going to work well as there are about 250 shades of gold that can be used to make the 3D M photo-realistic. Indeed, even when using the Indexed color depth (mode), the animation frames look like they are using 24-bit color (true color) depth, which is the point of using Indexed color.

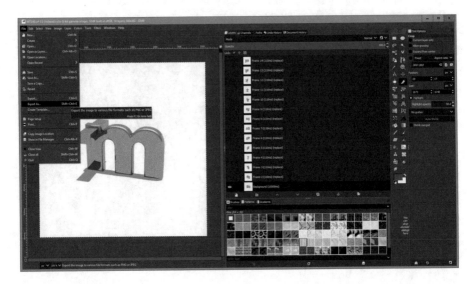

Figure 5-6. *Select the first animation frame layer and use File ➤ Export As menu*

The next step is to select one frame (layer) at a time, so we can keep track of what we are doing and show in GIMP what data we want to export into each numbered PNG8 animation file container.

Now that the Mode is set to Indexed, the work process for doing this for each layer would be to select the layer, use the File ➤ Export As menu to open the Export Image dialog shown in Figure 5-7, and export anim1.png through anim14.png files into the /**Assets**/**Animation** folder.

Also notice on the right side of Figure 5-7 that the drop-down selector in the Export Image as PNG dialog is set to the **automatic** pixel format (and not one of the RGB format options), to ensure that the PNG is exported using your project's Indexed color depth mode or format.

Figure 5-7. *Export the first frame anim1.png with automatic pixel format selected*

After you select layers 2 through 14 and go through the same work process to export (convert) aGIF asset frames to numbered PNG8 files which can be imported into Galaxy Watch Designer (as can JPEG), you will end up (on frame 14 export) with what is shown in Figure 5-8.

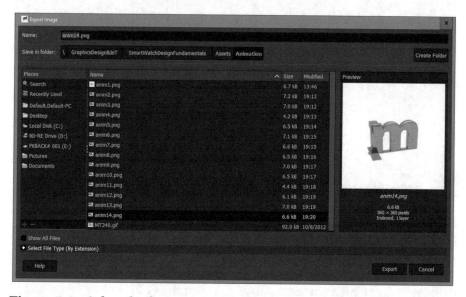

Figure 5-8. *Select the first animation frame layer and use File ➤ Export As menu*

You can click all 14 of the PNG frames in the dialog and use the preview on the right to check the animation logo position, resolution, and color depth data in real time, using the Export dialog's functionality.

Creating an Animated Watch Face

Now it's time to launch Galaxy Watch Designer and create an animated watch face design, as we have the assets in the optimized PNG8 format desired for creating animated watch faces. Notice when you start up the GWD software that it uses one of your previous watch face designs in the start-up screen, which is pretty cool, so I decided to showcase this in Figure 5-9 as it shows your watch face design in a real smartwatch. Notice I am using the latest beta version (1.6.1) which may get updated as I write the next nine chapters of the book at the end (Q4) of 2018.

Figure 5-9. *Launch GWD; notice the start-up screen shows your Hybrid Watch Face!*

This same Hybrid Watch Face design is also now shown in the **New Project** dialog which comes up after you start the GWD software, as you can see at the top of Figure 5-10.

Let's select **New**, at the top right, and create your new animated watch face from scratch, using animation as the watch face background and different Index and Watch Hand components, to get some practice building watch faces with this software. Name your animated watch face design project **CH5_Anim_Watch_Face,** and select Gear S2, S3, Sport, and Galaxy Watch 360 pixel format, and then click **OK** to create the project.

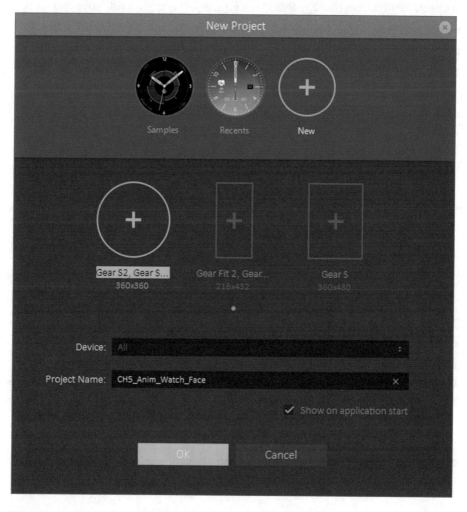

Figure 5-10. *Select the first animation frame layer and use File ➤ Export As menu*

The first thing to do is to click the Animation Component (I will forego an empty GWD screenshot which you can see in Chapter 1 in Figure 1-5 if you wish) to insert the Animation assets in the furthest back Z-order Layer in the Timeline pane (what I term the "backplate" in my other books covering digital compositing pipeline design).

The first dialog which you will encounter when you do this is the **Import Animation** dialog, shown in Figure 5-11, which informs you that the files appear to be a sequence of an image (which we learned is the definition of animation). Since this is correct, select the **Yes** button and continue on with the process of adding an animation to the layer stack.

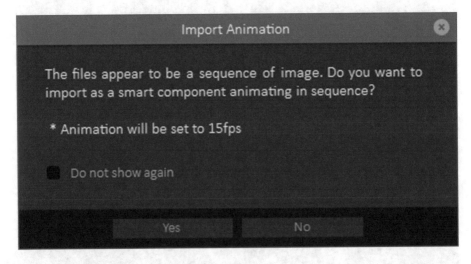

Figure 5-11. *Select the first animation frame layer and use File ➤ Export As menu*

Many savvy designer or developers out there will be wondering "since I have not shown GWD my numbered assets as yet, how does it know to display this (albeit correct) dialog?" The answer is contained in the next Open dialog which will come up, which is shown in Figure 5-12.

Figure 5-12. *GWD places us at the installed /res/Animation assets HDD location*

We can now see that GWD is configured to look in the resource (res) Animation folder for animation resources installed with GWD. Since we want to use our own animation, we need to navigate to your own assets folder and animation assets subfolder, shown in Figure 5-13 as far as my own HDD is concerned, and **Shift-Select-All** of these numbered files and then use the **Open** button to import this animation.

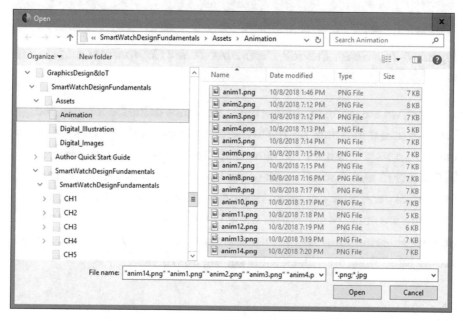

Figure 5-13. *Shift-Select the animation series files and click Open to import them*

Figure 5-14 shows the Animation 1 layer added to the Timeline pane and shows the addition of the 360_decorative Index Component as well.

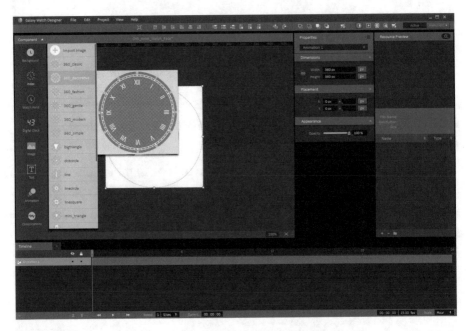

Figure 5-14. *Select the 360_decorative Index Component and add it to Timeline*

Next, we are going to change the appearance of the Decorative 360 Index to turn it into dark purple to match up better with the Gold MT logo animation, as you can see in Figure 5-15. To do this, as you've learned in Chapters 3 and 4, scroll down to the Appearance sub-section of the Properties pane after you select the Index 1 Component layer inside of the Timeline pane, which is also shown in Figure 5-15. Set the Hue to -60 degrees Hue rotation, and max the Saturation out at 100%, and darken the Purple by adding some black value setting this to -50.

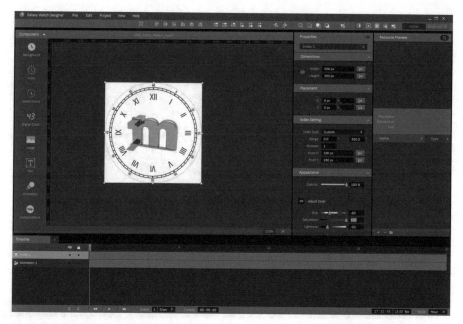

Figure 5-15. *Color the Index Purple in the Appearance section to offset the Gold*

Next, let's find some cool minimalist watch face hour and minute hands that will work with this design and not cover up the animation too much. The simple hour and minute hands are a thin line, outside of the middle of the watch face screen, so these will work well with this design, that is, with a couple of tweaks.

Click the Watch Hand Component icon to bring up the Watch Hand menu, and add a **simple_min** minute hand component, as shown in Figure 5-16. Let's use Opacity to help integrate this minute hand with the animation, so that the center pivot dot does not obscure the animation.

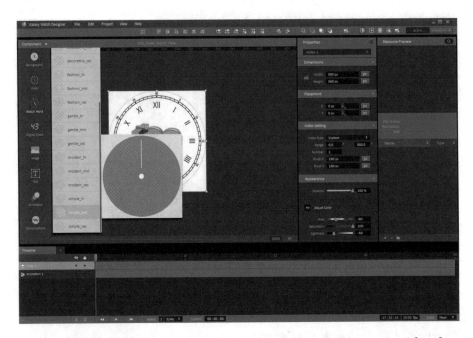

Figure 5-16. *Select the simple_min Watch Hand Component for the minute hand*

What is interesting to note about the nature of **Opacity**, and this holds true in Photoshop CS, GIMP 2.10.6, Fusion 9, Resolve 15, and many other compositing pipelines, is that the black will look transparent against the 3D rendered Gold Metal MT Logo, which looks great, and yet the Minute Hand line component still composites (renders) as black (or a super dark gray) against the white portions of this watch face design, which is precisely what we were all hoping would happen.

We want the Hour Hand to be Dark Purple so that we can see it overlay the Black Minute Hand (since they are both razor thin, which will look good with this particular Index and watch face design) and so that it matches the Solid Gold and Dark Purple (Los Angeles Lakers) colors.

To make the Minute Hand Black, move the Lightness slider over to Black to turn the White Minute hand Black. To reduce the Opacity, slide that slider to the left as well, until the Minute Hand still looks Black but the dot over the Animation Gold Logo looks as transparent as you can get it without the Minute Hand looking too gray. The optimal value was about 33%, or one third opaque, and two thirds translucent. Amazingly, even at only 33% opaque, the Minute Hand still looks Black!

Figure 5-17. *Make the Minute Hand Black and set Opacity to 33% and Lightness to -100*

Next, let's add the Hour Hand Component to this watch face design and make it dark Purple to match up with the Index Purple color we have opted to use (Dark Blue or Dark Green would work as well), and we will also make our matching Always-On Watch Face Design Green on Black with White Watch Hand analog components which will really "pop" off the screen, be quite readable, and transition well to Gold and Purple on White background color.

To make this next component an addition to the watch face design, click the Watch Hour Component, and select the **simple_hr** menu item to insert it into the design. Notice that the simple hour hand floats in the white areas outside of the Gold animated logo element and inside of the Roman Numerals of the antique-looking watch face index component.

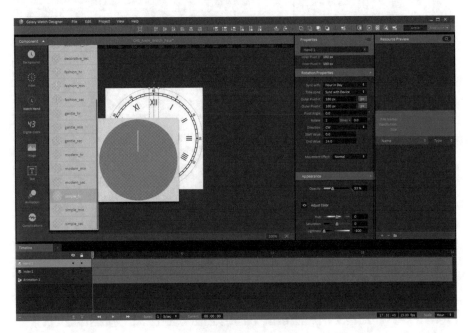

Figure 5-18. *Select the Watch Hour icon and the simple_hr Hour Hand option*

To color the Hour Hand dark Purple, we will again go into the Appearances section of the Properties pane and set the Hue slider to a rotational value of -35 degrees, while darkening the Lightness by 40% using a -40 value, and, again, by maxing the Saturation, to get the most Purple color possible, by increasing the Saturation by (to) 100%.

Notice I also renamed the Hour Hand and Minute hand layers as we learned how to do earlier in the book and left the Animation and Index Component layers with the names that Galaxy Watch Designer assigned to them, Animation 1 and Index 1, respectively.

I have chosen to use thin lines for the Watch Hour Components because a 3D animated background and roman numerals Index design components are somewhat "heavier" than our previous Hybrid Watch Face design components.

For this reason I wanted to "balance out" the watch face design by using the "lighter" Simple Hour and Simple Minute Watch Hand Components which were available in Galaxy Watch Designer for this design. You could also create and import your own Watch Hand components if you wish, which we'll look at how to do later on.

Figure 5-19. *Rename the Hour and Second Hand layer; set the Hour hand to purple*

Now that we have the watch face design matching the Animation Component (Frame) fairly well, let's set our focus back on the Animation and see how we get into the Animation Component assets (frames) and how we set the duration for these frames as well as how we preview the Animation as part of the watch face.

This first thing that will work is to drag the frame indicator at the top of the Timeline (gray bars) indicator (look for a small blue rectangle at the top-right corner of the Timeline layer stack). If you do this, you will see both the Watch Hand Components and the Animation assets will animate in the watch face Preview pane in Galaxy Watch Designer.

To really get a good look at your Animation Frame Assets, you will need to double-click the Animation 1 Layer, which will open that layer into its own pane at the bottom of GWD as shown in Figure 5-20.

Notice at the bottom of the Timeline area, there is a Repeat drop-down selector which is set to Forever. If you want to see the animation loop forever at 15 FPS, simply use the Play button at the bottom left of the Timeline area, and the animation will render smooth as silk in the Preview area for you.

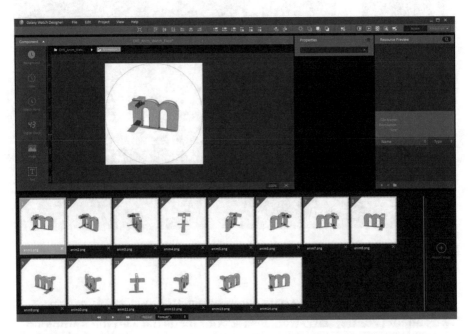

Figure 5-20. Double-click the Animation 1 layer to open it and see the frame data

Let's see what other options are available in the **Repeat** drop-down selector, by clicking on the right side and bringing up the menu of options, which is shown at the bottom of Figure 5-21, contained in a Red square.

As you can see, there are watch time-based options for changing the frames of the animation based on time elements. These include a once per second option, which I have selected, as well as once per minute and once per hour options. Expect more options to be added to this menu as the Galaxy Watch Designer software comes out with later versions, which it may have already by the time you get this book!

The latter two options would be great for animation frames that change during the hour or frames that change during the day, so that your watch face background is always unique. Pretty cool options in place already, if you ask me.

Remember that you can use the Play transport buttons as well as the interactive watch face design Frame Preview Slider at the top of the Timeline pane (looks like a little blue rectangle with a line coming down out of it but is only available when the Timeline has layers in it).

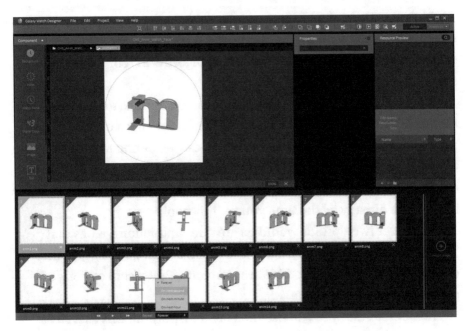

Figure 5-21. *Click the Repeat Mode Selector, and select on-next-second option*

Next, let's take a closer look at how to close up this Animation Component layer assets' viewing and editing mode and go back to the watch face design mode.

Notice at the top left of the Galaxy Watch Designer software user interface that a **CH5_Anim_Watch_Face ➤ Animation** selector has appeared in Figures 5-20 through 5-22 where the Animation assets editing was open. This is the path to close that open pane and return to the Timeline Layers pane.

Click the CH5_Anim_Watch_Face to return to the primary watch face editing view, which you can see back in place if you look ahead to Figure 5-22, where we start creating the necessary Always-On version of the watch face design, which we will create using Green and White Indexed 3-bit colors (since the watch hands use very few pixels) and using a mere 3.5% of OPR power overhead.

Since our 3D animation is likely to use a lot of power when the user is in the Active (wrist turned over) mode, we should include an optimized (low OPR) Always-On Low-color watch face mode with this watch face design to balance all power consumption for the watch face.

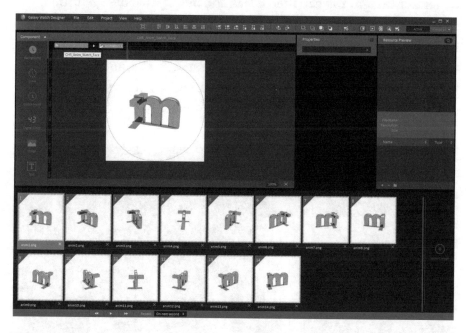

Figure 5-22. *To exit Animation Layer asset editing, click CH5_Anim_ Watch_Face*

Click the **Generate Always-On State** icon at the top right of the Galaxy Watch Designer software by Run, and select both the **Low Color** and **High Color** modes, in case you want to design both modes to span all Gear and Galaxy watch models, and then click the blue **Enable** button.

This will enable the **Always-On button** on the upper right of the GWD software, so that it will drop down the menu for selecting between Low color and High Color modes, as we did in the previous chapter, so that you will be able change the watch face design mode that the GWD software is in, by simply clicking on that button as we did in the previous chapter. What happens when you click this icon is that the Galaxy Watch Designer software uses the current (Active) watch face design, currently the Animated Watch Face project, and creates the matching Always-On watch face design. You can then tweak and modify that design further, as you please. In this case, an Always-On face with Red Hour hand and a Black Minute Hand and Black Index was created, so I had to modify the appearance of these, to use White for the Watch Hands, and Green for the Index. Therefore, the Green turns to Purple, and the White turns to Black, when Active mode kicks in (when the user rotates their wrist).

Figure 5-23. *Click the Enable Always-On Mode icon at the top right of GWD*

Once you click this Always-On Watch Face Generation and Enabler button, a Notice dialog, shown in Figure 5-24, will appear. This will advise you that this Always-On watch face will be created using the current watch face design and that you can then modify that as needed.

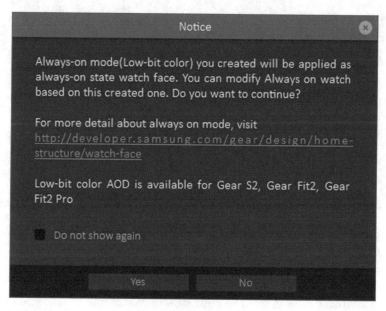

Figure 5-24. *Click Yes in the Notice dialog, to create Always-On*

The Always-On watch face that GWD created for me was not an optimal design, so I selected White for the Watch Hands, as they used very few pixels, and Green for the Index, as it does use a lot of pixels, and using RGB values use the least OPR. Green is the brightest of the RGB pixel colors on a Black background, as you can see in Figure 5-25.

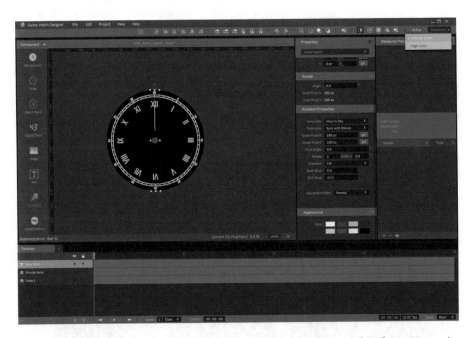

Figure 5-25. *Create Always-On with Green Index and White Hour/ Minute Hands*

Use File ➤ Save on the CH5_Anim_Watch_Face project, and answer **Yes** to the Notice dialog, seen in Figure 5-26, which will advise you of the version compatibility between GWD 1.6 and earlier versions.

Figure 5-26. *Save Anim_Watch_Face project by answering Yes to Notice dialog*

Congratulations, you have created an Animated Watch Face. Although this is a fairly advanced watch face design, there are many more advanced features in the Galaxy Watch Designer which we have yet to cover in the next nine chapters of this book.

Even though, in only five chapters, you have created Analog and Digital watch faces already, as well as Hybrid and even Animated watch faces, there are still many far more advanced features to cover over the next nine chapters, including weather, sensors, conditional features, and of course testing and deployment, among other things.

As you can see, becoming a professional watch face designer and developer is not quite as easy as it looks!

Summary

In this chapter, we took a closer look at how to accomplish adding animated elements into your watch face design. We use an animated GIF image that I used for my Mind Taffy logo. We first looked at animation concepts and formats used in the first sections of the chapter, where we learned about frames, FPS, PNG8, and animated GIF, as well as animation mathematics which basically affect playback speed. Next, we looked at how to extract frames from an animated GIF asset in GIMP 2.10 and ready them for use in Galaxy Watch Designer as PNG8 Indexed color image assets.

Next we looked at how to create an animated watch face design by importing these PNG8 animation frame assets, as well as how to edit these individual animation frames using these PNG8 assets inside the Timeline pane and how to set playback characteristics for these assets.

Finally, we create an Always-On watch face design, so that we can publish the animated watch face onto an actual watch or to the Samsung RTL (Remote Testing Lab) website.

CHAPTER 6

Smartwatch Design Testing: Software and Hardware Testing

In this sixth chapter of the *Smartwatch Design Fundamentals* book, let's look at testing your watch face design. There are several ways of testing your watch face design, including inside the Galaxy Watch Designer software using the **Run** (**Play Icon**) feature, in a Samsung Tizen Developer Testing Website (which is considered software-based testing) called **The Remote Test Lab**, and on Samsung smartwatches.

The first part of the chapter will go over software-based testing, which can be done in the Galaxy Watch Designer software. We'll look at the Run (Emulator), Run (Smartwatch), Build, and Distribute (Store) icon group at the top right of the Galaxy Watch Designer software package.

After that we will take a look at how to sign up for testing in the Remote Test Lab online, which is hosted by Samsung Electronics. This is available to registered Samsung Tizen Developers (up to 20 hours of usage per day across a variety of Samsung devices including tablets, smartphones, iTV Sets and smartwatches) running the Tizen and Android OSes.

© Wallace Jackson 2019
W. Jackson, *SmartWatch Design Fundamentals*,
https://doi.org/10.1007/978-1-4842-4369-5_6

After that we will look at a far more complicated testing process, using actual Samsung smartwatch hardware. This involved connecting the smartwatch to Galaxy Watch Designer through Wi-Fi, which means setting up IP addresses, and similarly complex networking protocols.

Software Testing: GWD and Online

If you don't have a Samsung Smartwatch, such as a **Galaxy Watch**, or a **Gear S3 Frontier**, for instance, you can still test the watch face design using a **simulator**. Those of you who are Android WEAR2 watch face designers may be familiar with using the simulators in Android Studio 3 (Intelli-J IDEA), for smartphones, tablets, smartwatches, and iTV Sets.

Galaxy Watch Designer (or Tizen Studio 2.5, for more advanced design) also has a built-in simulator for testing smartwatches, which can be accessed via the **Play** icon next to the Create Always-On icon, which we used in Chapter 5. We look at this in the next section of this chapter.

There's another way to test smartwatch designs via the Internet, on Samsung's Remote Testing Lab (RTL) website. We will be looking at all of these tools in this chapter, for those readers who do not have access to Samsung (Gear S, Gear 2, S2, S3, Fit, Fit2, or Galaxy Watch) smartwatch hardware that they can test on. Testing on hardware is also more advanced (difficult), as it involves setting IP settings (networking), so that the smartwatch hardware can be "seen" by the GWD software.

Testing in the Galaxy Watch Designer

The fastest and most seamless way to test your watch face design is right there in your Galaxy Watch Designer, where you are working on creating your watch face. There are a collection of five icons, grouped together at the top right of the software, which allow you to test, build, and distribute your Always-On and Active watch face designs with the click of a button (well, it's an icon, actually). Let's start the Galaxy Watch Designer and select the **CH5_Anim_Watch_Face** project from the **Recents** section of the New Project dialog, as is shown in Figure 6-1. Now that we have created more watch faces, the dialog is getting better at loading previous watch face design projects we have created, and you can open them back up, with a click on the watch face, which is really handy for this chapter covering testing your watch face designs.

Figure 6-1. *Open the CH5_Anim_Watch_Face project in the New Project dialog*

At the top right of the Galaxy Watch Designer software, shown encircled in red in Figure 6-2, are the five publishing-related icons. To test the watch face design in GWD, use (click on) the second one from the left, which has a Play transport (right-facing arrowhead) on the icon. The four icons next to that are to **Run on Device** (third icon), **Build** the Watch Face (fourth icon) executable, and **Distribute** to Store (fifth icon) so that a watch face design can be sold to the public once you're done.

Figure 6-2. *Icons for Testing, Building, and Distributing (Store) are at the top right*

Click the **Run** icon, to test the in-software testing emulator, seen in Figure 8-3. The emulator is tall and thin, with a screenshot (left) and an Always-On state selector button at the top, under that is a simulation of the watch face design running with your current system's time and date, along with some pixel resolution and device (and your OPR percentage, if you are in the Always-On mode) information underneath that.

In the light gray (bottom half) of this watch face emulator (a Run dialog) are sliders for testing: Time, Year, Month, Day, and 12 Hour and 24 Hour modes. At the bottom of the Run dialog there is a **Close** button, which does much the same thing as using the (white) round "X" closing the dialog icon, always located at the top-right-hand corner of the dialog.

I clicked the **Always-On to Active Mode Toggle** icon (half white and half black/gray), and I observed (in the first two panes of Figure 6-3) that **both my Hour and Minute Hands** were referencing the same time. To fix this bug, which showed up here in testing mode, I used the **Close** button and returned to the Galaxy Watch Designer software to fix this.

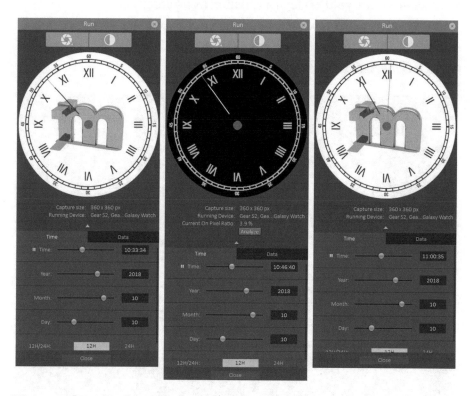

Figure 6-3. *Use the Run Icon to test Active and Always-On watch face modes*

To see where the problem is in the GWD software, you will need to click both the Hour Hand and Minute Hand layers in your Timeline pane, and look in your Properties pane, under the **Rotation Properties** sub-section, as seen in Figure 6-4. Notice that for the Minute Hand the Rotation Property for the selected Minute Hand is **Sync with: Hour in Day**, instead of set to be **Sync with: Minute in Hour**, as it should be.

Set this to the correct value using the drop-down menu selector, and again click the Play (Run) icon at the top of GWD to test the design in the emulator dialog. As you can see on the right-hand side of Figure 6-3, the watch face now has a purple minute hand and a black hour hand, which emanate from the gold 3D logo animation as desired.

We need to make sure (as you learned in Chapter 4) that any changes made to the Active watch face design also get made to the Always-On watch face design. Let's do this, and test it next.

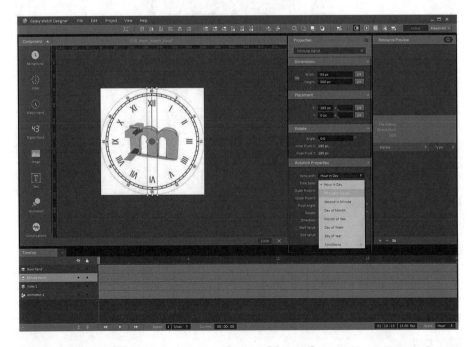

Figure 6-4. *Fix the Active Second Hand layer by setting Minute In Watch rotation*

To see if there is a problem with the Always-On state in the GWD software, you will need to select Low-bit Color from the Always-On button menu and then click both the Hour Hand and Minute Hand layers in the Timeline pane, and look in the Properties pane, under the **Rotation Properties** sub-section. Notice that for the Minute Hand the Rotation Property for the selected Minute Hand is **Sync with: Hour in Day**, instead of set to be **Sync with: Minute in Hour**, as it should be.

Set this to the correct value using the drop-down menu selector, and again click the **Play (Run) icon** at the top of GWD to test the Always-On design in the emulator dialog.

It is no surprise that you will need to make the same corrections that you made in the Active state version to the Always-On version of this watch face design. As you can see, in Figure 6-5, the same correction needs to be made for the Always-On version to show two different watch face hands at two different times when you test the watch face using the Run (Play) icon. Do this now.

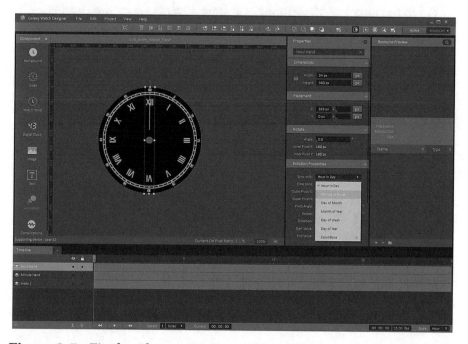

Figure 6-5. *Fix the Always-On Second Hand layer using Minute In Watch rotation*

As you will see, your Always-On watch face design now has two different hands for Hours and Minutes, rather than both hands being stacked on top of each other and locked together, so we've fixed this problem and are ready to go to the next step in watch face testing!

Developer Certification: Required to Test

To be able to use the Samsung Remote Test Lab online, you must be signed up as a Samsung Developer. There are two levels, one is singular (private person, or individual developer) and the other is corporate (group of people creating Tizen, and/or Android watch faces and apps, for sale to the public). You can sign up without having to declare your commercial (or noncommercial) status, which we will do next, so you can use Samsung RTL (not the same as the Right-To-Left language direction) if you wish. You can convert your status at any time!

Go to the `https://developer.samsung.com/signup` page, and click the "Join Samsung Account now" link, seen at the bottom of Figure 6-6.

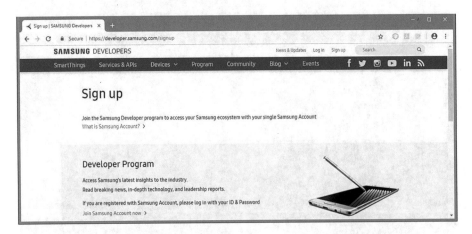

Figure 6-6. *Fix the Always-On Second Hand layer using Minute In Watch rotation*

Read through the Terms and Conditions, Terms of Services, and Samsung Privacy Policy (all provided as links), and then click the blue **AGREE** button, as shown in Figure 6-7, to begin your sign-up process.

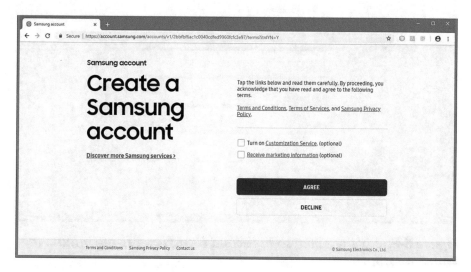

Figure 6-7. *Fix the Always-On Second Hand layer using Minute In Watch rotation*

Fill out the form, seen in Figure 6-8, and then submit it to Samsung.

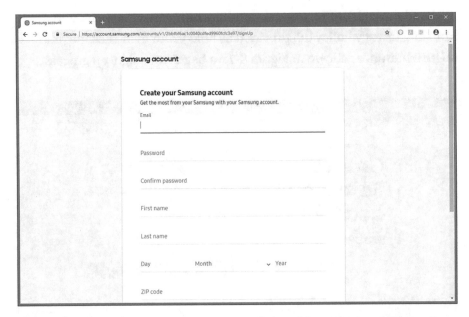

Figure 6-8. *Fix the Always-On Second Hand layer using Minute In Watch rotation*

After you verify the personal data in the form by clicking the link sent to your e-mail address, you will see the page shown in Figure 6-9.

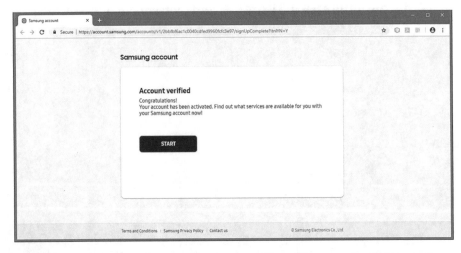

Figure 6-9. *Fix the Always-On Second Hand layer using Minute In Watch rotation*

Once you click the blue **START** button shown in Figure 6-9, you will be taken to the Cloud Device Farm, as shown in Figure 6-10, where you'll click the Galaxy Watch section to go to a Remote Testing Lab, for Galaxy Gear Sport, S3, Gear Fit 2, and Galaxy Watch hardware testing.

Figure 6-10. *To access Galaxy Watch on the Cloud Device Farm, click its icon*

As you can see in Figure 6-11, you can test on Samsung's Gear Sport, S3, Fit 2, and Galaxy Watch. Let's learn how to build a TPK next, as this is what is used for RTL tests, as well as testing on real watches.

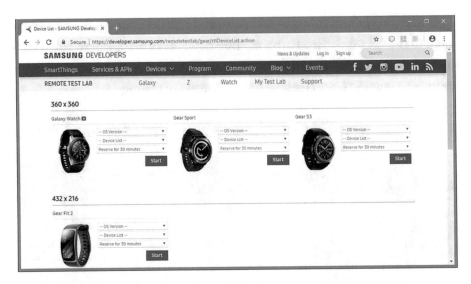

Figure 6-11. *A Remote Test Lab allows you to test TPK builds,
remotely, online*

Frames also contain pixels, for each image frame, which means that
the animation asset also has a resolution, as well as an aspect ratio, and
a color depth. All of the frames in any 2D animation asset usually use the
exact same resolution, aspect ratio, and color depth, though it's possible to
mix different file formats and color depths.

Hardware Testing: Gear S3 Frontier

There are two testing icons at the top of GWD, and both use a Play (DV)
transport icon to signify a Run (Test) of the watch face design. The in-
software one (which we covered already) is just the Play arrow, and the
other, Test (Run) Using a Hardware Device, shows a Play icon on a watch
face, shown encircled in red in Figure 6-12, along with the dialog it brings
up to connect via Wi-Fi with your device directly. This part is a bit tricky,
so I'll step you through what it took for me to connect GWD to my Gear S3
Frontier visually (in Figures 6-12 through 6-20) in this section.

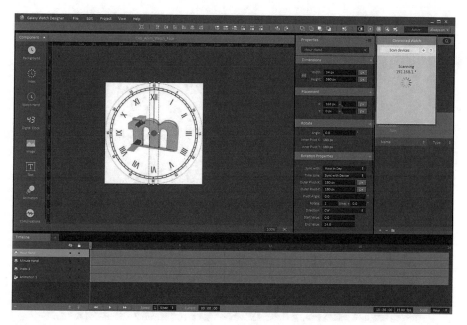

Figure 6-12. *Click the Run on Device Icon and then the Scan Devices button*

Click the **Scan Devices** button, and the dialog for connecting external hardware devices will look for your watch. If you haven't turned on debugging mode, in both the smartwatch and its paired smartphone, you might get this Notice, seen in Figure 6-13, until you have done the six things listed in the notice. Pair your phone via Samsung's Gear app, which you download into your iPhone or Android or Tizen smartphone.

Figure 6-13. *If the scan does not find device, go through the six steps in the Notice*

To get the connection working, I went into the watch gear (settings) area and found the Debug Mode and turned it on, telling the watch to work directly with the GWD software. I tried connecting again, and when that did not find the watch, I googled LGE K20V phone debug mode and followed the "tap seven times on Build Number in Phone ID section of Settings" and put my paired Android 8 phone in developer mode as well. I also made sure the watch was on (Active Mode) and tried again. Once I saw the Figure 6-14 dialog, I knew I had connected!

The reason why connecting smartwatch hardware to Galaxy Watch Designer causes battery drain is because using Wi-Fi and sending "data heavy" TPK files around takes a lot of dedicated processing, memory and Wi-Fi component power to send, receive, process, and load the watch face into memory and then put it up on the watch face screen.

Figure 6-14. *Once GWD finds the device, you'll get a battery drain warning dialog*

Select the device you want to test on, as shown in Figure 6-15.

Figure 6-15. *When the watch is connected, its model number will be shown*

Once you select your smartwatch model number, in my case one of the Gear S3 Frontier models, the GWD software will talk to the Samsung server, and see if the device has been registered. If it has not, you will see the Distributor certificate dialog shown in Figure 6-16.

Figure 6-16. *Distributor certificate dialog asks you to request Distributor certificate*

Complete and submit the Distribution Certificate Request Device Profile form seen in Figure 6-17. Note **Connected Device ID** at the top.

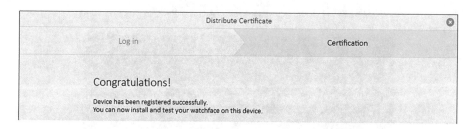

Figure 6-17. *Request Device Profile Distributor Certificate dialog you will fill out*

Once you've submitted this form with your Samsung Developer ID (e-mail) and password, you will see the dialog shown in Figure 6-18.

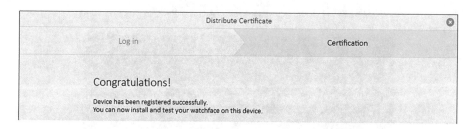

Figure 6-18. *Device submitted successfully form allows you to test on the device*

Now that you and your device are registered for development, if you click the model number you want to test, you will get the dialog called ThreadInstall tpk Check as seen in Figure 6-19. You will see this the first time you test any watch face design if a TPK (Tizen Package) has not been created for that watch face design as yet. Click the **Yes** button to create a .TPK file, and send it over to the smart watch device.

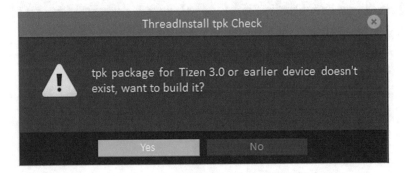

Figure 6-19. *If no TPK exists, GWD will build one for you, inside the GWD folder*

Once you create the Tizen Package file, Galaxy Watch Designer will automatically send it over to the smartwatch hardware, as well as install it and launch the watch face design on your smartwatch (in my case, a Gear S3 Frontier Model 760) for review and testing. My gold 3D animating logo spins smooth as silk on a Gear S3. I showed it to several clients, who were blown away at the quality level afforded by a Gear S3.

Figure 6-20. *You will see a progress bar of the Build, Install, and Launch Process*

At this point in time, you will have a watch face playing on your smartwatch device; in my case it was an animating Mind Taffy logo in the background of a Roman numeral watch index with thin hour and minute hands.

Online Testing: A Remote Test Lab

Now that we have a .TPK generated, let's try to get the online Remote Test Lab (Hybrid Testing) working. This is the most difficult testing solution to get working, because it starts at the GWD and also has a server-based component engineered at Samsung that has to be made to work via a JNLP app that comes from Samsung's server and runs on your desktop to create a simulation of a real smart watch. Let's revisit the Remote Test Lab, shown earlier in Figure 6-10, that we saw after we registered as developers on the Samsung website. It looks easy to utilize, but at this stage of its development, it is still a work in progress. Since I tested on my real Gear S3 Frontier smartwatch in the previous section, I chose the Gear S3 SM-R765A-KR1 (E35F) option and Tizen 3 in the Grea S3 section as well as the "Reserve for 30 minutes" option, as can be seen at the top of Figure 6-21. Click the dark blue **Start** button (1), and look at the bottom left of your browser window, where you'll see the **JNLP Web Start** file. Click the **Keep** button, and then right-click and **Open** the JNLP to launch the Java emulator application, which will call the Java 1.8 RunTime (which you need to have installed) and bring up the **Java Launch** dialog, before showing the **Remote Test Lab** dialog.

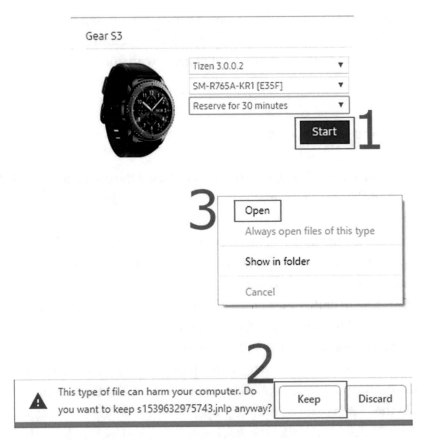

Figure 6-21. *Start the Emulator (1), Keep the JNLP download (2), and Open it (3)*

The Remote Test Lab dialog, shown in Figure 6-22, tells you the custom JNLP Web Start Application specifics, including Device Model, Tizen OS Version Used, Location, Time Duration, and Credits Taken from your developer account for usage. The JNLP will disconnect from Samsung's server after 30 minutes and shut itself down so pick a longer time if you need it. This JNLP application (like the Android Studio AVD emulator) emulates a smartwatch hardware device, including memory, O/S, storage, apps, your TDK application, and its screen display output in memory, and to do this takes a massive amount of memory and CPU resources (processing cycles), so don't be surprised if your production workstation's cooling fans kick into overdrive while the JNLP is running.

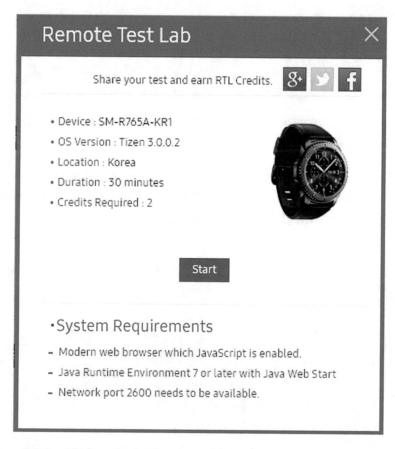

Figure 6-22. *Click a dark blue Start button to load the JNLP into system memory*

Click the dark blue Start button seen in Figure 6-22, to download the JNLP, as is seen in the **Starting Application** dialog in Figure 6-23.

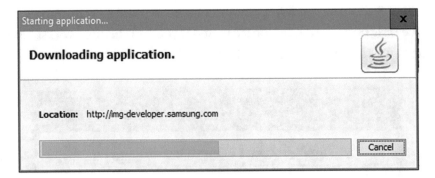

Figure 6-23. A progress dialog shows JNLP file loading into the system memory

The Java Runtime Environment (JRE) will then ask you if you want to run the application, as seen in Figure 6-24. Click the **Run** button to run the JNLP, which loads the JNLP from HDD into system memory.

Figure 6-24. The JRE will then ask you if you want to run the JNLP application

The RTL start-up screen will then appear as seen in Figure 6-25, once it's loaded in system memory, and will then connect to the RTL Server.

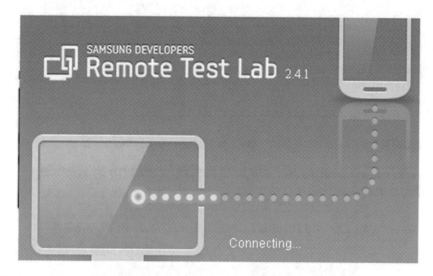

Figure 6-25. *The RTL application running from memory connecting to its server*

Next you will see a Warning dialog advising you that the service provides you with remote access to a real device and that no personal information will be collected from the device. There are bullets which tell you what NOT to do, like using personal information, PIN numbers, and the like. Click the "I understand and wish to proceed" button, seen in Figure 6-26, to launch a functional version of an emulator on the screen.

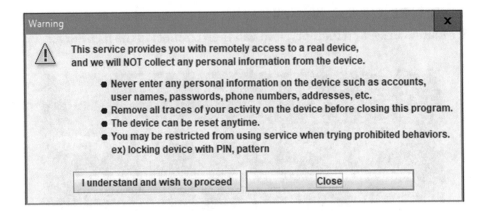

Figure 6-26. *Agree to not use personal information in Warning dialog presented*

Select your desired **Device Language**, as shown in Figure 6-27.

Figure 6-27. *Select a language from the Device Language dialog and click OK*

To load your watch face's .TPK (Tizen Package) file, which we created in Figure 6-19 and Figure 6-20, right-click the watch face and select **Test ▶ Install Application**, as is shown in Figure 6-28.

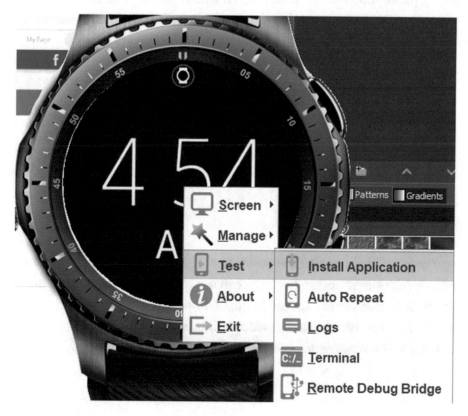

Figure 6-28. *Right-click the watch face, and select Test ▶ Install Application*

To find the TPK, which should be located in your workstation's C:/ Users/PC-Name/GearWatchDesigner/workspace folder, as shown in Figure 6-29, open your File Management Utility (for Windows this is the Windows Explorer File Manager Utility), and enter ***.tpk** in your Search field (shown highlighted in light blue at the top right). This asterisk is a "wildcard," which means "all files," whereas a question mark symbol will replace only one letter. So, to find all Android and Tizen Packages, use ***.?pk** as your search string, which would translate to mean: all files with the .apk (Android Package) or .tpk (Tizen Package) file extension.

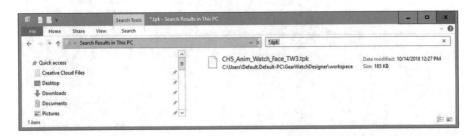

Figure 6-29. *Search your PC for *.tpk, or all files ending with the .tpk extension*

Once you have located the watch face .TPK file you want to test on your development workstation, you can use the **Open** dialog, shown in Figure 6-30, and select it for use in the Remote Test Lab application. Select the **CH5_Anim_Watch_Face_TW3.tpk** file, and click the **Open** button to load it into the **Application Manager** dialog for installation.

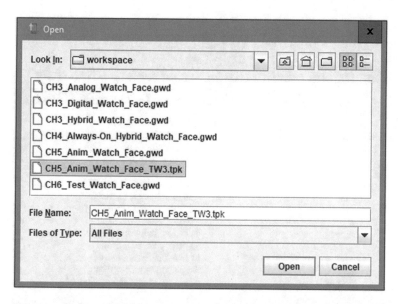

Figure 6-30. *Select TPK file for watch face design you want to test, and Open it*

The Application Manager should really list this TPK, which was just loaded into it (notice selected blank entry at the end of Figure 6-31). You'll have to use "developer smarts" and click the **Install** button to load the TPK; that's the intelligent thing to do at this point in the test process.

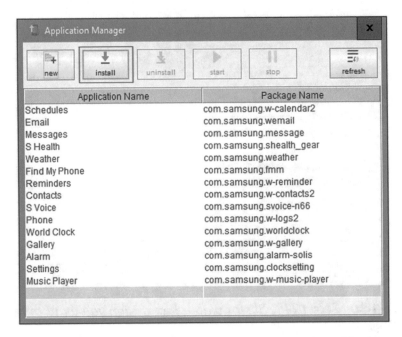

Figure 6-31. *Click the Install button, to install the TPK file that you just Opened*

Alas, I am still getting an error, shown in Figure 6-32, which is preventing me from emulating the .TPK on the RTL JNLP application.

Figure 6-32. *I'm getting errors when I run TPK, continuing to try and figure it out*

I did a search on the keywords "Samsung's Remote Testing Lab Won't Run TPK" and found a few things that others suggested in getting the emulator to work, which I need to do before I close out this chapter on testing and which doubled the figures from 22 to 45. The first thing suggested was to have (install) the latest Java, shown in Figure 6-33. This just jumped from v181 to v191, so I decided to do this next, and try again. There are some other suggestions we can try, after that upgrade.

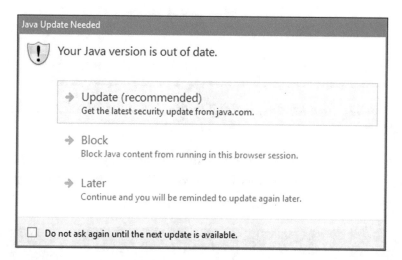

Figure 6-33. *Let's try updating Java to the latest security update from java.com*

As you can see in Figure 6-34, Java 8 Update 191 is available!

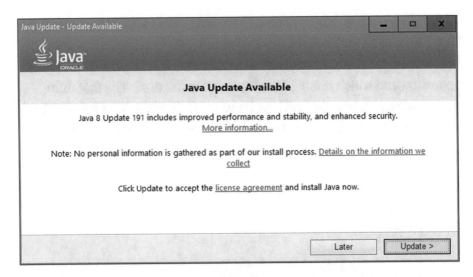

Figure 6-34. *Run Java Update; if a Java Update is available, then Update it*

Click the Update button to open the Downloading Java Installer dialog, which will show you a progress bar tracking the download of the Installer onto your hard disk drive, as shown in Figure 6-35.

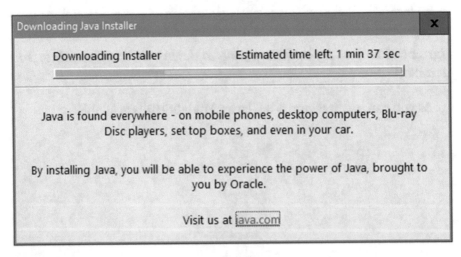

Figure 6-35. *Download the Java Installer, which is indicated by the progress bar*

Once the download finishes, you'll get a **Java Setup – Progress** dialog, showing you an Installing Java progress bar seen in Figure 6-36.

Figure 6-36. *Install the latest version of Java, also indicated using a progress bar*

I again ran the emulator with the Tizen 3 TPK (see Figures 6-21 through 6-31) and got another error message like the one shown in Figure 6-32. So I went back to Google and noticed there was a Port 2600 enablement issue I had not tried, so now I'm going to cover how to do this as well. I am not going to stop, until I have the emulator working!

In Windows, go into the **Control Panel**, and enter the **Windows Defender Firewall** Icon. Click the Advanced Tab (Button), and enter the **Advanced Security** area, where you can set up "Rules" for this firewall.

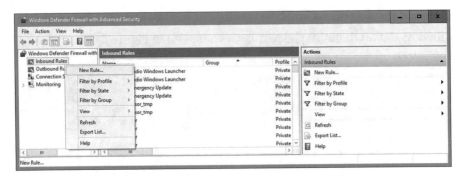

Figure 6-37. *Use Control Panel ➤ Windows Defender Firewall ➤ Advanced dialog*

Select Rule Type of **Port** and click **Next**, as seen in Figure 6-36, to define a Rule regarding **Port 2600** to open up that port in the firewall.

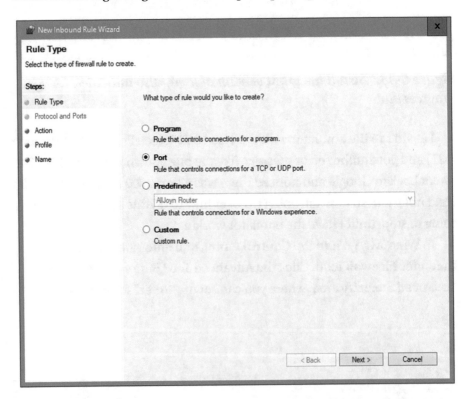

Figure 6-38. *Select the Port Rule Type, and click the Next button to continue*

Select **TCP**, specify Port **2600,** and click **Next**, as in Figure 6-39.

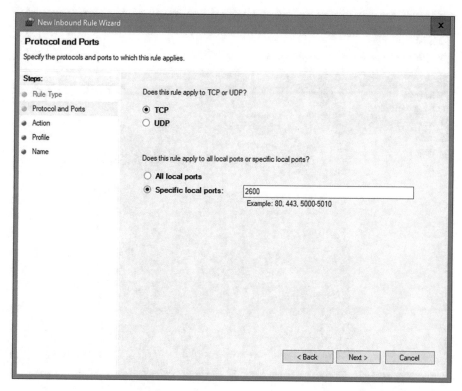

Figure 6-39. *Select TCP, specify local Port 2600, and click Next*

Click "Allow the connection" and click **Next**, seen in Figure 6-40.

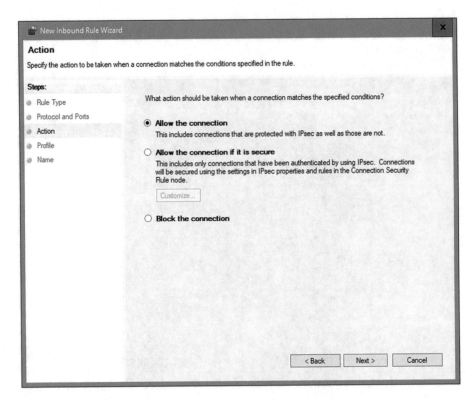

Figure 6-40. *Select "Allow the connection," and click Next to continue the setup*

Select Domain, Private, and Public, as is shown in Figure 6-41.

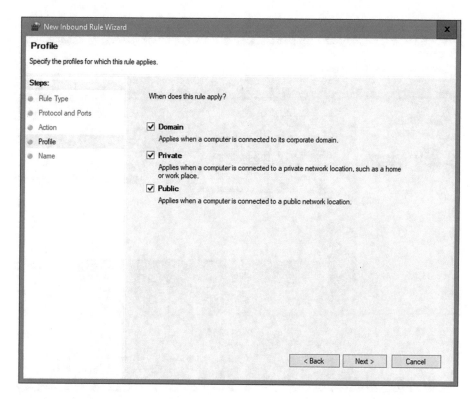

Figure 6-41. *Select Domain, Private, and Public to apply rule everywhere*

Name rule "Samsung_RTL_Port_2600," as seen in Figure 6-42.

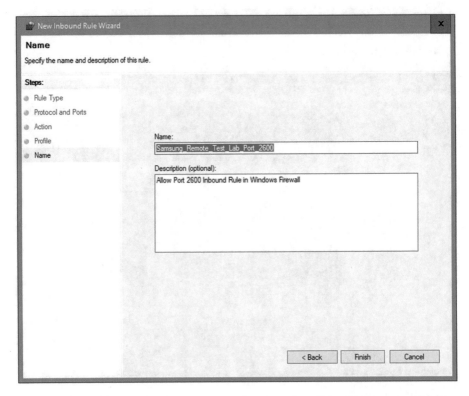

Figure 6-42. *Finish by Naming the Inbound Rule "Samsung RTL Port 260"*

Your rule will now be listed in the **Inbound Rules** pane of the **Windows Defender Firewall with Advanced Security** window, as is shown selected in blue at the top of Figure 6-43.

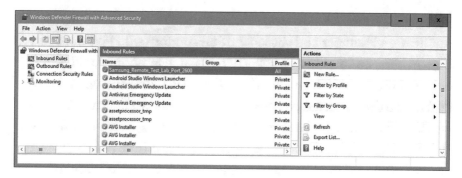

Figure 6-43. *Showing your Samsung Remote Test Lab Port 2600 Inbound Rule*

To use the latest Tizen 4.0 TPK file, I entered the Galaxy Watch Designer and generated the CH5_Anim_Watch_Face project as a Tizen 4.0 file (using the **Build** icon) to try that later version on a Galaxy Watch emulator (see the top-left hand of Figure 6-11). I also utilized the **Opera** browser this time (I had also tried Firefox previously, with zero success) and the new Java 8 u191, loaded in Figures 6-33 to 6-36. This time I got the "**App was successfully installed**" dialog, as is seen in Figure 6-44.

Figure 6-44. *After building and testing a Tizen 4 watch face, I'm getting success!*

I clicked on the **OK** button and the Galaxy Watch emulator then appeared on the screen, with its default chronometer watch face which comes preloaded with the Galaxy Watch. Maybe there is something I need to load from the Application Manager, shown on the left side of Figure 6-45, to be able to access the loaded TPK via Clock Settings.

I highlighted **com.samsung.clocksetting** at the bottom of the
Application Manager and clicked the **Start** button (with Play transport
icon, in blue) and suddenly a collection of watch faces appeared, and I
swiped these to the left, and found the CH5 watch face and tapped it to
load it, and then took the emulator screenshot, shown in Figure 6-45 on
the right-hand side. I needed to get this working to be able to finish this
chapter on testing, as there are three different ways (in GWD software, on
the hardware, and in an emulator online) to test watch face designs!

Figure 6-45.   *To select the watch face, run clocksetting application,*
and select it

As you can see, becoming that professional watch face designer
and developer is not quite as easy as it looks, given that it can become
fairly difficult to test (and install, in a store), due to watch face developer
certifications, firewalls, using Java 8 and JNLP, allowing JavaScript in a
browser, different browser versions, different servers, hosted in different
countries (KR is Korea, PL is Poland, US is USA, see Figure 6-21, top, next to
the red number one), IP settings, Enabling Developer Debugger Options on
smartwatches and smartphones, and many similar "technical landmines"

to testing on smartwatches and in emulators covered in this chapter. Smartwatch, smartphone, and iTV Set application development can be very challenging, for a number of reasons, covered in my books!

Summary

This chapter showed you how to test your watch face designs using both software (Galaxy Watch Designer Emulator and Online Samsung RTL website) and actual device hardware (in my case the Gear S3 Frontier Smartwatch from Samsung). This includes the Galaxy Watch Designer Run (emulator) Icon and dialog as well as the Samsung RTL or Remote Testing Lab, which is online, and my own Samsung Gear S3 Frontier Smartwatch device (hardware). We also looked at the work process for the **Run on Device** function for testing on a real smartwatch device, if you happened to have purchased one!

I use the Galaxy Watch Designer **Run Emulator** as well as the Samsung RTL **Remote Test Lab** website to show clients (in 3D) what their watch face design was going to look like, by running these tests, using the System **Print Screen** Key (and GIMP 2.10 Create ➤ From Clipboard), and then sending the client the screenshot, so all of this great material covered within this chapter can be utilized in your day-to-day watch face design workflow! All of the information in this chapter is important to become familiar with and to master for this very reason!

In the next chapters, we'll continue to learn about more Galaxy Watch Designer features, as well as about third-party tools, such as GIMP 2.10.8, to see how external programs can aid in your watch face design skillset and workflow.

CHAPTER 7

Smartwatch Watch Face Layer-Based Design Using GIMP

In this seventh chapter of the *Smartwatch Design Fundamentals* book, let's take your watch face design skills thus far and develop a watch face design from scratch, using all new elements that we design in GIMP 2.10.10. What we want to do is synchronize the layer compositing pipeline in GIMP 2.10 with what we are doing inside the Timeline pane in the Galaxy Watch Designer.

In the first part of the chapter, we will take that vector background that we learned how to find as a Creative Commons Zero (CC0) asset, and rendered in Inkscape in Chapter 2, so that we will have one custom background which is not part of Galaxy Watch Designer. We will design custom watch minute and seconds indicators, and hour indicators to go with these, so that we can achieve a 100% custom watch face design, which we will learn how to assemble in the next chapter of this book.

We will create this design using GIMP 2.10 compositing layers, with the same names and compositing order as we will use in the GWD Timeline pane. In this way, you will see how to use a professional image compositing software package to design and preview watch face design concepts, keeping your components in their own layers, so they can be exported for assembly inside of your Galaxy Watch Designer software.

© Wallace Jackson 2019
W. Jackson, *SmartWatch Design Fundamentals*,
https://doi.org/10.1007/978-1-4842-4369-5_7

Layer-Based Watch Face Design

Let's take a look at how to create our own custom watch face components using PNG8 and PNG32 formats. We can use an Indexed PNG8 file format for the background, as it does not need antialiasing, and then use RGBA PNG32 file formats to import the layer compositing overlays with alpha channels (for perfect compositing) for the Hour Numbers, which we will install later on, inside the Galaxy Watch Designer.

To do this we will open the vector file we optimized in Chapter 2 first, which will put it on the bottommost (background or backplate) layer in GIMP 2.10.6. Then we'll add 12 (Hour) 3D ring background elements and the Arial Black hour numbers in GIMP, align these using GIMP grid alignment tools, and finally export them as PNG32 hour indicator assets.

Creating Composite Layers in GIMP 2.10

The layer (rendering) order is important; so that is the order we will be creating using the GIMP compositing stack, with the 8-bit vector background graphic as the "backplate," or bottom layer, with the 1 through 12 hour indicators, each on their own layer, so that they can be exported as their own PNG32 files, later on in the process. Minute and Seconds indicators will be created later and placed into GWD in a way so they don't go behind your Hour Indicators (which are larger) on a watch face.

Backplate: Background Image in the First Layer

Launch GIMP, and use the **File ➤ Open** menu sequence to use the **Open Image** dialog, seen in Figure 7-1, and find the **Vortex360x360_8bit** PNG file we optimized using Inkscape and GIMP in Chapter 2. Since this is an Indexed file format (to optimize it down to 60 KB, or hundreds of times smaller than the original 4 MB vector asset), this will place GIMP into the **Indexed (8-bit) Color Mode**.

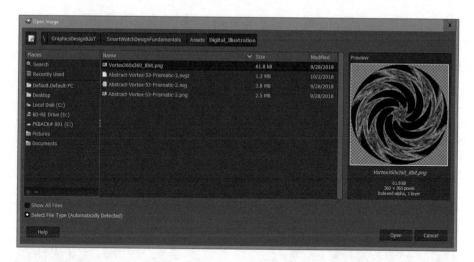

Figure 7-1. *Open the Vortex360x360_8bit PNG as the background layer in GIMP*

Later on in this work process, we'll switch GIMP 2.10 back into a 32-bit (RGBA) color mode, as your hour indicators will use a **PNG32** file format and not the PNG8 file format. Next, let's import this 32-bit black number background with a 3D steel ring around it and use it as an Hour marker (indicator). You'll find this in the **/Assets/3D/** folder in this book.

Hour Indicators: Compositing Hour Markers

To add the Hour Indicator graphic as a layer above the backplate (bottom layer), GIMP has a cool **File ➤ Open As Layer** command, seen in Figure 7-2, which will insert a 32-bit compositing element above any selected layer that you are currently working on. In this case, this is the bottommost vector graphic layer. This will place the 32-bit steel-ring black background element, and its surrounding alpha channel (transparency), right above the watch face vector background, giving you a background over which to put Hour numbers (text), which we will be creating using the GIMP Text tool, using a **32** pixel **Arial Black** font setting. This will be on the layer above the PNG32 hour marker layer, so that the hour number text can be edited as to its position, color, size, and so forth. This is the inherent power of layer-based editing. Once this is in place, you can then use the **Layer ➤ Duplicate Layer** command to create the other 11 hour markers, in a relatively short period of time.

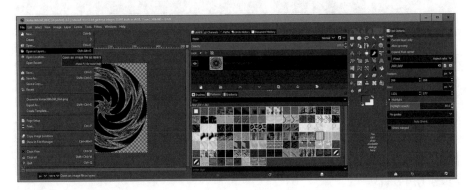

Figure 7-2. *Use Open As Layer, and add the Hour Indicator background element*

Use the **Open Image as Layers** dialog seen in Figure 7-3 to find and select the **blackhoop64.png** file in the book repository, which, as you'll see in the preview on the right, is a 3.6 KB, 64 x 64 pixel, RGBA (RGB + alpha) single-layer file. Click **Open** to insert this as Layer 2.

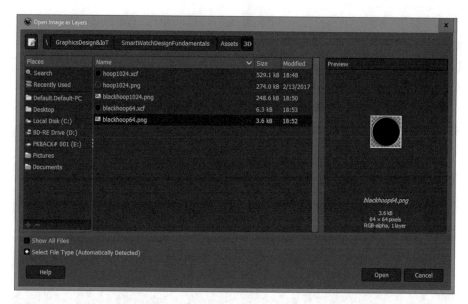

Figure 7-3. *Find the blackhoop64 PNG 3D ring with black interior color and click Open*

Click this second layer and select it, and use the **Move** (the four-arrow icon) tool to click and drag this PNG overlay on top of your watch face design, as seen in Figure 7-4. Then click the **A** (text) tool in GIMP, to add a **Text Layer** above the **blackhoop64.png** layer. Select an **Arial Black** font, set a **32** pixel size, and type **12** for the first top hour number.

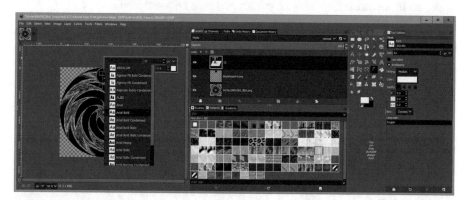

Figure 7-4. *Add Text Layer above the hour indicator; add Arial Black Hour number 12*

Next, let's duplicate what we just did, to create a 1 Hour Marker. Select the second layer, and use your **Layer ➤ Duplicate Layer** menu sequence (or right-click the Layer and use the context-sensitive pop-up menu) as shown in Figure 7-5, to duplicate this layer, and its PNG32 graphic element, on the next layer up. Select and drag this layer up, so that it is right above your 12 (Hour) Text Layer in the compositing stack.

Figure 7-5. *Use Layer ➤ Duplicate Layer command to duplicate the hour marker*

As you can see in Figure 7-6, you will now have the background image and two sets of hour marker layers to create the 12 and 1 O'clock hour markers. Once you've selected the second PNG layer, click the **A** (text) tool again, to insert another Text Layer above this second PNG.

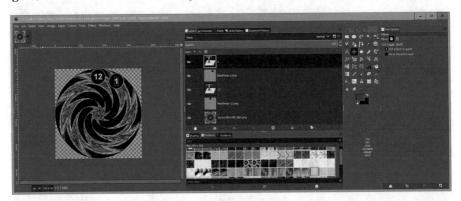

Figure 7-6. *Drag the second PNG32 layer above the Text Layer; rename both 1 and 12*

Use the now familiar **Move** tool to move the second hour marker
PNG32 asset into place at the 1 O'clock location, as seen in Figure 7-6,
and **rename** both PNG32 layers steel-ring assets as **blackhoop-1.png** and
blackhoop-12.png, and add **blackhoop-2.png** seen in Figure 7-7. The
Text Layers will **rename themselves**, after you enter your 1, 2, and 12 hour
number indicators, so you will not have to do this manually! GIMP Layer
naming works as it does in GWD (double-click and type in name).

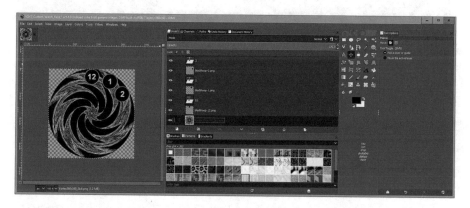

Figure 7-7. *Repeat this entire process again, to create the 2 O'clock
hour marker*

I used the **Layer Preview Size** option that you learned about to
decrease the layer icon size, so we could fit more layers in the screen
shot, and duplicated four more layers, to create six hour markers, seen
in Figure 7-8. The Text and PNG32 layers were dragged into the correct
compositing order, selected, and then positioned using the **Move** tool. Be
sure to click the Move tool on the image component you want to move,
before dragging.

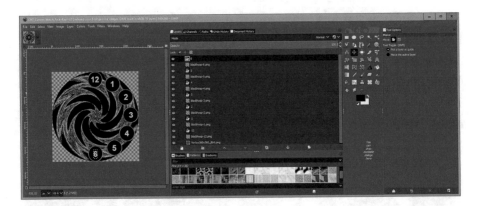

Figure 7-8. *Duplicate the first six layer pairs to create the first half of your design*

Let's close those tabs in the Patterns (Gradients, Brushes) pane, using that same small arrow which opens the Layers pane configuration options, and make room for the next 12 layers. As you can see in Figure 7-9, you can use the **Close Tab** option to close your Patterns, Gradients, and Brushes tabs. This will completely remove the bottom pane UI area, making more room for the Layers pane to expand downward to fit what we are creating there for the second half of your watch face design.

Figure 7-9. *Use the Patterns pane configuration arrow, and close the three tabs*

I'll go ahead and duplicate and roughly position all 12 of the hour markers, which you will soon see (Figure 7-10 in the next section of this chapter). This section covers using GIMP 2.10 **horizontal** and **vertical** "guides," which can be "pulled out" of the top and left "Rulers" using the **Move** tool. This allows developers to visually position (i.e., "tweak") watch face design elements within a layer-based compositing pipeline.

Aligning Watch Face Hour Elements in GIMP

To pull out alignment guides into your GIMP Preview area, seen on the left in Figure 7-10, select the Move tool (a four-tipped, NSEW arrow icon), and drag out a **dashed line** from the middle of the top ruler, as seen in Figure 7-10. I selected the Text Layer named 11 and used this Move tool to click the 11 marker and then used the arrow keys to "nudge" this number 11 hour marker into an alignment with the number 1 hour marker, one pixel at a time (each Left-Right-Up-Down arrow key tap will equal one pixel of movement of your selected image or Text element).

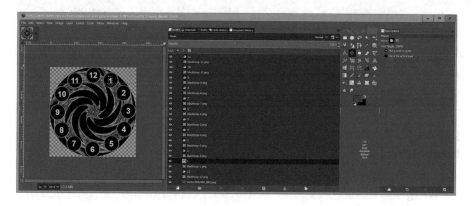

Figure 7-10. *Use a Horizontal Guide Line to align numbers 1 and 11 at the base*

Next, drag this horizontal guide exactly halfway down your watch face, by pulling on this guide line using the Move tool. Do this while you are watching the X, Y coordinates at the lower left-hand corner of GIMP, as is shown encircled in red in Figure 7-11.

When the Y coordinate reads **180**, let go of your guide, and stop the drag operation, leaving the guide line at 180 pixels, which is half of 360 and which is also shown in Figure 7-11. Next, use this watch face design horizontal centerline to position your 3 and 9 O'clock Hour Indicators, and then center the PNG32 steel-ring backgrounds and the 3 and 9 number indicators, aligning them directly across from each other.

Next, let's add a vertical center indicator so we create the center (cross) intersection of guides over our watch face design and use these to align watch face hour markers, so we have help tweaking positioning.

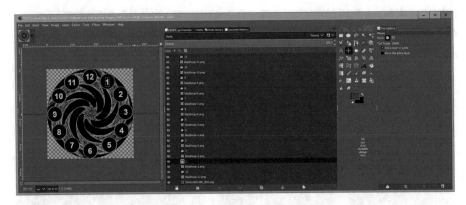

Figure 7-11. *Add a Horizontal Guide Line at Y: 180 using the lower-left pixel readout*

Next, add the vertical guide at the exact center of the watch face design by dragging a new guide out of the left-hand-side ruler, and then watch the lower left-hand corner of GIMP and position that guide at **180 X** and any Y value (in this case, 93), and drop this second guide at the exact center of your watch face compositing project. You can use this to align your 12 and

6 O'clock hour markers, and numbers, as is shown in Figure 7-12. Next, we'll add eight more guides to this watch face design compositing project, and we will clean up this new design even more.

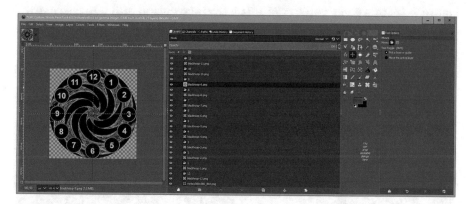

Figure 7-12. *Add a Vertical Guide Line at X:180 using the lower-left pixel readout*

As you can see in Figure 7-13, I have pulled alignment guides out of the top ruler for all of the hour markers and numbers, and these are spaced evenly apart. If you like, you can also position these by an exact number of pixels apart from each other using the technique you just learned about previously (watching the X, Y pixel position readouts).

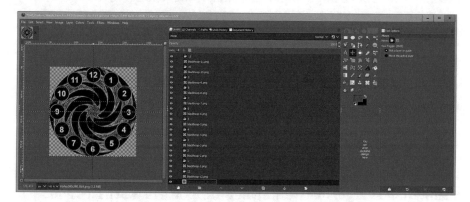

Figure 7-13. *Add five horizontal guide lines to align hour indicators (top to bottom)*

Finally, let's do the exact same thing and add four new vertical positioning guides pulled out of the left-hand ruler and position them similarly to align the hour markers vertically as well. As you can see, in Figure 7-14, this gives you a custom watch face design grid you can use to position your 1 through 12 hour indicators on your watch face design.

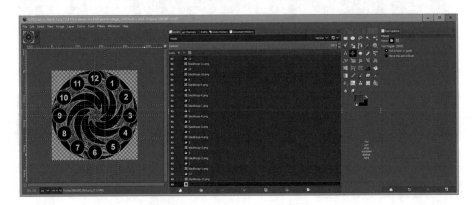

Figure 7-14. *Add five vertical guide lines to align your hour indicators (left to right)*

Once you have tweaked your hour markers into the positioning that you want to use for your watch face design, you will then be ready to export PNG32 assets with a larger alpha channel, which will serve to align these assets perfectly inside the Galaxy Watch Designer, which we will be doing in the next chapter. Remember, you can use your X, Y position readout in GIMP to perfectly position the components before you undertake the exporting process, so be sure not to start this file exporter process (seen in the next section) until your design is absolutely perfect!

Exporting PNG32 Watch Face Hour Elements

Let's clear the guides from our composition so we can see the **alpha channel** (and image) that we are going to export as a watch face hour indicator asset more clearly. GIMP has a handy **Image ➤ Guides ➤ Remove All Guides** command, which is seen in Figure 7-15, to do this.

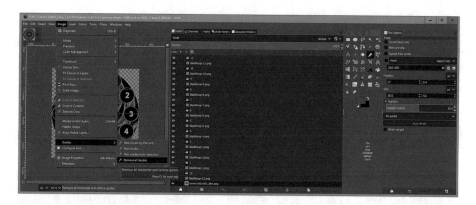

Figure 7-15. *Use Image ➤ Guides ➤ Remove All Guides to clear guides in the project*

GIMP is smart enough to look at your **Layer Visibility** during its **File ➤ Export As** work process, so what we want to do is to turn on only the layers we want to export for each hour indicator asset. Turn off your background layer at the bottom, and turn on the 12 O'clock layers, as is seen in Figure 7-16. Notice the PNG32 Alpha Channel (a checkerboard pattern) is what positions your hour indicators in the watch face design.

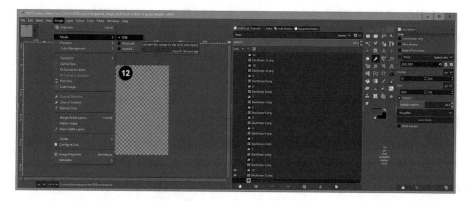

Figure 7-16. *Be sure to set Image ➤ Mode ➤ RGB (32-bit RGBA color hour hand)*

Make sure that **Image ➤ Mode ➤ RGB** (24 bit with alpha channel export of hour indicator assets is needed) is set, as seen in Figure 7-16. Use the **File ➤ Export As** menu sequence to open up an **Export Image** dialog, as shown in Figure 7-17, and make sure that you are exporting 8 bits per channel **RGBA** (32-bit: PNG32) assets, for optimal compositing quality in the Galaxy Watch Designer. Then click the **Export** button to save.

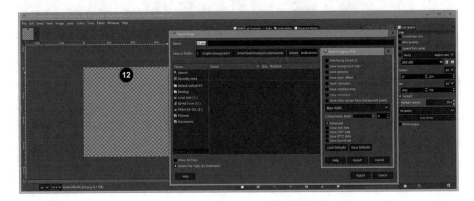

Figure 7-17. *Export the numbers to /Assets/Indicators/ folder, as PNG32 RGBA*

Follow this exact same work process for all of the hour indicator layer pairs so that the only thing that you see in each preview will be the alpha checkerboard pattern and the hour indicator asset which you are exporting. Name each asset **1.png** through **12.png**, so that they can be easily identified in the Galaxy Watch Designer, when we later assemble the assets which we are creating using GIMP 2.10.6 in this chapter.

As you can see, in Figure 7-18, when you export your last asset, all 12 PNG32 assets will be in the export dialog, where you can click each one and see it in a dialog **Preview** on the right-hand side. You can click the asset names and watch the hour indicator animate around the perimeter of the watch face much like we will be doing in the Galaxy Watch Designer when we assemble this design using that software later on. This will allow you to visually understand how powerful the approach we are taking here is, especially given how powerful this alpha channel compression is, as far as PNG32's compression algorithm is concerned. What is really cool is that you're learning how to combine these two very powerful programs (GIMP and GWD) into a watch face design workflow.

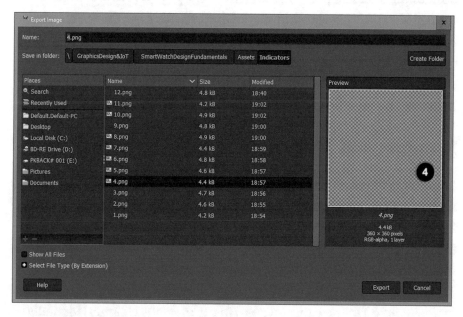

Figure 7-18.   *Click down the list of files and watch the preview animate the hours*

It's important to notice that a PNG32 image codec (Compressor-DECompressor) is doing all of the key data footprint optimization for us here, as it can turn most of the alpha channel area into just a few bytes of data due to the way a compression algorithm handles unused areas.

Notice that we are using this alpha channel data for pixel-precise positioning of our watch face design elements in GIMP, instead of using GWD Properties pane sections, with little to no data footprint "overhead" associated with this watch face component asset positioning approach!

What is also significant is there is less processing overhead by the smartwatch and Tizen 3.0 (or 4.0) code, regarding pixel positioning within the watch face design code, as the alternate way of doing this, which you can also try, to gain more experience with the Galaxy Watch Designer software, is to export these hour indicators without this alpha channel positioning data and position them in GWD using the Properties pane (using its X and Y pixel positioning setting). In this case, the watch face code will calculate and position the hours instead of overlaying the image composite layers at 0, 0 (as these are all 360 pixels) and having the assets do the positioning. Next, let's create your Seconds and your Minutes Indicators for your unique watch face design, also using GIMP.

Seconds and Minutes: Other Indicators

Let's create the seconds indicator using a 3D blood red sphere which moves around the perimeter (edge) of the watch face and then the minutes indicator, which will be a 3D gold arrowhead, which also moves around the perimeter (edge) of the Galaxy Watch, which has minutes printed on the watch bezel, which this gold arrowhead will point to. This will be a **Tizen 4.0** watch face, since that is what is currently working as an emulator in the Remote Testing Lab, as we saw in the previous chapter. Hopefully everything will be working more smoothly once this book is released in 2019. So let's fire up GIMP 2.10.6 and get started!

The Second Hand: Process a Red 3D Sphere

I rendered a red sphere (since second hands are red) on a gray background as a 380 KB **seconds.bmp** file and used the **File ➤ Open** menu sequence to import it into GIMP. The sphere can be seen at the left side of Figure 7-19 and will need to be **extracted** and placed onto transparency, so that it can be composited within the watch face design.

Click the **Fuzzy Select** (Magic Wand in Photoshop) **tool**, and select the
antialiasing option; set **Threshold to 15**, and select the **Draw Mask**
option. In the **Select By:** drop-down, select **LCH: Lightness** (Luminosity
Channel Lightness, to designate selecting gray values only), and then
click the gray area surrounding the sphere, as is seen in Figure 7-19.

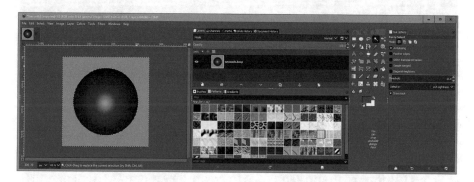

Figure 7-19. Use the Fuzzy Select (Magic Wand) tool to select gray
background

Since it's only this sphere we want to select (to extract it), we will
need to invert the selection (sometimes it is easier to select the opposite
of what you really want). Use the **Select ➤ Invert** menu sequence, seen
in Figure 7-20 (with the selection shown already inverted to save figures
used), to select only the sphere. Use the **Edit ➤ Copy** menu sequence to
save only the red sphere to the clipboard, so we can paste it over some
transparency, so that we have only the sphere as our seconds indicator.

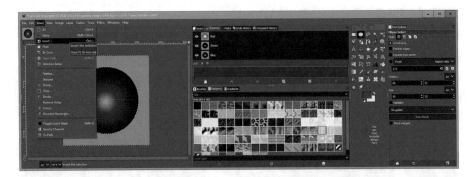

Figure 7-20. *Use Select ➤ Invert menu sequence (select sphere, instead of gray)*

To place this red metal sphere data, now in your workstation's **clipboard**, into a new file with a transparent background, use the **Create ➤ From Clipboard** menu sequence to create a new empty (transparent) file with this sphere in it. This can be seen, circled in red, in Figure 7-21.

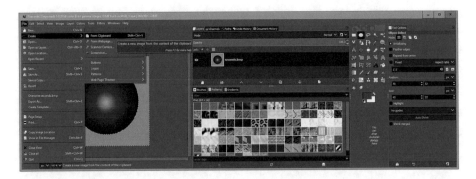

Figure 7-21. *Use Create ➤ From Clipboard to place sphere copy in transparency*

Use the **Image ➤ Scale Image** menu sequence, shown in Figure 7-22, to scale the sphere from 270 pixels (a 1:1 square), to be **15** pixels.

Figure 7-22. *Scale the 3D Sphere down to 15 pixels, to use as seconds indicator*

It's important to consider a **pivot point** for the seconds indicator, when you're creating the asset **width dimension** (in pixels) for both the minutes and the seconds graphics since the Galaxy Watch Designer will put this pixel in the center of the graphic and pivot the graphic around it!

This is why I used 15 pixels, rather than 16, because with 16 there would be 8 pixels on each side and the seconds (and minutes) indicators would be off by one pixel in either direction, no matter where the code puts the center of the graphic as pivots can't be between pixels.

By using an odd number of pixels, there will be a "center pixel" in that dimension, upon which your seconds asset will rotate, with an **even number** (7 and 7) of pixels on each side of this one pixel center. Later, when we extend the alpha channel transparency in the other dimension, we will use a 360 pixel dimension for the smartwatch face physical size.

We used **Image Size** to reduce the size of the Seconds indicator, and we will use **Canvas Size** to put it around the edge of our watch face design, by changing the asset dimension, from 15 x 15 to 15 x 360, as you can see in Figure 7-23. We will again use this alpha channel data, to do the positioning of the seconds indicator around the watch face perimeter for us, similar to what we did with the watch face number indicators for this new watch face design that we are learning how to create in GIMP.

Notice that we did not have to use the **Offset** data fields, to push the sphere to the bottom of the new asset dimension as we want it at 12 O'clock (High Noon) for the watch face design starting point. The small image pixel dimension and large alpha channel will make this file under one kilobyte. This is extremely small (only 760 bytes used for the data).

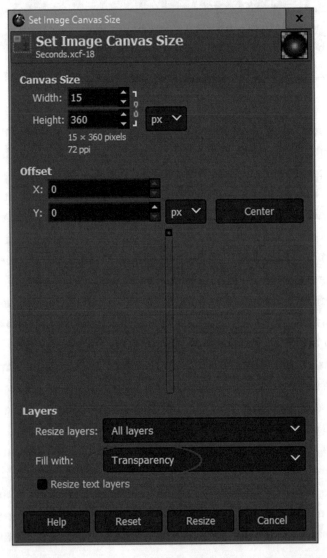

Figure 7-23. *Set Canvas to 15 x 360 pixels; Fill with Transparency*

Use the **File ➤ Export As** menu sequence to export the seconds indicator asset as a PNG32 asset, and place it with your 12 number indicator assets in the /**assets/indicators/** folder, as is shown in Figure 7-24. Once your **seond.png** seconds indicator is in this folder, you can use the **Preview** window to see how the second asset and the 12 asset line up together. Depending on how we assemble the **Z-order** of these assets in the Galaxy Watch Designer, the seconds indicator can go on top of, or behind, the number indicators for your watch face design.

Figure 7-24. *Use File ➤ Export As to export seconds indicator to an assets folder*

Next, let's create the 3D Arrow for your minutes indicator, just to show how you can use any 3D software package such as the open-source Blender 2.8 or paid software such as Autodesk 3D Studio Max, which I used in the next section of the chapter to create this 3D asset.

215

The Minute Hand: Process a Gold 3D Arrow

The easiest way to create this asset in a 3D software package is to **extrude a font**, in this case a font called "WingDings" that contains shapes such as the upward pointing arrow we are looking to use as our minutes indicator. To do this, I entered 3D Studio Max and added a Text element and set that to the **WingDing** font, as you can see on the right in Figure 7-25. To find the correct WingDing, I used the **Character Map** Utility, also shown at the left in Figure 7-25, to locate and copy the up arrow character in the font, which I then pasted in the text field in 3D Studio Max. This gives me a 2D lines (spline) vector representation of the arrow, which I can then apply an **extrusion** (in this case, the **Bevel Modifier**) to in order to make it into a three-dimensional (3D) arrow. After that I can do the same work process we did with the sphere in GIMP 2.10 (or GIMP3 in 2019) and put it on a transparent 21 x 360 PNG.

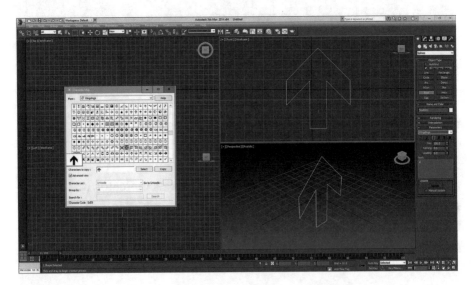

Figure 7-25. *Using WingDing font in 3D Studio Max to create the 3D Arrow asset*

As you can see in the Modifier Stack seen on the top right of 3D Studio in Figure 7-26, I have added a **Bevel Modifier** to make the arrow 3D and bevel it, as well as a **UVW Map** modifier, so that I can apply the gold **texture map** to this 3D object, so it will render as gold (or whatever texture map I decide to apply to it later on to make it look cool). You can see a blue **Material Editor** window overlay on the left side of the figure.

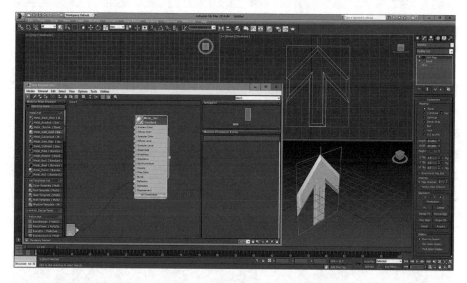

Figure 7-26. *Applying Gold Metal Texture to the 3D Arrow, using Materials Editor*

Next, we're going to practice the work process which we learned earlier in this chapter in Figures 7-19 through 7-24, only we will be using the minutes asset rather than the seconds asset. Figure 7-27 shows the minutes (arrow) asset at 210 by 270 pixels using a unique gold and blue texture on top of the alpha channel (transparency) data. Since we want an odd number of width (for a single-pixel pivot point in the middle), we will resize the 210 by 270 graphic 1000% (10X) down to 21 by 27 pixels and then extend your alpha channel data 333 pixels (down) to create a 21 by 360 minutes indicator PNG32 asset, this time in under 2 kilobytes.

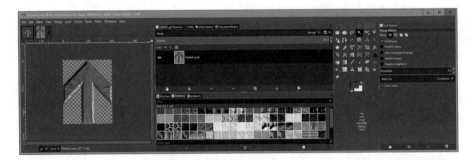

Figure 7-27. *Once you've placed the minutes indicator on transparency, resize it*

Set the same options in your **Set Image Canvas Size** dialog, as is shown in Figure 7-23, except that your resulting image canvas dimensions should be **21 by 360**. Be sure and fill the bottom of this new canvas with transparency (alpha channel). This will extend the checkerboard pattern as seen in Figure 7-28 and push the arrow out to the edge of the watch face design, where the Galaxy Watch has a bezel with minutes on it.

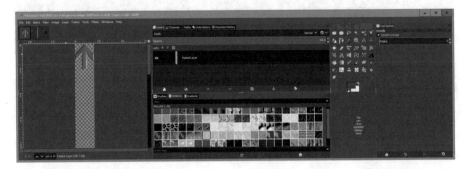

Figure 7-28. *Resize your minutes indicator asset to 21 pixels (odd width) by 360*

Once you've saved **minute.png** out to your **/Assets/Indicators/** folder, you should have 14 PNG32 assets in this folder, with which you can create a new and unique watch face design, which we'll be doing in the next chapter, covering how to use the Timeline pane for conditional watch face design, as well as some more practice with using the GWD layer-based watch face design compositing, using assets developed using GIMP 2.10.6 (or later, if available for download on GIMP.org).

Let's learn how to see what the data footprint is for all of these PNG32 assets you have created using 3D Rings, Spheres, and Arrows. We are shooting for less data used than the 60 KB background vector asset we optimized down from almost 4 gigabytes earlier in the book.

To accomplish this, use your OS's **File Management Utility**; for Windows 10 this is called the **Windows Explorer File Manager**, which is represented by a manila folder icon and which is seen in Figure 7-29.

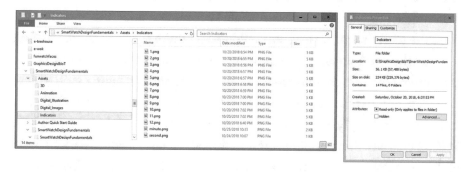

Figure 7-29. *Right-click the Assets/Indicators folder to select Properties (dialog)*

You can right-click this **/Assets/Indicators/** folder to get a **context-sensitive menu** of options. One of these is at the end of this menu, which is the **Properties** option, which will give you a dialog (shown at the far right in Figure 7-29) with several tabs regarding the properties of the files in the folder. One of these, size, tells you the size of all of the files which are in the folder, in this case **56 KB**, which is 5 K less than the 61 K background asset, so the watch face design is now using less than 120 K of total PNG8 (background) and PNG32 (component asset) data. This is quite impressive, given how clear the watch face design is going to be, which we will see in the next chapter covering using the Timeline.

Summary

This chapter shows how to use the external open-source software (GIMP 2.10.8) to add layer-based watch face design capabilities for the reader to use with the Galaxy Watch Designer software package. This is why I had the reader download several popular open-source software packages, including GIMP 2.10, Inkscape, Audacity, and Blender 3D, in the initial chapters where we set up your watch face content production workstation.

We started by learning about layer-based design using GIMP 2.10, which is available for free at GIMP.org. We placed a "backplate" image in the bottommost layer and added layers with Hour Indicators above that to simulate our watch face design while keeping the hour assets separate from the total design, so that we could export them at a later time. We then learned the work process for exporting these hour indicator assets and then create the minute hand asset as well as the second hand asset, which we will install in the next chapter when we create our custom watch face from scratch. Finally, we exported the second and minute hand assets as PNG32 files which we could import in the next chapter, when we assemble all of these PNG32 assets that we created in this chapter inside the Galaxy Watch Designer 1.6 software package.

CHAPTER 8

Smartwatch Conditional Design Using the Timeline

In this eighth chapter of the *Smartwatch Design Fundamentals* book, let's take your watch face design assets we created in GIMP in Chapter 7, and use the Galaxy Watch Designer Layers and Timeline to develop a watch face design from scratch, using all new 2D and 3D vector elements that we created and optimized using 3D Studio Max and GIMP. What we want to do in this chapter is show you how to leverage PNG8 and PNG32 assets you created in a layer compositing pipeline in GIMP, and how these design assets are assembled into a watch face design using the Layers and Timeline panes in Galaxy Watch Designer.

In the first part of the chapter, we will start to build the watch face design, adding **black background** color (Z-Order = 0), a **vector image** acquired, rendered, and optimized in Chapter 2 (Z-Order = 1), then your **Minutes Indicator** (Z-Order = 2) on top of that, and the **Seconds Indicator** (Z-Order = 3) on top of that, so the seconds tick over the minutes arrow.

© Wallace Jackson 2019
W. Jackson, *SmartWatch Design Fundamentals*,
https://doi.org/10.1007/978-1-4842-4369-5_8

We will then add **Hour Indicators** with conditional logic, set up using the Timeline so that each hour indicator appears in the watch face design during the hour in which it should be actively shown. In this way, when a user looks at the watch, the hour, minutes, and seconds are all easily viewed. In later chapters, we'll add sensor features to this design.

Building the Watch Face Foundation

Let's build a watch face foundation that allows us plenty of opportunity to leverage conditional logic, later on in this chapter, as well as in chapters which follow it later in the book. Since the Vector Image we optimized from a 4-MB SVG to a 61-KB PNG8 has transparency (alpha channel) data in it, the logical thing to do is to first create a Background element, initially black, like the design, which can be shifted to be any color using conditional code. Using the alpha channel and opacity data for the rest of the graphic, this allows us to color the vector graphic with any color (Hue) that we wish, allowing millions of different backplate images to be created by using only two layers (Background, plus Vector Image). Then you can add the minutes and seconds assets after that, and finally, the 1 through 12 hour number assets, to complete the basic design. In later chapters, we can add compliments, in the middle of the spiral rays. We can even animate these rays with this design approach, which puts background color, image, minute, second, and hour elements each on its own layer. Let's take a look at advanced watch face design!

Adding the Background Color and Image

Launch Galaxy Watch Designer, and use the **New Project** dialog, seen in Figure 8-1, to first click the **New Project** (watch face with a plus + sign in it) option, shown encircled in red on the left half of the figure, and then select the Galaxy Watch (or Gear S2, Gear S3, Frontier, and Sport) 360 x 360 pixel resolution round watch face design template, as is shown on the right side of the figure, also encircled in red.

Name a new project **CH8_Conditional_Watch_Face**, and click the **OK** button to launch Galaxy Watch Design software. The first thing we need to look for is a uniform black background color just like the one we used for the Always-On watch face design we created in Chapter 4. Click the Background component to see if there is one that fits this need for a uniform RGB 000 black color. I see an option named **ch_bg_c_04**.

Turns out Background_Color_4 is RBG 0,0,0 value (Black) color!

Figure 8-1. *Open the Galaxy Watch Designer, select New, and Round 360x360*

Select **Background ➤ ch_bg_c_04** as seen in Figure 8-2 to add this "Background Color 04" setting as the **Background 1** layer in GWD.

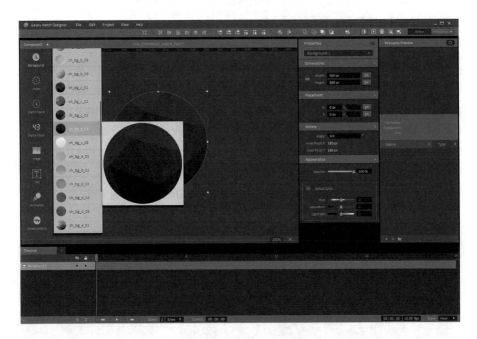

Figure 8-2. *Select the Background ➤ ch_bg_c_04 black background color setting*

Next, select the **Image** component (encircled in red in Figure 8-3). The first thing you'll see is the **/GearWatchDesigner/res/Image/** folder, which Galaxy Watch Designer opens for you, to select default imagery.

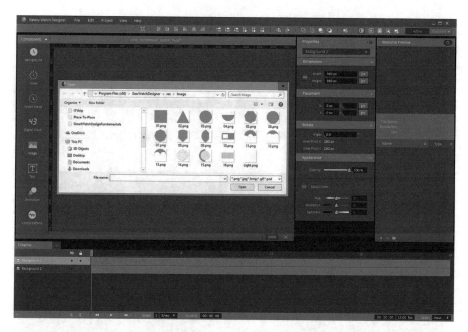

Figure 8-3. *Add an Image asset above the Black Background (opens / res/Image)*

Since you don't want to use existing assets, navigate into your **Assets** folder and **Digital_Illustration** subfolder, as seen in Figure 8-4, to double-click the **Vortex360x360_8bit** PNG file, to open it in GWD.

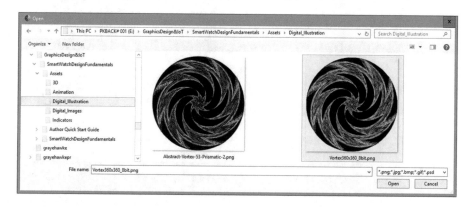

Figure 8-4. *Navigate to /Assets/Digital_Illustration/ folder; open Vortex360x360*

Right-click, and **Delete** the **Background 2** added to your layer composite, as seen in Figure 8-5. Rename your remaining two layers.

Figure 8-5. *Delete Background 2 layer added with Image layer; rename layers*

Select the Vector Illustration layer, and set the Image Properties to **0, 0**, as shown in Figure 8-6. Note that GWD initially sets this to 5, 5.

Figure 8-6. *Set placement of Image at 0,0 (inserted at 5,5) to center over black*

Adding Minutes and Seconds Indicators

Now that we have the two layers in place which hold the background color and background image, we can add the next two layers which will hold the seconds and minutes indicators used to tell the precise time of day. This is done using the Watch Hand Component icon seen on the left side of the Galaxy Watch Designer in Figure 8-7, encircled in red. Since we are using our own custom PNG32 asset created in Chapter 7 for a Minute Hand Indicator, we select the **Import Image** menu option, shown at the top of the Watch Hand Component menu in blue in Figure 8-7. Find the **/Assets/Indicators** folder to double-click the **minute.png** file and add a minute indicator asset to the top left (at pixel position 0,0) of your watch face design. This will put the minutes arrow to the left side of the watch face design preview initially, so you'll have to center it. We will do this next using the **Placement** portion of the **Properties** pane, and configure how it works with the smartwatch time readout by using the **Rotation Properties** portion of the Properties pane.

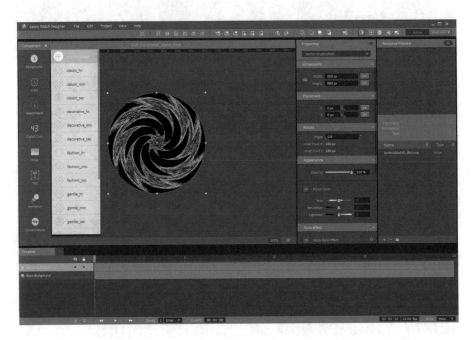

Figure 8-7. *Add Watch Hand ➤ Import Image and find the minute. png indicator*

I dragged the minutes arrow over to halfway, seen in Figure 8-8, which equated to the **X** value of **172** pixels in the **Placement** section of the Properties pane. Later, you will use the **Run** icon (emulator), at the top of the GWD software, and make sure the Minute Indicator is rotating around the perimeter of the watch face design correctly. Be sure to set **Sync with: Minutes in Hours** in the **Rotation Properties** section of the **Properties** dialog. Next, let's add the Seconds Indicator, so that the red sphere is on top of the gold arrow whenever it passes. The red sphere should not disappear behind the gold arrow, if it happens to occupy the same minute or second position in time around the outside of the watch.

Figure 8-8. *Position the Minute Indicator in the middle of your watch face design*

Since we're using a PNG32 asset created for your Second Hand Indicator, we again select the **Import Image** menu option, shown at the top of the Watch Hand Component menu, in blue in Figure 8-9. As seen in the **Open** dialog, we locate the **/Assets/Indicators** folder and double-click the **second.png** file to add a seconds indicator asset to the top left (at pixel position 0, 0) of your watch face design. This will again put your seconds indicator at the left side of the GWD watch face **Preview** pane.

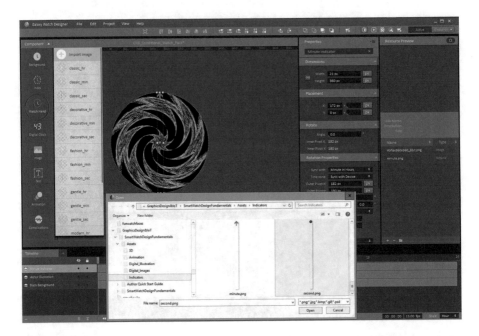

Figure 8-9. *Add Watch Hand ➤ Insert Image /Assets/Indicators/ second.png asset*

I dragged the Second sphere over halfway, seen in Figure 8-10, which equated to the **X** value of **176** pixels in the **Placement** section of the Properties pane. Later, you will use your **Run** icon (emulator), at the top of the GWD software to make sure the Seconds Indicator is rotating around the perimeter of your watch face design correctly.

Now we have your core watch face design, with the ability to change the watch face color, and the minutes and seconds time indicators, all in only four layers in your Timeline pane. This is optimal, because we are going to need three times that many Timeline Layers (one for each hour 1 through 12), to add your Hour Indicator assets, along with their conditional logic. This conditional logic will tell each of these hour assets to display themselves only once during the hour (if 24 hour mode is on), or twice (if the 12 hour mode is used) during the 24 hour day.

Finally, we will again need to set the time value for this seconds
indicator in the **Rotation Properties** section of GWD's Properties
pane. This time, we will utilize the **Sync with: Seconds in Minute**, and
again use the **Time zone: Sync with Device** option in the drop-down
selector menus. This will tell the watch face design what to do with this
indicator.

Figure 8-10. *Center Seconds Indicator on top of Minute Indicator
using Properties*

Next, let's test the minutes and seconds indicators and see if they spin
around the outside of the watch face design as we have set them up to!
Click the **Run** (Play) icon at the top right of the Galaxy Watch Designer
software to open up the in-software emulator, so you can test what we have
implemented thus far by using only four layers.

As you can see in Figure 8-11, this watch face design thus far is looking exactly as we intended it to look, from the black (backed) vector background image asset, to the gold Minute Hand indicator (left side of the figure), to the red Second Hand indicator (right side of the figure).

To test the Minute Hand indicator, the best method is to drag the top **Time** slider (click and drag the ball handle to the right) to watch your Minute Hand indicator asset spin around the perimeter of the watch face design. Remember, the Galaxy Watch has minutes printed on its bezel!

To test the Second Hand indicator, the best method is to use the Play/Pause Transport icon, located next to this Time slider (and shown encircled in red on the right in Figure 8-11). This animates your watch face Second Hand indicator asset, by attaching its movement frames to time expenditure, moving the second hand around the watch face perimeter!

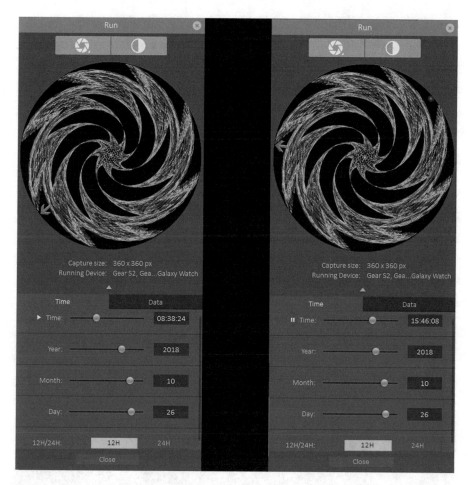

Figure 8-11. *Test the Seconds and Minute Indicators by using the Run emulator*

Next, we are going to add the 12 Hour Indicator assets to the design, using 12 more layers. The reason we are doing these Hour Indicators individually is that we only want to display the current hour in the day to the watch face user, to make it that much easier to read the time value. The hour indicators will still be in position on this watch face (where the user expects to see them), but this design leaves more space on the watch face

233

surface for content display without watch face design elements getting the way. Therefore, this should be a great design if you are doing photographic imagery watch faces, for instance, as eleven twelfths (92%) of your watch face background area will be left unobscured. Hours, minutes, and seconds indicators stay out of the way!

Adding in the 12 Hour Indicators

Since the numbers are the watch face Index, select the **Index ➤ Import Image** menu sequence seen in Figure 8-12, and add the **1.png** file from the **Assets/Indicators** folder. Note that if you add these as Watch Hand Components, program logic will be attached to them that will move them as time passes, and we want to make sure these remain fixed in place.

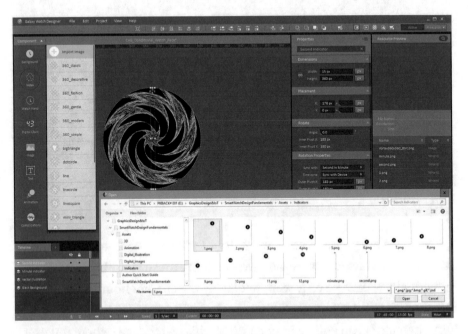

Figure 8-12. *Add the first Hour Indicator as an Index Component by using 1.png*

As you can see in Figure 7-13, I have renamed the **Index 1** layer to **Index Hour 1**, so that it is clear what that layer does later on. I will do this for each of these 12 Index Hour indicator layers as I will create each one using the same work process, shown in Figures 8-12 through 8-14.

Notice in Figure 8-13 that as I add additional Hour indicators, I set an **Hour** "resolution" for the timeline, using the bottom-right corner drop-down, encircled in red. I am doing this because after we add all 12 of these Index Hour indicators, we'll be setting **visibility conditions**, which affect these Hour indicators on an hourly basis (hence the Hour setting).

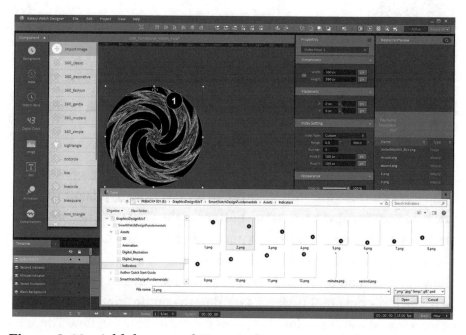

Figure 8-13. *Add the second Hour Indicator as an Index Component using 2.png*

As you can see in Figure 7-14, I've added seven hour indicators!

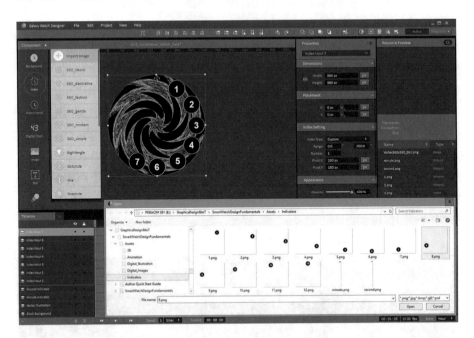

Figure 8-14.   Add each of the 1.png through 12.png assets, renaming each layer

Once you've imported 12 Hour indicators as Index Components, Galaxy Watch Designer should look like what is shown in Figure 8-15. I resized the Timeline pane at the bottom of the GWD by dragging the top Preview portion up, using the pane resize tool which you'll get when you put the mouse (cursor) between the black line above the Timeline pane and under the Preview pane. I did this so that I could see all of the layer data in this watch face design composition, as we will be working on the conditional settings for the hour indicators. These will be accessed with the gray blocks, displayed for each of the day's 24 hours in each layer's timeline, since we set the timeline resolution to Hour (see Figure 8-13).

Figure 8-15. *Resize your Timeline pane to be half of your GWD working area*

To test the Watch Face Design, use the Run (Play) icon at the top right of GWD, and drag the slider in the Hour portion of the emulator, as is seen in Figure 8-16. Notice Seconds and Minutes indicators spin around the perimeter of the watch face and the Hour Indicators remain fixed. Note that if you had added your Hour assets using a Watch Hand Component, the Hour Indicators would also move around the perimeter, so you need to be careful how you design using the GWD components.

Figure 8-16. *Test a watch face design using Run icon once all assets are added*

Now that the watch face design layers contain the correct assets and positioning data (from the GWD **Properties** pane, for your seconds and your minutes, and from GIMP asset alpha channels for your hours), we can switch our focus over to the area (the timeline) to the right side of the Layers compositing stack, where we can now apply conditions to each Hour Indicator based upon what hour in the day (which square in the layer's timeline) you wish to apply a condition to. In this case, we're using the Show and Hide conditions to affect an Hour Indicator visibility.

Applying Conditional Logic in Timeline

The work process to apply conditional logic to an hour time slice for any given layer in the compositing stack (left side) is to click to select that hour (block) in the timeline area to the right of the layer, so that it turns green, indicating it's being working on. After it is turned on for editing, you can then right-click it to get a context-sensitive menu, to change **attributes** for that layer's component, in this case, **visibility** (Show or Hide menu option). What we're going to do is **Hide** (black square) each hour in time periods in which the Hour Indicator should not be showing and **Show** (gray square) the Hour Indicator during the correct hour.

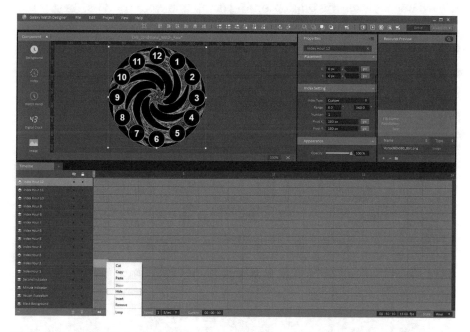

Figure 8-17. *Click Hour 2 layer timeline square, so it turns green, and then right-click*

When you select any square, in Figure 8-18, I've selected Index Hour 4's layer during a 3 O'clock time period, the time marker jumps to that hour, to show the design during that time. In the case of this figure, I have right-clicked the square and highlighted the **Hide** menu option to hide the Hour 4 indicator when it is 3 O'clock. Since I have not clicked the Hide option as yet, all squares after the timeline shuttle indicator are gray, so all Hour indicators are visible in the Preview. If I were to pull the **Timeline Shuttle** (in blue) to the left at this point, the 2 and 3 Hour Index layers would turn off (Hide), as a line that comes down from the shuttle handle passes by them. This ability to test designs is similar to what you get if you use the **Run** icon as we did in Figure 8-16 (see the right side).

You can see that a **stair-step pattern** is beginning to form using this Show-Hide logic we are implementing using this work process. As you'll see when we're finished, you'll have suspended stairs which serve to turn on each Hour Indicator only during an Hour time slot within which that Hour indicator should be displayed (Show menu option) to a watch face viewer. Pretty straightforward, but I'm going to show you the whole process, in the remaining pages of this chapter, as it is complex.

Figure 8-18. *Right-click and hide Index Hour 4 indicator, during 3 O'clock hour*

In Figure 8-19 I'm hiding Hour 8 during all other hours. I dragged the timeline shuttle to zero, showing which indicators have been hidden.

Figure 8-19. *Drag timeline shuttle indicator to the left, and watch the hours hide*

Let's continue hiding your Hour 8 Indicator, by selecting (green) and right-clicking (select the Hide option) the conditional squares in that layer's timeline, for zero (Midnight) through six, as shown in Figure 8-20 to continue building our stair-step pattern. You will continue turning off the visibility of the 9, 10, and 11 Hour Indicators as you continue moving up the timeline conditional matrix, making sure only hours which need to show an hour marker are set to **Show** the Hour indicator, using the gray square. If during this Show/Hide attribute setting process you drag the timeline shuttle indicator, you will see the hour indicators disappear, as the shuttle moves to the left of the timeline (toward the Midnight zero hour). Do this as you create the stair-step pattern, so you see how this conditional time-based (in this case, using Hour resolution) logic works.

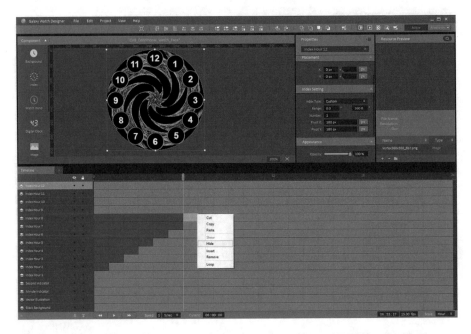

Figure 8-20. *If shuttle is past hidden indicators, all Hour indicators will be visible*

As you can see, in Figure 8-21, I have finished the upper half of the stair-step pattern and selected the Midnight hour marker in the layer timeline, to make sure it says "Show," for the 12 O'clock Hour indicator. As you can see in the figure if you mouse-over the green selected box, it will tell you the hour (zero, or 0,0, in this case), which needs to show 12.

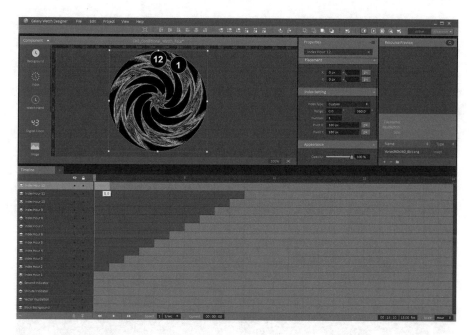

Figure 8-21. *Make sure Hour indicator 12 is shown at Hour Marker 0 in timeline*

As you can see in Figures 8-21 and 8-22, I pulled the timeline shuttle indicator all the way to the left, and only the 12 O'clock Hour indicator should be showing, but the 1 O'clock Hour indicator is also showing, which means that I started with the 2 O'clock indicator and need to turn off a stair-stepped row of blocks underneath my current stair-step pattern, so that when I pull the shuttle to the left all Hours will turn off except for Midnight/Noon (the 12 O'clock Hour indicator).

To do this, I need to click-select, then right-click-select, **Hide** for layers **Index Hour 1** through **Index Hour 11**, moving up the stair-step pattern just underneath the current gray stair-step pattern. I have shown this process, started in Figure 8-22, with Hiding Index Hour 1 during the 0,0 (12 O'clock) time slot. The completion of this work process can be seen in Figure 8-23, where I turn off visibility for the Hour 11 indicator during the

10 O'clock hour (column), which is shown selected in green, just before the **Hide** option is selected from the context-sensitive menu.

Now all that we have left to do is to Hide your 12 O'clock Hour indicator during the 1 O'clock through 11 O'clock hour slots along the very top of this current stair-step pyramid that we have been building.

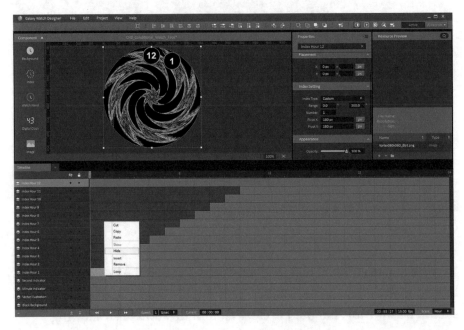

Figure 8-22. *Drag timeline shuttle to left to clear all hour indicators except for 12*

Figure 8-23 shows a completed top half of the stair-step pattern, except for hiding the 1 to 11 O'clock blocks for the Index Hour 12 layer.

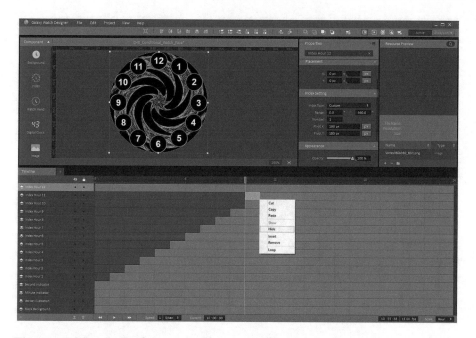

Figure 8-23. *Complete stair-step pattern so the 1-11 numbers will disappear at 0*

Select (to green), and right-click and **Hide** the timeline blocks for the **Index Hour 12** layer from the 1 O'clock hour through the 11 O'clock hour (which is shown highlighted in green in the middle of Figure 8-24, about to be Hidden by using the right-click ➤ Hide work process).

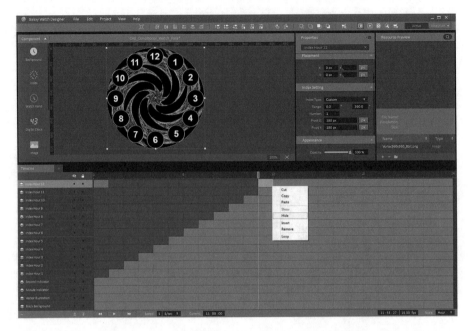

Figure 8-24. *Here is one half of a stair-step hour indicator pattern showing conditional logic*

Once you have completed your stair-step pattern, which can be seen in Figure 8-25, you will be able to drag (left) your Timeline shuttle icon at the top of the Timeline pane, and turn the 12 hour indicators off, as you move the shuttle head toward the left side (0,0) of the Timeline conditional time portion of the display (the other portion of the Timeline pane on the far left contains the component layers themselves).

Whereas having black blocks on one side of a stair-step pattern equates to turning the indicators (all) on or off, as you drag your timeline shuttle, as you may have surmised, having black blocks on BOTH sides of a stair-step pattern equates to having all numbers appear individually (turning themselves on and off) whenever you drag your timeline shuttle back and forth over the finished left half (the hours 0 through 11) of the Timeline pane. Let's turn all the squares under the steps black next.

Figure 8-25. *Drag timeline shuttle side to side to watch hours appear/disappear*

Now do the same Hide (black square) process on the underside of the stair-step pattern you've created thus far, as seen in Figure 8-26.

Figure 8-26. *So only one hour appears each hour, hide bottom half (under stairs)*

Hide Hour 1 for hours other than 1 O'clock shown in Figure 8-27.

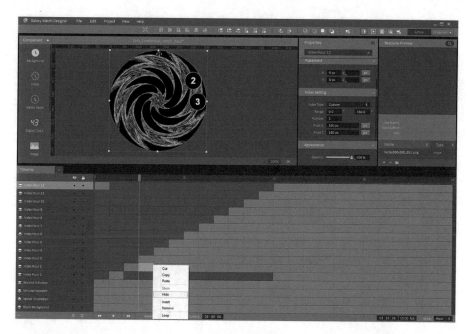

Figure 8-27.   *Hide Index Hour 1 for all of the hours other than the 1 O'clock hour*

Hide Hour 10 in 11 O'clock block to finish, shown in Figure 8-28.

Figure 8-28. *Hide last Hour 10 indicator during 11 O'clock to finish step pattern*

Once you isolate your stair-step pattern as a diagonal row of stairs on a black background area, drag the Timeline shuttle head (also called a playback head in digital video editing software packages), and your number indicators will turn on and off during the appropriate time of day, as can be seen in Figure 8-29. The next thing we would need to ascertain is whether this design we have now crafted (possibly only half crafted) is going to work twice a day (is it sufficient for 12 Hour mode, or do we have to do the work for 24 Hour mode to have this 12 Hour mode working twice a day). To ascertain the answer to this question, you will have to use the Run (emulator) icon, to see if the Galaxy Watch Designer is smart enough to duplicate the left side of this Timeline conditional area twice a day, or do we have to do this work ourselves (to get some more practice with conditional programming in GWD using the Timeline pane).

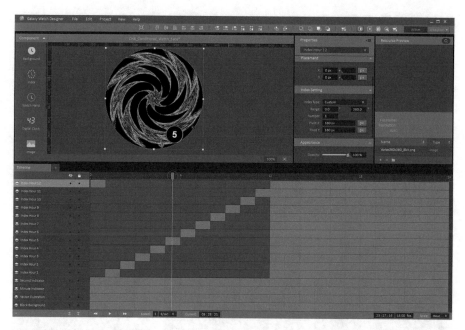

Figure 8-29. *Drag timeline shuttle; see hours appear one at a time on watch face*

Click the Run icon and drag the Hour slider bar from the left to the right. As you can see in Figure 8-30, from Midnight (zero hour) to 11 O'clock, the Hour indicators behave as desired, but in the afternoon, all of the Hour indicators come on at the same time (see middle of the figure).

Figure 8-30. *Use Run (emulator), and see if 12 hour conditions apply to 24 hours*

What this indicates is that we will need to duplicate what we just did on using the left-hand side of this Timeline conditional time pane on the right-hand side of the Timeline pane as well.

This time, instead of working from left to right, and turning off the entire layer for each hour indicator, we will work from the bottom to the top, turning off each hour column for each nonmatching hour indicator while leaving the matching Hour indicator block gray.

This time, as you can see in Figure 8-31, as you select and then right-click and Hide each Index Hour indicator layer (working from 1 at the bottom to 12 at the top), it will then disappear from view in the GWD Preview area at the top of the software package.

Since in Figure 8-31 we are in the Noon hour column, we will be "disappearing" your Index Hour 1 through Index Hour 11 indicators, as we work our way up the column using this new vertical work process.

In this way, you will see both ways of approaching this Hour hide process, and get a better visual feel and understanding for how this time conditional programming for watch face components is implemented.

Figure 8-31. *Create Index Hour layer stair-step pattern for Hours 12 through 23*

Right-click the 12 Hour block at the top of the 1 O'clock column to Hide the Hour 12 indicator, shown in Figure 8-32, leaving only the 1.

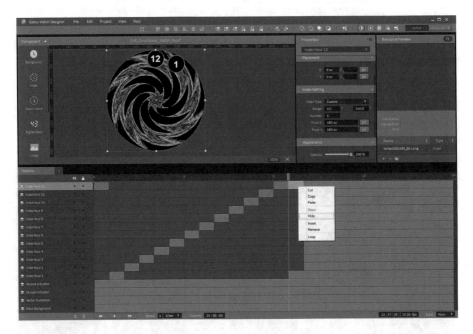

Figure 8-32. *Hide the Hour 12 indicator, at the top of the 1 O'clock time column*

Turn off the Hour 1 indicator at the bottom of the 2 O'clock time column by selecting (green) and right-clicking and Hiding Index Hour 1. This work process can be seen in Figure 8-33 as we begin to build the stair-step gray blocks for the second half of the 24 hour time period.

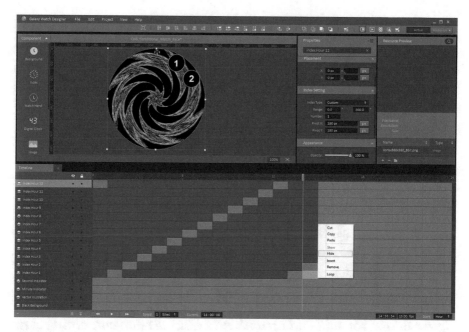

Figure 8-33. *Be sure to hide underneath portion of your stair-step pattern as well*

You will continue to turn off all of the blocks around your second gray stair-step construct on the second half of the Timeline pane, which I have done already, and which you can see in Figure 8-34. As you may have imagined, this is a duplicate of the first half of the Timeline display, and these sections could essentially be "tiled" together on out to infinity.

I wanted to focus on how these conditional time elements are to be implemented within Galaxy Watch Designer by positioning elements using alpha channel data created in packages outside of GWD such as GIMP, Fusion, Corel Draw, Paint Shop Pro, or Photoshop. The reason for this is because many existing designers (new readers of this book) will have multi-layer composites that they will want to immediately drop into watch face designs, so I focused this chapter on conditional design and how to use previously created composites (Chapter 7) inside GWD.

Figure 8-34. *You will end up with a 24 hour version containing stair-step patterns*

In the next chapter, we will explore more advanced settings in the **Properties** pane as well as continue to learn how to design more complex 24 Hour designs in a chapter covering 24 Hour watch face design. In this way, we'll have a more logical learning progression in regard to the Galaxy Watch Designer features and capabilities. After that, we will get into even more complex topics such as compliments, sensors, weather, and other advanced design elements.

Summary

In this chapter we looked at how to assemble the watch face design assets we created using GIMP 2.10.8 and 3D software in Chapter 7, and learned how to use the conditional area at the right side of the Timeline pane in Galaxy Watch Designer to show the Hour Indicator (3D hoop overlays with Hour) markers only during the hour in which the watch face time was occurring. First, we built the watch face design foundation and added a background color and vortex image, which we created using Inkscape and optimized for file size using GIMP 2.10.10.

We then added the 3D minutes and seconds indicators, which will be used to circle the perimeter of the watch face design, without obstructing your primary background design, in this case, the vector illustration pinwheel located in the center of the Watch Face Design.

We then added in the 12 Hour Indicator assets, so that we could implement the conditional programming into the design by using the Timeline pane area (right) of the Galaxy Watch Designer software.

Next, we learned how to right-click frame blocks in order to apply conditional logic to the hour indicators using the blocks (called **frames** in Galaxy Watch Designer) which we can select (they turn green), and right-click to set a **Show** or **Hide** setting, which will make sure that the correct Hour Indicator asset is shown only during that hour of day.

Hidden Hour Indicators are shown as black in the Timeline view, and Shown Hour indicators are shown as gray, resulting in a stair-step pattern which implements the hour indicators being shown at the proper time of day (and also making it easier for the designer to see what is being accomplished with this conditional logic application).

We also looked at how to test the design, by using the **Run (emulator) Icon** so that we could see exactly how this conditional logic which we were implementing works! As you will see in future chapters, implementing other logic in the Timeline pane area works in a similar fashion, so this chapter gives you a foundational overview of how things are accomplished in the Galaxy Watch Designer 1.6 software package.

We then finished implementing a **stair-stepping** pattern for your Hour Indicators so that each Hour Indicator asset is showing only during the hour that it should be. Doing this allows the watch face designer to showcase artwork (imagery, weather, illustrations, animation, logo, etc.) using the majority of the 360 pixels in your watch face, where the Hour,

Minute, and Seconds Indicators show around the perimeter of the watch face design, without obscuring any of the subject matter of the watch face design. At the same time, we took an in-depth look at the complete work process for implementing conditional logic using the Timeline pane in the Galaxy Watch Designer software package. Our mission for this chapter has now been accomplished!

CHAPTER 9

Watch Face Battery or Steps Taken: Percentage Conditional Design

In this ninth chapter of the *Smartwatch Design Fundamentals* book, let's build upon your watch face design assets we created using GIMP 2.10 in Chapter 7 and use the Galaxy Watch Designer Layers and Timeline in Battery Power Mode to develop a watch face design that turns red as the battery power drains from the smartwatch. What we want to do in this chapter is show you how to alter the PNG8 and PNG32 assets you created in Chapter 7 using different tools in GIMP, to create the PNG assets which will turn your watch face from black to red as power fades.

In the first part of this chapter, we'll enable the GWD watch face battery power percentage conditional grid, using the Plus (+) icon to the right of the Timeline Tab, to see how to add different conditions to GWD, such as Steps Taken, Battery Power Percent, or Kilometers Traveled.

We will then modify the Vector Illustration, so that it will turn red as the battery dies, using some new tools in GIMP 2.10.6, so you'll get some more practice with digital image editing and compositing software.

© Wallace Jackson 2019
W. Jackson, *SmartWatch Design Fundamentals*,
https://doi.org/10.1007/978-1-4842-4369-5_9

We'll then take a close look at the work process in Galaxy Watch Designer for turning a background image from Black (full battery) to Red (less than 20% battery life), so that the watch face will let the user know when his battery starts to fade, without having to use any complications.

Adding Different Conditions to GWD

You may have noticed a tiny + Tab next to the Timeline Tab at the very bottom of the Galaxy Watch Designer. This currently allows you to add four additional types of watch face design conditions to the Time-based conditions which we covered in Chapter 8. There are conditional grids of blocks for Battery Percentage (Battery Life Indications), Steps Percentage (Steps Taken), 12 or 24 Hour Mode, and Miles or Kilometers Traveled. What we are going to do in this chapter is to turn the watch face background into a visual battery condition (charge) indicator, so that it lights up red as the smartwatch battery dies. We will go into GIMP and create dark red, medium red, red, and light red (illuminated) areas in the black vector image so that the black background glows more and more red, as the smartwatch battery dies. This is a pretty cool concept, and I have not seen it implemented in a watch face design thus far, so it is a good way to show how to design conditional watch faces based on battery life, without having to use space on the watch face design to add a complication (we'll cover complications in a later chapter in this book).

Figure 9-1. *Click the Plus (+) Tab next to the Timeline Tab to open a Battery Tab*

Modifying the Vector Background Color

Launch GIMP 2.10.6 (or later) and use the **File ➤ Open** menu sequence to open the **Assets/Digital_Illustration/Vector360x360_8bit PNG8** asset. Select the Fuzzy Select tool (Magic Wand in Photoshop) and set the **Threshold** to **Zero**, select the **antialiasing** option and **Select By Composite,** and finally select the **Draw Mask** option, as seen encircled in red in Figure 9-2.

Figure 9-2. *Launch GIMP, open vector.png, and use Fuzzy Select on Black areas*

Click the sixteen all-black areas in the vector image, which will turn purple on mouse-down (click the mouse and hold to see this color a bit longer). To select all of these black areas at one time, hold down the Shift key between each of the 16 selections until you see the + (ADD NEXT SELECTION) next to your fuzzy select tool mouse pointer. Once you select all of the black areas (which we are soon going to color-shift, lighten, and saturate, to go from Dark Red (80% Battery) to Bright Red (0% Battery)), open the **Hue Saturate** dialog by using the **Colors ➤ Hue-Saturation** menu sequence.

Select **Lightness** slider and increase it by 50% and rotate the **Hue** to Red by -100, as seen in Figure 9-3, to create a **Dark Red** color where the black color used to be. As the watch loses power, it will now start to turn into red color, which we'll continue to lighten by 33.3% until bright red.

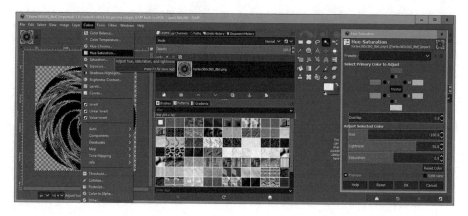

Figure 9-3. *Use Hue-Saturation dialog; adjust Lightness by 50% and rotate Hue by -100*

Notice in Figure 9-4 that the Image Color Mode is still set to 8-bit color (Indexed Color Mode) rather than 24-bit (True Color Mode). We will want to use 24-bit color space to shift Hue, Saturation, and Lightness as we'll want to shift between 16,777,216 colors, rather than 256 colors, so we get a smoother shift between Medium Red, Red, and Bright Red. So select the Image ➤ Mode ➤ RGB menu sequence to switch GIMP into a finer color translation mode before you do the next three Hue-Saturation implementations to create Medium Red (Vector360x360_p50_8bit), Red (Vector360x360_p25_8bit), and Bright Red (Vector360x360_p0-8bit) file versions. After you color-shift all four assets, be sure to change GIMP back to Indexed Color Mode using Image ➤ Mode ➤ Indexed, so that the File ➤ Export dialog optimizes them down to 61 KB, instead of 185 KB.

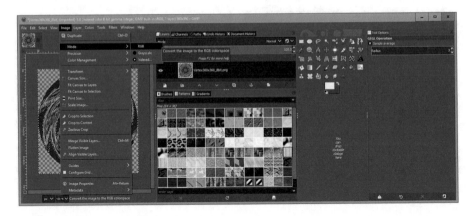

Figure 9-4. *Switch Image ➤ Mode ➤ Indexed (8 bit) to Image ➤ Mode ➤ RGB (24 bit)*

Use the **Hue-Saturation** dialog to shift the Dark Red areas into Medium Red, by shifting **Lightness** up by **33%** and increasing **Saturation** of the Red color by **100%**, seen in Figure 9-5. Next, **File ➤ Export** each version, using the **Vortex360x360_pNum_8bit** PNG8 file name format.

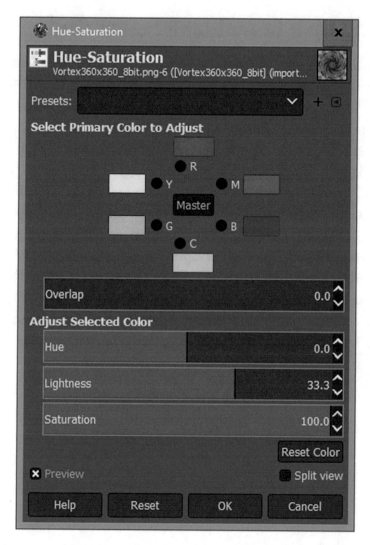

Figure 9-5. *Increase Lightness by 33% and Saturation by 100% three times*

Now we're ready to start building a GWD conditional power grid.

Setting Up a Conditional Power Grid

The first thing we want to do is to add the four new image component layers in the Galaxy Watch Designer and rename them to Vector 0% Power through Vector 100% Power so we know what they represent as we are building our Conditional Power (Battery) Percentage (left) indicator watch face design. Click the **Image Component**, seen encircled in red on the left side in Figure 9-6, and add the **Vortex360x360_p75_8bit.png** file (Dark Red) and rename the layer **Vector 75% Power**. On top of that in the layer stack (you can drag the layers to arrange them from dark to light or select the correct layer before the Insert Image Component operation), add the **Vortex360x360_p50_8bit.png** file representing 50% battery life and then the **Vortex360x360_p25_8bit.png** file representing 25% battery life and finally the **Vortex360x360_p0_8bit.png** file for no battery life (0%) power left. These will be added using the **Open** dialog seen in Figure 9-6 to open the files from the **Assets/Digital_Illustration** folder. Rename each layer right after you open each image asset.

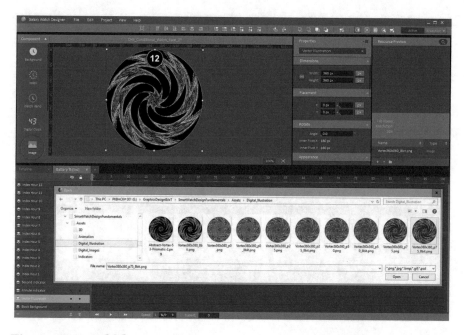

Figure 9-6. *Add four image component layers using 8-bit versions of new images*

Select each Vector Illustration layer, and set Image **Placement** Properties to **0, 0**, as you did in Chapter 8. Notice that GWD initially sets this to 5, 5; so you need to **recenter** all four new layers, as well as rename them, as is shown encircled in Red in Figure 9-7. Make sure the layers are in the right layer order with a Black Vector Illustration (100% Battery Percentage) on the bottom of the layer stack, with the 75% through 0% increasing red colors on top of the black image, and in the proper order, as is shown in Figure 9-7.

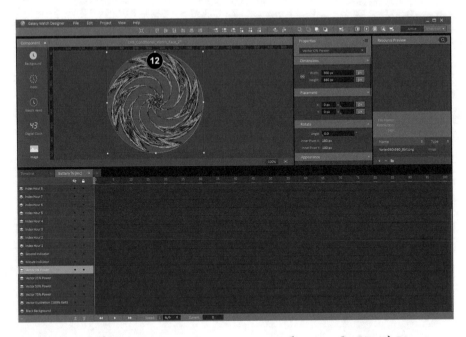

Figure 9-7. *Set placement of Image at 0, 0 (inserted at 5, 5) to center over black*

When I first started playing around with this conditional battery power feature in the Galaxy Watch Designer, my first inclination was to select the layer percentage block in green and then try to set the Hue, Saturation, and Lightness sliders in the Properties pane in the top part of GWD, hoping that the software would save these values in code, and change them accordingly for each conditional block (stage). Alas, the software is not yet this advanced (at least not as of Version 1.6.1), and so we must use Show and Hide with Imagery, which is why we created four new background images using GIMP in the first part of this chapter.

As you can see in Figure 9-8, the Show and Hide options can be accessed (they become blue on mouse-over, not gray) by selecting and right-clicking each percentage block, just as we did in Chapter 8 for time conditions. Just like with time conditional blocks, as you'll see in Figure 9-8, these can be selected individually, and shown as blocks turning gray, and hidden blocks will turn black.

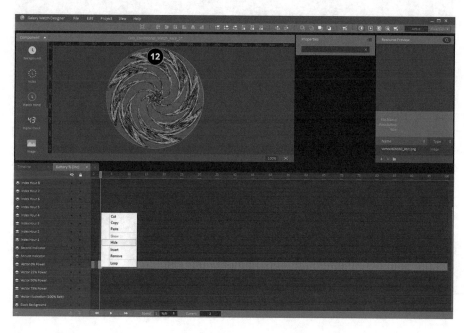

Figure 9-8. *Battery Power is indicated visually, using Show and Hide for each %*

Notice in both Figures 9-8 and 9-9 that all of the blocks in the 0% Battery columns are selected. Just so you don't think I selected, right-clicked, and showed all of these, as I did not, you can preselect the entire layer (row) for usage, by right-clicking a block on a selected row (any block will do) and using the **Activate** option, shown in Figure 9-9. Notice I'm doing this in the Vector 25% Power layer (row) in Figure 9-9 (I did it for Vector 0% Power layer (row) in Figure 9-8), and I'm about to show you how to **Multi-Select** (dragging a marquee around all of the areas that you want to select) blocks, so that we can speed up this work process significantly, without having to select, and then right-click, over a hundred individual blocks. What a relief that I found this nifty feature!

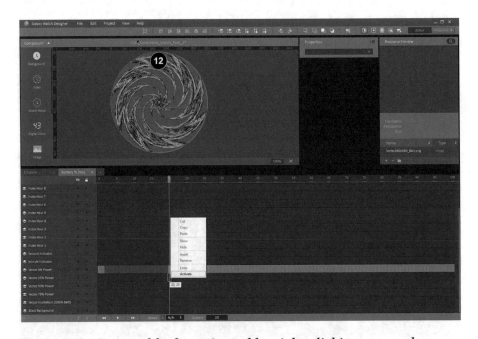

Figure 9-9. *Battery blocks activated by right-clicking one and selecting Activate*

I expect this works in other conditional views as well, so we will utilize this moving forward and greatly speed up our conditional timeline editing setup work process for the other types of conditions, including those currently available (seen in Figure 9-1) and those that are added to the Galaxy Watch Designer in the future.

As you can see in the GWD watch face **Preview** pane, the Red (Power is Low) background images will show, unless we hide them using conditional battery power logic in blocks attached to layers above the original (black) background. Right now, there is no such logic that has been implemented as yet, so the preview at the top of GWD is Red.

Let's now select the blocks at the right side of the top 0% Battery Power layer, using the Multi-Select feature, to drag a marquee around these blocks, as can be seen in Figure 9-10.

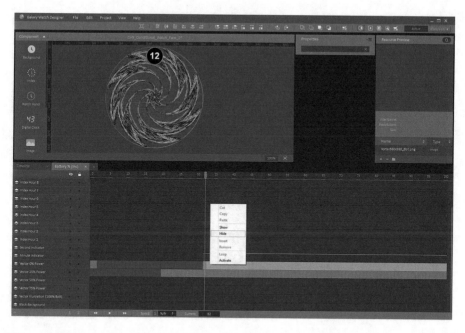

Figure 9-10. *Select the rest of the first row (0%) blocks to right-click ➤ Hide them*

Right-click anywhere on the selected group of blocks, and click the **Hide** option, which will hide each of these blocks using the battery power percentage level columns in which each block resides. Since we have already activated the 25% Power layer in Figure 9-9, let's multi-select the blocks on that layer as well to define the 25% battery power.

Since we want blocks in the 20% to 41% Battery % (Power) columns to be gray for the Vector 25% Power Layer (second from the top of the red to black vector background asset containing layers), we will next multi-select the 42% through 100% blocks in that layer, to select (turn them green) so that when we right-click to Hide in the context-sensitive menu, it sets the Hide option for each of these blocks individually. You can see this multi-select being implemented in Figure 9-11, as we set 60 blocks to Hide with one simple drag-select and one simple right-click ➤ Hide move. I like to call each step in a work process used to implement a "move," as you may have noticed.

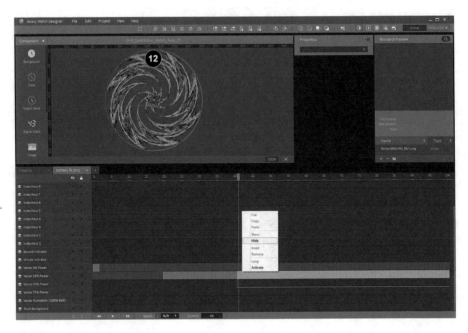

Figure 9-11. *Select 41% through 100% blocks in the 25% layer/row to Hide them*

We now have a section of blocks set to "Show" for the 25% power graphic from 20% through 41% Battery Percentage. Since we are only using five graphics (of 60 KB each, or 300 KB total asset data footprint overhead), you want to have these at (approximately) 0% to 20%, 20% to 40%, 40% to 60%, 60% to 80%, and 80% to 100%. Then the correct level of red, which signifies "I need to be charged" to the watch face user, will grow in visual intensity the lower the battery power runs, which is the objective of this particular watch face design.

Next, let's activate the third (out of five battery power indicator asset layers) Vector 50% Power Image Component Layer, by clicking any of the 100 Battery % blocks in that layer and right-clicking it to select the Activate option, which will turn each of the blocks in that layer to "Show" and turn them all into gray color.

As you can see in Figure 9-12, activating a layer of blocks also brings up a warning dialog which states "This action will delete all frames of other conditions. Do you want to continue?" The answer is to click the Yes button option, which is not intuitive at first, because as you will see, when you do this, all of the conditional frames in your other layers (and in your Timeline time conditions) will in fact NOT be deleted!

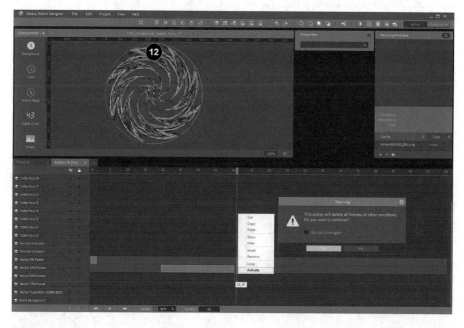

Figure 9-12. *Select any block on 50% Layer (3) and then right-click and Activate*

In future versions of Galaxy Watch Designer, this warning dialog should be modified to instead read: "This action will delete all frames of other conditions located on this Layer. Do you want to continue?"

It is also important to note that GWD is calling what I have been calling "blocks" (for what they appear as) "frames." As long as you know how they work, I'm sure that these can be called "squares," "blocks," or "Frames." Let's continue our Activation and Multi-Select work process.

To show you how to get even more mileage out of your Multi-Select feature, let's also click one of the "frames" of the **Vector 75% Power** layer and **Activate** that layer's conditional Battery Percentage frames as well, so that we can select two rows of frames at a time!

As you can see in Figure 9-13, I have multi-selected the 0% Battery frames through the 41% Battery (Power) frames for the Vector 50% Power and the Vector 75% Power layers, to adjust the Show-Hide selection for 82 frames, using one right-click ➤ Hide work process move!

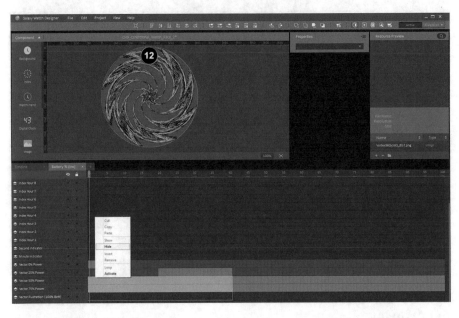

Figure 9-13. *Right-click + Activate 75% layer, to block select 0% to 41% and Hide*

This leaves only the 41% to 60% for the Vector 50% Power layer to be shown (Hide 60% to 100% frames) and 60% to 80% for the Vector 75% Power layer to be shown. Much like what we did in Chapter 8 with Time Conditional layer settings, this creates (wide) stair-steps for each of the five levels of power (red) indication for the watch face.

If you want to fade the black to red more gradually, you can create ten different assets (600 KB) or fifteen different assets (900 KB). This is a data footprint optimization at the end of the day, if you think about it. If GWD allowed us to attach code (HSV slider settings) to the conditional blocks, fade could happen gradually, using no extra assets.

As you can see in Figure 9-14, I have multi-selected the 40% to 60% blocks of the **Vector 75% Power** layer to **right-click ➤ Hide** them.

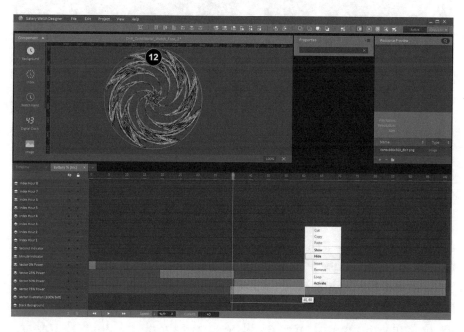

Figure 9-14. *Select 40% through 60% of 75% Layer and right-click to select Hide*

As you can see in Figure 9-14, GWD will pop-up an overlay that tells you what frame, or range of frames, has been selected, in case you have a need to be superaccurate regarding your frame numbers. Now we have to select frames 80% to 100% for Vector 75% Power and Hide those so that only the correct block (step) of frames is shown.

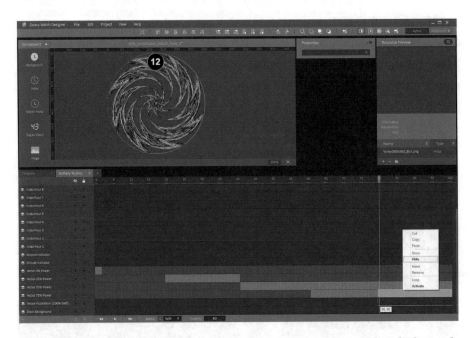

Figure 9-15. *Select 80% through 100% of 25% Layer, right-click, and select Hide*

Only a couple more moves need to be executed to complete the setup of a visual battery power (left) watch face design. The next thing to do is to **Hide** frames 60% through 100% for the Vector 50% Power layer, so that the middle block of steps is isolated in the staircase you are building in this project. Note that since the Vector Illustration (100%) is the default bottommost layer, it will be shown simply by hiding the other three layers above it, and it does not have to be activated, multi-selected, right-clicked, and shown in order to be seen as the default watch face design background, as it will be shown anyway when the Battery Power Percentage conditional layer hiding is implemented. So until a battery is 75% (25% drained), a black vector background is seen. As the battery power drains, the other (Red) backgrounds are shown.

Finally, select the **3% to 20%** (black, hidden) frames for **Vector 0% Power** to right-click ➤ **Show** these so the background is Red when the smartwatch battery drops below 20%, as is shown in Figure 9-16.

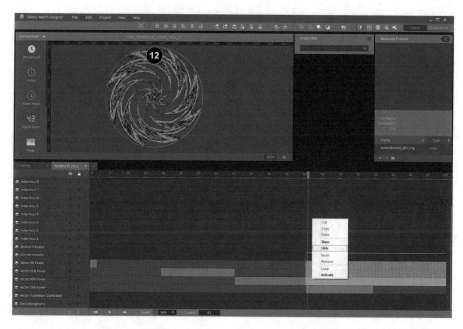

Figure 9-16. *Select 60% to 100% blocks for 50% battery layer, right-click, and Hide*

Now that the watch face design layers contain the correct assets and visibility data (directed by the GWD Battery % Tab frames that we have just set-up), it is time to test this watch face design, by using the **Run** icon (emulator).

Figure 9-17. *Select Hidden blocks on 0% Power Layer, right-click, and Show*

This process can be seen in Figure 9-18, where the left frame is currently showing 0% battery power, because the Battery Power slider goes from 0% to 100% battery charge in the emulator for testing. Click the **Data** Tab, encircled in red in the far-left panel, to switch from Time-based testing to Sensor Data-based testing.

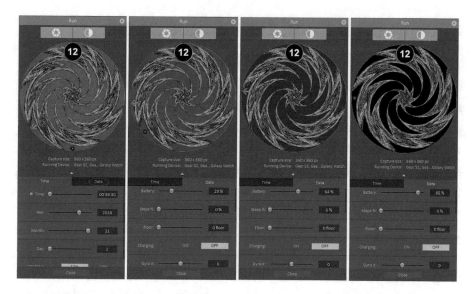

Figure 9-18. *Test Conditional Battery % logic, using Data Tab, in Run (emulator)*

As I drag the Battery slider to the right, shown in the other three panels, from 29% to 64% to 85% battery power, the background image darkens from bright red to black, showing that our conditional battery % (power) percentage-based conditional setting works as intended.

There is another of these conditional percentage types, which we are covering in this chapter, for Steps %, as you may have noticed in Figure 9-1. This works in exactly the same way as Battery % does, using 100 blocks or frames to define what happens (Shows or Hides) for each of the 0% to 100% of your Walking (Steps) workout target.

I'm not going to duplicate the first part of the chapter now that you know the work process to implement this, as it is largely the same, but we can go over how to do a Steps % Watch Face Design before we finish up with this chapter so you can create a visual steps taken watch face design and get some practice implementing conditional percentage-based smart watch design in Galaxy Watch Designer.

Setting Up a Conditional Steps Grid

To set up a Steps-based visual watch face design, create about ten watch face background assets in GIMP going from bright blue (Blue Ribbon First Place) or bright gold (Gold Star for Goal Achievement) just as we did using the work process shown in Figures 9-2 through 9-5. Then select the Steps % Condition Tab as shown in Figure 9-1, and add the ten asset layers (and rename them) as shown in Figures 9-6 and 9-7. Next, implement ten steps (levels) of color saturation as your steps goals are completed by hiding the brightest color assets from 0% to 10% down to the brightest color background asset, indicating that the steps goal has been achieved.

Notice that this is the opposite of what we did regarding battery power usage, where we went from bright red at 0% power to black at 100% power. Steps will go from 0% Steps Taken Goal being black to 100% Goal Achieved being bright blue or bright gold. This means that the layers will have to be in the opposite order for Steps % Conditional design, with the Bright Color asset on the bottom layer and the black vector asset on the topmost layer, so that 0% (Black) turns to Dark Blue (10%) to Navy Blue (20%) to Medium Blue (30%) to Blue (40%) to Cornstarch Blue (50%) to Light Blue (60%) to Dark Cyan (70%) to Cyan (80%) to a Lighter Cyan (90%), and so forth.

The other conditionals are all-or-nothing (12-Hour or 24-Hour or Kilometers or Miles) and are therefore much wider blocks and easier to implement compared to Time (using Hour or Minute Resolution Setting) or Percentage Conditions, which use 12, 60, or 100 blocks (frames).

Summary

This chapter shows Galaxy Watch Face developers how to implement conditional logic; in this case, we are going to make the watch face design turn from black to red as the battery power runs out, that is, from 100% down toward 0% battery charge. The first thing that we do is to look at how to use the latest version of GIMP (2.10.10) to create a few watch face pinwheel background assets using our black vector pinwheel asset, and then how to implement the conditions (Battery Power Percentage) which are necessary to change this background asset as the battery power runs out on the smartwatch.

Next, we reinforced how to implement conditional logic using the Timeline area of the GWD, this time to **block-select** or **multi-select** the multiple frame elements in the Timeline, so we can more rapidly implement our conditional logic related to **Battery Power Percentage** (ranging from 0%, or zero, to 100%) requiring 100 frames (or blocks) in the Timeline Editor pane. This is an important concept, and technique, for Galaxy Watch Designers to learn how to implement, so that they can more quickly and efficiently utilize the Galaxy Watch Face Design 1.6 software package. We will continue to explore advanced concepts such as this in Chapters 10 through 14 throughout the remainder of this book.

CHAPTER 10

Watch Face Complication Design

In this tenth chapter of the *Smartwatch Design Fundamentals* book, let's get into designing those little "watch faces within a watch face," called "complications." These are very common on watches typically referred to as "chronograph" watches, although with the proliferation of different sensors on smartwatches; these little subdials often contain information regarding steps taken, heart rate, battery power used, altitude, and so on. There is a special Complication Component at the bottom of the Component pane, and you could think of this as a "subroutine" for a watch within a watch, since you can design component faces much like you can design a watch face, which we will see later on in this chapter.

In the first part of this chapter, we'll outline the several different types of components which you can utilize in your watch face designs, and what each of these compliment types can show on the surface of your watch face design, and how you can add layers to decorate them.

We will then show you how to add a simple **Steps %** component to your Chapter 8 Vector Illustration watch face, since we showed you how to use the Conditional Timeline Frames to do this in Chapter 9.

We will then look at how components that have been added can be modified so that you know that you can create custom compliments, just like you can create custom watch faces. We will learn how to use the Text

© Wallace Jackson 2019
W. Jackson, *SmartWatch Design Fundamentals*,
https://doi.org/10.1007/978-1-4842-4369-5_10

component, and rearrange, reconfigure, and test (Run) added compliment assets, by using the **Layer** pane and the **Properties** pane.

Watch Face Complication Types

There are five categories of watch face complications, ranging from the simple complications (text readouts) to those which are more complex (those with moving parts tied to smartwatch hardware sensors). Let's cover these first, so that you have an overview of what can be added to your watch face design to inform the smartwatch user about additional data and features, such as Altitude, Temperature, Steps, or Heart Rate.

Text-Based Complications

Text complications are the simplest type of complication, as they only show information using font resources (numbers and letters). Thus, the font type, color, and size are the most important design characteristics.

Text Combined with Icon Complications

Text with an icon complication indicates the information type using an icon and then shows the current sensor data in real time using text and numeric values. For this type of complication, your icon graphic, icon color, and font type, size, and color used are the most important watch face design characteristics.

Icon Only Complications

Icon (only) complications provide an indication to a feature state (musical note that indicates music is playing) or the presence of an available feature (envelope indicates mail waiting for review) through an icon with no accompanying text or data value. If an icon changes to show a data value (such as a battery icon that shows itself charging up), then it becomes a "Gauge" complication, which we will cover next. These Gauge and "Hands" complications are the more complex types.

Gauge Complications

Gauge complications show data values as a percentage without using what look like watch face hands (so does not look like a speedometer or meter type of display). This could be done by using an icon that changes (animates) such as a battery outline which fills up with green as it charges or loses green as it drains. This can also be done by using a solid color circular progress bar or a rectangle that fills with color, or a 3D asset that changes its shape according to the status of a given data value, oftentimes hardware sensor inputs to a complication.

Hands (Metered) Complications

Hands complications look more like a meter, or a gauge in an automobile, with markings around the perimeter which have a hand or hands pointing to the value at hand (taken out of a range of values). This serves to show a relative level of a data value as compared to a whole range of possible data values. Note that for a Hands Complication, this is accomplished by using tiny watch face hands. There is actually a sixth type of complication, which I am going to show you how to create in this chapter, which is the "Hands Plus Icon" type, where I combine the Steps Icon with a Hand that goes from a 0% to 100% Steps Goal, and add a few numbers (0, 25, 75) to indicate this progress visually, turning the complication into a Steps Progress Meter.

Adding a Watch Face Complication

Let's start out by launching the Galaxy Watch Face Designer software package and using the New Project dialog that appears on start-up to open the project we created in Chapters 7 and 8. If you wanted a power indicator feature in the design as well, you can even open CH9's project, and use that, if you wanted to include the **Conditional Battery %** logic.

Use the New Project dialog, shown in Figure 10-1, to open the **CH8_Conditional_Watch_Face** project by selecting it (shown in blue), and then click the **OK** button, also shown highlighted in blue.

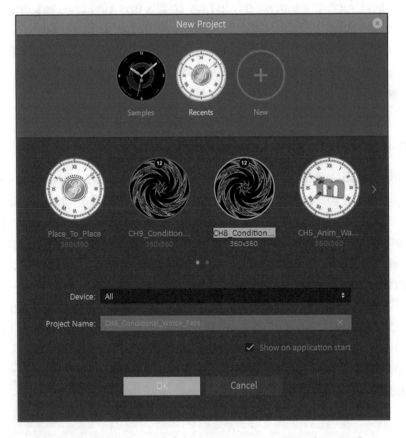

Figure 10-1. *Click the Plus (+) Tab next to the Timeline Tab to open a Battery Tab*

286

Click the **Complications** option in the **Components** pane on the left side of GWD, and select the **Workout** menu and **Speed_Analog** sub-menu. These are seen in Figure 10-2, encircled in red and highlighted in blue. The Galaxy Watch Designer will put three layers for this Hands Plus (Steps) Icon complication at the very top of the layer compositing stack.

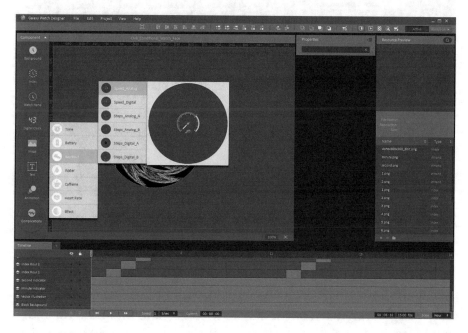

Figure 10-2. *Click Component ➤ Complications and then Workout ➤ Speed Analog*

As you can see in Figure 10-3, the current Analog Steps Speed Complication has been designed using alpha channel (transparency) for all three of its layer-based components (currently Hand 1, Image 1, and Background 1, until we rename those layers during our work process).

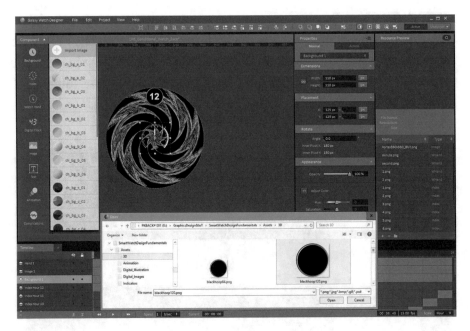

Figure 10-3. *Locate the blackhoop120.png to use as a complication*
background

The center of our Vector Illustration artwork is far too busy to be
used as the background for this complication, so we will need to add in a
solid background (we'll use the one we used for Hour Indicators, back in
Chapter 7), so that we can see this complication more clearly, located at
the very center of the new watch face design.

To do this, we will highlight (select) Background 1 and use the
Background icon in the Component pane and select the **Import Image**
menu item, seen in blue at the top of the menu option list in Figure 10-3.

Locate the **blackhoop120.png** file in the **/Assets/3D/** folder, and click
Open to insert it in the Complication as the new background image asset
as shown selected in blue at the right side of an Open dialog seen at the
bottom of Figure 10-3. This will place it at the top left (X/Y: 0, 0) of your
watch face design, as you will see if you look ahead to Figure 10-4.

Figure 10-4. *Drag Background 2 Layer on top of (under) your Background 1 Layer*

The first thing that you will want to do is to reorder your Layer compositing order, by dragging **Background 2** on top of **Background 1** to tell Galaxy Watch Designer that it should composite (show or render) it as being underneath the rest of the complication design elements.

Dragging the Background 2 layer on top of a Background 1 layer will cause Background 1 to illuminate, and be outlined in blue, indicating that it is the target layer on top of which you are dropping Background 2 in order to change the layer order, do this so you can see the added complication design details (the Hand, Steps Icon, and Meter Markings background).

Once the Background 2 is underneath Background 1 in the layer order compositing stack, you can grab (click and hold) this background asset, and drag it underneath the new complication, so that you can see it clearly using the black background color, with a silver hoop around it.

You can look ahead to Figure 10-5 to see what this looks like if you wish. Next we will use the arrow keys on the keyboard to fine-tune the pixel positioning of the background around the complication interior design components. If it's a pixel off, I put a blackhoop1024.png asset in this book's assets repository, so that you can resize a 119 pixel version.

I used a 119,119 pixel Placement setting as seen in Figure 10-5.

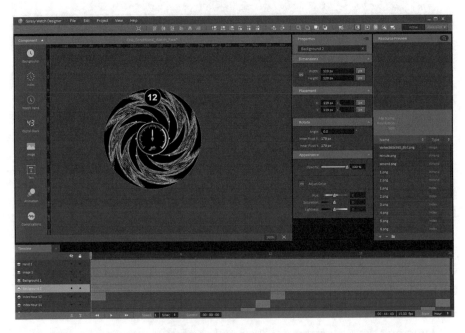

Figure 10-5. *Center Complication in Background 2 using Properties* ➤ *Placement*

Next, I saved the work done so far adding a complication to the Chapter 8 watch face design, by using the **File ➤ Save As** menu sequence, seen at the top left in Figure 10-6 to open the **Save As** dialog, and gave the project a new name of **CH10_Complication_Watch_Face**. I will do this before I use the **Run** icon (emulator), to test what we have in place so far, and before we change the functionality of the complication, and turn it into a **Steps %** Complication, by changing its design component layers and settings in the next section of this chapter.

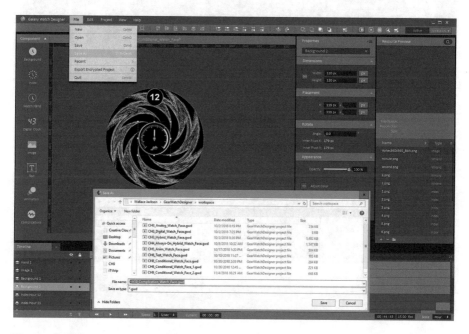

Figure 10-6. *Use Save As to save new CH10_Complication_Watch_ Face project*

Next let's select the **Hand 1** layer for the compliment and set the Steps % function, so that it tracks the percentage, from 0% to 100%, of your **Steps Goal**. To do this, we go into the **Rotation Properties** section of the **Properties** panel, and select the **Sync With:** drop-down selector option for **Conditions ➤ Steps %** as is shown selected in Blue in Figure 10-7. This will make our Hand rotate from High Noon (0%) back around to 100%. This means that we will need to hide, or even remove (delete) the default Background 1 (speed gauge marking) from the complication design at some point, and add our own, which we will be doing next.

Figure 10-7. *Set Sync with Conditions ➤ Steps % in the Rotation Properties pane*

When you select the **Steps %** (as well as the Step counts, and Speed options, which I tried and tested but were not yet implemented), you may get a **Warning** dialog, shown in Figure 10-8, which advises you that certain features do not work with other features as of yet, as this software package is still under development. I expect that Samsung will get their code working for these Galaxy Watch Designer conditions and complications, which implement things like Weather and Sensors into your watch face design process, sometime in early 2019, around the time that this book has been released. I ignored this warning, and instead used the **Run** (emulator testing) icon, to test and to see which conditions would work as complications in my watch face design, and decided to use the Steps % feature, to show you how to custom modify added complications to better suit your custom watch face designs.

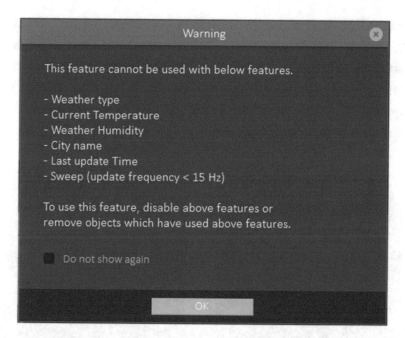

Figure 10-8. *Take note of all Warning dialogs, and exit them using the OK button*

Since smartwatch models all implement different sensors and features, watch face design can be a bit of a moving target, especially for the programmers working on the Galaxy Watch Designer software. As the Team at Samsung adds features and removes bugs, releasing new versions every month or two, warnings like this should fade away.

Next, let's test the existing complication as added, before you start modifying it to be a custom complication which suits your **Steps %** needs. To do this, we will use the **Run** (inside Galaxy Watch Designer emulator) Icon, located at the top right of the Galaxy Watch Designer.

As you did in Chapter 9, click the **Data Tab** on the right-hand side of the Run emulator window, and switch over to the testing modes that are for testing sensors and all the other **Non-Time-Based** features.

You will see the **Steps % Slider Bar** as you scroll down through the testing options using your mouse scroll wheel or the drag-bar on the right side of the Run window. I encircled it in red in Figure 10-9 so that you could see that I had dragged it 15% of the way over and that this Steps % was showing in the Hand rotation of the **Speed_Analog** complication design, which we will be showing you how to change to be the **Steps %** Complication design. We will do this by modifying and adding new layers into the layer compositing stack inside of the Galaxy Watch Designer.

Figure 10-9. *Use Run* ➤ *Data Tab to drag Steps % Slider, and test complication*

What I want to do to "transmute" (change across layers) this new complication into a Steps % Complication is to move that **steps icon** up, turn it into gold, get rid of those speed gauge markings (Background 1), and add **Text** Component design elements (since we haven't used Text Components in our design work as yet) to create **0, 25**, and **75** markings (at High Noon, 3 O'clock, and 9 O'clock positions) as well as a **Steps % Text** readout element at the bottom of the complication, in the 6 O'clock position. We will also see how to use the Galaxy Watch Designer **color picker** dialog to color the text elements, so lots of new features to learn!

Design a Watch Face Complication

Let's start redesigning the complication by selecting a **Step Icon (Shoe)** layer, shown highlighted in blue, and encircled in red, in Figure 10-10. Set the color sliders to Hue **50**, Saturation **75**, and Lightness **20**, giving the shoe icon a golden color, which looks pretty cool. Use the **up arrow** key on your keyboard to move the shoe up a few pixels (to **Y** of **115**) closer to the Hand. The Properties settings can be seen encircled in red in Figure 10-10, and once we delete Background 1, we will have room for number calibration around the inside of the complication edge, which we will add next, after we make room for it by deleting the **Background 1** speed calibration markings, which don't work correctly with Steps Percentage.

Figure 10-10. *Select Steps Icon layer and position at 115 Y up underneath the Hand*

Click the dot in the Eye column of the **Background 1** layer, to turn off its visibility in the **Preview** area, to make sure that this is that speed calibration marking asset (in the complication) you wish to delete. If it is, right-click the layer, and select a **Delete** option, and remove it.

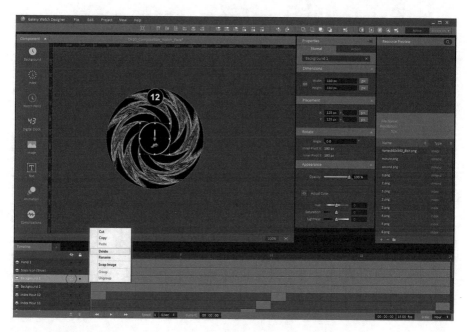

Figure 10-11. *Hide Background 1 layer (to make sure) and then right-click ➤ Delete*

Click the **Steps Icon (Shoe)** layer, to make it the active layer, and click the **Text Component**, shown encircled in red in Figure 10-12, to insert the Text asset into the complication design. Select the **Steps %** Text asset, which will insert a Text asset which will **update** as the Steps Percentage increases, from 0% of Steps Goal to 100% of Steps Goal.

Figure 10-12. *Add a Text Component for Steps % above the Background 2 layer*

Therefore, there are Text assets which are connected to code and which update dynamically (let's call these **dynamic** Text assets) as well as Text assets which are simply fonts that you can set to font name and font style and define the text value by typing in your own character values (let's call these **static** Text assets). We will use both of these in our design modifications in this section, so that you have some experience using both types of Text Components in your designs.

When you add a Text Component, just like all other components, it appears at the top left of the watch face design, at a 0,0 pixel location. If it is a Text Component, and you click it, the text value highlights in blue, and you can type in your desired value, if it is static Text. If it is a dynamic Text component, it updates its own values, like in the **Steps %** Text we just added, so all that you need to do is to drag it into position.

Let's drag the Steps % dynamic Text component into position, underneath the Steps % Shoe Icon, and let's also **decrease** its font size down to 20 pixels, from the default 24 pixel size. We may decrease this even more, later on, to match the static Text component indicators that we will be adding at the 3 O'clock, 9 O'clock, and High Noon positions on the revised complication, to indicate 0%, 25%, and 75% on the Steps % gauge complication we are creating here.

Drag the dynamic Text Steps % indicator to the **125, 185 - X, Y** position location underneath the Steps % Shoe Icon, as shown encircled in red in Figure 10-13 along with the Font Size adjustment. As you can see, the 20 pixel font size is still a bit too large to fit comfortably under the Steps % (shoe) icon, so we may adjust this size downward a little later on during the tweaking (adjustment) of this complication design modification. We will also take a look at how to color the static Text markers to better match the gold show, starting at Yellow (0) and getting warmer (orange for 25 and then red for 75). We will leave the dynamic Steps % readout at the bottom of the complication under the shoe at White, to match the Hand color, which we will also leave White.

Figure 10-13. *Drag Steps % Text under the shoe icon, and set Font Size to 20*

Since we're tweaking this design, I'm going to move the opening on the gold shoe to a **127,111 X,Y** location, to center the shoe under the hand, as seen in Figure 10-14 encircled in red in the Properties Placement pane.

Figure 10-14. *Adjust positioning of Gold Shoe to 127,111; center under hand*

Let's use the **Run** (icon) to access the smartwatch emulator in the Galaxy Watch Designer software, and see just how our watch face design looks, as well as how it responds to **Steps % Slider** movement. This can be seen in Figure 10-15. As you can see on the left, the Steps % Font Size is a bit too big for the design, and it looks like we should reduce it by another 4 pixels, from 20 pixels to 16 pixels, which we will do next, and the results of which share this screenshot on the right-hand side of the figure, which shows the new font size and colors.

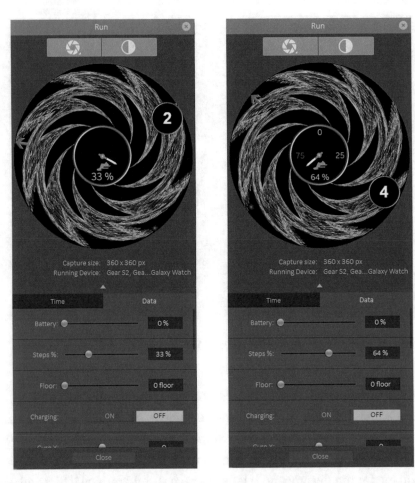

Figure 10-15. *Test Font Size, Text Position, Color, and modifications using Run*

You will see that the Hand points to the correct Steps % around the perimeter of the complication, as you drag the **Steps % Slider Bar** under the **Data Tab** to test whether or not this has now been "wired up" correctly in the **Properties (Sync with:)** drop-down selector widget.

Next, let's add some static **Normal Text Components**, and add three markers to the top center (0), right (25), and left (75) of the new Steps % Complication which we are currently designing. To add the zero indicator at the top of the complication, click the **Text Component**, seen encircled in red in Figure 10-16, and select the **Normal Text** option, shown highlighted in blue.

Figure 10-16. *Add a static Normal Text Component to show percentage markers*

This places the Text asset at the top left of the watch face design at 0,0. Click this and type in a **Zero (0)** character, and then click and drag the zero Text asset into place, at the top center of the complication. If you look ahead to Figure 10-17, you can see what this should look like before we also color the zero a bright yellow, by using the Color Picker. In fact, let's do that next and learn how to use the **Color Picker Tool**.

Figure 10-17. *Click a Yellow area of the Color Picker to set the zero Text color*

Notice in Figure 10-17 that I have encircled the **Color Appearance** Properties section, which has a **hexadecimal** representation, which you will text edit to specify precise color values, as well as the rectangular, clickable, **color swatch**, which you can click to open a Color Picker.

Let's do that now, and click the rectangular (it's initially white) color swatch, and open the **Color Picker** dialog, shown in the middle of Figure 10-17. Click the bright yellow area between green and red, so you can visually set the yellow **#FFFB67** color value you clicked. The Color Picker is a much loved tool because it allows you to set values for coding visually, as many would not be able to come up with a #FFFB67 value to get this yellow-gold color, without using this Color Picker Tool.

The next things that we need to do, all shown in Figure 10-18, involve setting the **Font Size** to **16**, positioning the zero at **127,102** to better center it under the (vertical) Hand component, and clicking the (static) Text

Component and again selecting **Normal Text** to add the **25** percentage indicator at a 3 O'clock position in this new design. Set a **25** value in the Text component, and drag it into place (see Figure 10-19).

Figure 10-18. *Reduce Font Size to 16, Position 0 at 127,102, and Add Text*

As is shown, encircled in red, in Figure 10-19, color your **25** Text **Orange**, position it at **165,150**, and set the **Font Size** to **16 pixels**.

Figure 10-19. *Set Font Size to 16, Position 25 at 165,150, and set Color to Orange*

Next, let's add the 75 marker using a Text value of 75, a **Font Size** of **16**, and a **Properties Placement** of **87, 147** at the 9 O'clock location. Click the Color Swatch and open the Color Picker dialog, and click the Red area to set a Red color, as shown in Figure 10-20. Now our 0, 25, and 75 markers are balanced (16 pixels each) and grow from Yellow to Orange to Red in color warmth the more the Steps Goal is achieved. The only thing that we have to do now is to shrink down the Steps % Text object to match the rest of the complication design; let's do that next!

Figure 10-20. *Set Font Size to 16, Position 75 at 87,147, and set Color to Red*

As you can see in Figure 10-21, encircled in Red, I renamed the static **Text Component** Layers 0% Marker through 75% Marker, and selected the **Steps % Text** layer, the **Font Size** pop-up menu, and then the **16 pixels** value to match the three perimeter marker Text assets. I also grabbed the 75 Marker and aligned it with the 25 Marker using the purple alignment lines, and I moved it a few pixels closer to the steel ring surrounding the Complication using the left arrow key on my keyboard to "nudge" the 75 into a better position at 9 O'clock.

Figure 10-21. *Set Steps % Dynamic Text to match Font Size of 16 in drop-down*

Next, let's make this compliment **clickable**, so that it opens up the **Samsung Health App (Steps Section)**, so I can show you how to make your complications clickable (make them into a **Button**) next.

Making a Complication into a Button

To set up a Complication to become a button (to be able to be clicked to open an application), you will want to right-click the top-right corner of the Properties pane, as is shown in Figure 10-22. The context-sensitive menu that appears has a "Set as Button" option, which turns blue when selected (as shown). I selected the Background 2 Layer before invoking this option; it has the largest area to be clicked as far as the Complication's design elements (components) are concerned. You want to attach this clickability to the largest component of the complication (not the shoe icon, numbers, or hand design elements), so that the user has the best chance of opening the application when they touch the complication itself on the watch face.

Figure 10-22. *Right-click the corner of the Properties pane; select Set as Button*

Select the **Action ➤ Open App** option as shown in Figure 10-23.

Figure 10-23. *Select Action option for Open App to add an Open App drop-down*

Select the **Samsung Health ➤ Steps** application, in the **Open App** drop-down selector, as is shown in Figure 10-24.

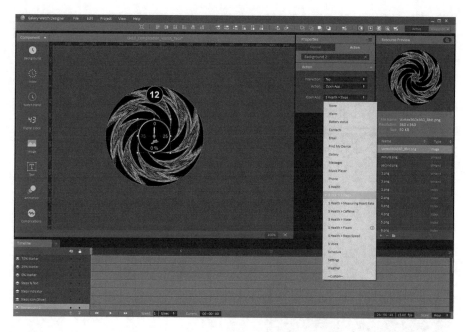

Figure 10-24. *Select Samsung Health ➤ Step, in Open App drop-down selector*

Let's use the **Run** icon to test the complication, and see how it looks and what happens when one clicks the complication itself. As you can see in Figure 10-25, the Galaxy Watch Designer pops open a dialog which informs the developer that the **Samsung Health ➤ Steps** application has been opened and suggests testing the watch face design on a "Real Device" hardware using the **Run on Device** icon at the top right of the Galaxy Watch Designer.

Figure 10-25. *Use a Run icon to test the complication in Galaxy Watch Designer*

Watch face designers serious about watch face design will most likely purchase a Gear or Galaxy Smartwatch in order to test watch face and complication designs. Fortunately, I can test most of the cool features in the Galaxy Watch Designer using the Run (emulator) icon, allowing this book to educate readers on most of the features.

As you can see, designing a Complication is in many ways like designing a watch face. You have now learned how to use static Text

Components as well as dynamic Text components, which can be used in watch face design as well as in Complication design.

In the next chapter, we'll get into even more advanced aspects of watch face design.

Summary

In this chapter we took a look at how to add premade "complications" provided by the Galaxy Watch Designer, as well as how to create your own custom complications, by modifying an existing complication. We also looked at how to make a complication clickable and how to test a complication using the Run (emulator) Icon. A watch face complication is like a miniature watch face design within a larger watch face design, so in coding terms, it is like creating a subroutine for your watch face design (visually).

We started out by looking at the different types of complications that you can utilize within your watch face designs, and then we looked at how to add an existing watch complication by using the **Component ➤ Complication** pane, found on the left side of Galaxy Watch Design 1.6 software package.

After that, we looked at how to add our own (image) assets and different types of static and dynamic Text assets to the complication, in order to create a custom complication designed for the center of our pinwheel watch face design. This is visually impressive for our pinwheel design, so that if we ever spin our pinwheel, it will rotate behind this centered complication. In this case, the complication is for steps goal percentage achievement.

Finally, we looked at how to make a complication clickable, as well as how to test our custom complication and its clickability, using the Run (emulator) Icon. We will continue to address advanced topics in the final four chapters of this book.

CHAPTER 11

Watch Face Gyroscopic Design: Using the Gyroscope

In this eleventh chapter of the *Smartwatch Design Fundamentals* book, let's get into designing what are called "Parallax" watch faces with gyroscopic or gyro-based watch face components, called "gyroscopes," which was a recent feature added in **V.1.5.2**. These are used on watch faces that are customized, that is, those which use components dragged out of the GWD **Components (Left Pane) ➤ Complications (Bottom Icon) ➤ Effects (Pop-out Menu) ➤ Gyro Effects (Autobahn | Cube | Gyro_Effect | Leveler | Light_Effect | Sub-Menus).**

In this chapter, you will learn what the **Properties ➤ Gyro Effect** dialog is and where it can be implemented in your watch face design components.

In the first part of this chapter, we'll outline the several different types of gyro effects which you can implement in the Gyro Effect dialog.

We will then show you how to add basic gyro animation (a spin) of the black vector illustration background pinwheel we created by using Creative Commons Zero, open source Inkscape, and GIMP 2.10.10.

© Wallace Jackson 2019
W. Jackson, *SmartWatch Design Fundamentals*,
https://doi.org/10.1007/978-1-4842-4369-5_11

We will then look at how components that have been added can be modified so that you know that you can create custom Gyro Effects compliments such as the **Compliment ➤ Gyro Effect ➤ Light Effect**.

Applying Gyro Effects to Components

There are seven categories of gyroscopic effects, ranging from **rotation** to **scale** (called **Dimension**) to **movement** (called **Pivot Point X and Y**) to translucence (called **Opacity**). Each set of fields (text inputs/readouts) takes to and from values which will **interpolate** based on **X or Y or XY** gyro sensor movement of the smartwatch. This determines how the watch face design component (Watch Hand, Image, Index, Complication, etc.) will behave when it is controlled by the gyroscope sensor in the smartwatch using these 15 data fields in the **Gyro Effect** control panel, which we will be exploring in detail in this chapter to see how you can use it to apply these 3D special effects. Note that this is a very advanced area of interfacing your watch face design with one of the most advanced sensors in the smartwatch, and therefore the only real way to master it is through repeated entry of data values in the Gyro Effect dialog and testing (and tweaking) the results on the Run emulator as well as on real smartwatch devices.

Range (-Degrees to +Degrees)

This determines the range of movement (rotation) from degrees to degrees as well as the number of times (which is why there are three data fields in this first or topmost section of the Gyro Effects dialog).

Dimension X (Scale 0% to 100%)

The second section of the Gyro Effects dialog determines the X Dimension (Scale) of the component, from 0.0 (0%) to 1.0 (100%).

Dimension Y (Scale 0% to 100%)

The third section of the Gyro Effects dialog determines the Y Dimension (Scale) of the component, from 0.0 (0%) to 1.0 (100%).

Inner Pivot X (0 pixels to 0 pixels)

The next two sections of the Gyro Effects dialog determine the X Pivot (Movement) of the component, from 0 (pixels) to N (total number of pixels of movement).

Inner Pivot Y (0 pixels to 0 pixels)

The fifth section of the Gyro Effects dialog determines the Y Pivot (Movement) of the component, from 0 (pixels) to N (total number of pixels of movement).

Rotate (Degrees to Degrees)

The fourth section of the Gyro Effects dialog determines the Rotation (to and from) of the component, from 0 (pixels) to 360 (degrees of rotation). This is used to rotate a watch face component around its pivot point (center)

Opacity (0% to 100%)

The fifth section of the Gyro Effects dialog determines the Opacity (translucency) of the component, from 0 (opaque) to 100% (solid). This is to fade the component in and out of view, as you will see later on in this chapter when we apply a light reflection to the watch face design using a Component ➤ Complication ➤ Effect ➤ Light Effect menu.

Adding a Watch Face Gyro Rotation

Let's start out by launching the Galaxy Watch Face Designer software package so we can use the New Project dialog that appears on start-up to open the project we created in Chapter 10 and make the background pinwheel rotate using the Gyro Effect dialog Rotate setting.

As you can see in Figure 11-1, to apply the Gyro Effect to the CH10 project, we select the Vector Illustration (image) Layer and click the icon to the left of the **Gyro Effect** section of the **Properties** dialog, which you can access by scrolling down in the **Properties** pane, using your middle-mouse wheel or the pane's right-side scroll bar.

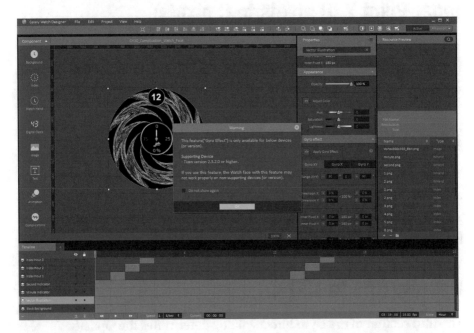

Figure 11-1. *Click OK to Tizen 2.3 or later; enable the Gyro Effect dialog for use*

A **Warning** dialog will appear, advising that Tizen 2.3.2 watches or higher are required to use the Gyroscope feature and that it may not work on older Samsung smartwatches. Click OK to acknowledge this **Warning** dialog, and it will vanish, and we will continue to set Rotation values for the Gyro Effect. As you can see (encircled in red) in Figure 11-1, there is a button to the left of the Gyro Effects section title that can be clicked to enable the Gyro Effect.

Notice that the default Gyro Effect rotation Range is set from -90 degrees to +90 degrees from zero degrees in the dialog. This should be fine for our background pinwheel to spin around behind the Steps % Complication we added in Chapter 10. Let's get the Gyro Effect and the Steps % Complication working together in the same watch face design now!

The first thing that you will want to do is to enter 90 in the Range section of the dialog, as seen at the top of Figure 11-2. I tested this in the Run (emulator) and it did nothing on gyro rotation, so I entered the Rotate section of the dialog next and specified 90 -0- to 90 degrees and then tested it again in the **Run ➤ Data Tab ➤ Gyro X Slider** to see if it was working. It was, and the Vector Illustration was spinning when the watch's X Gyro Tab was used. Since the code is currently hidden in the Galaxy Watch Designer, the best way to test features such as the Gyroscope is to set your data values and then use the **Run ➤ Data Tab ➤ Gyro X and Y Sliders** to test your watch face design.

Figure 11-2. *Set Rotate to 90 degrees of Range, and Rotate the data values*

You can look ahead to Figure 11-2.

Test the 90 degree **Placement ➤ Gyro Effect ➤ Y Tab** setting, seen in the Run (emulator) in Figure 11-5. The **Steps %** works as well, as you can see on the right side (**Steps % Slider** works) of Figure 11-3.

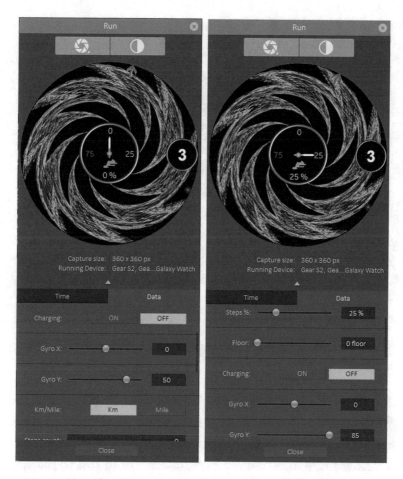

Figure 11-3. *Test the Gyroscope using Run ➤ Data*

Next, I saved the work done so far adding a Gyro Effect to the Chapter 8 watch face design, by using the **File ➤ Save As** menu sequence, seen at the top left in Figure 11-4 to open the File ➤ Save As menu sequence, and gave this Gyroscope project the new name of **CH11_Gyroscope_Watch_Face**. I will do this before I use the **Run** icon (emulator), to test what we have in place so far, and before we change the functionality of the complication, and turn it into a **Steps %** Complication, by changing its design component layers and settings in the next section of this chapter.

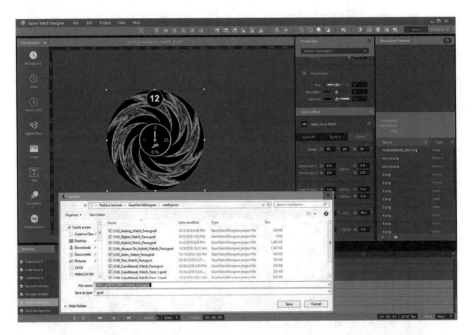

Figure 11-4. *Use Save As, to save new CH11_Gyroscope1_Watch_
Face project*

Next, let's add a **Components ➤ Complication ➤ (Gyro) Effects
➤ Light_Effect** layer for the compliment and set the watch face effect
that puts a ray of light reflection complication on top of the watch face,
so that it looks more three dimensional, rotating from 15% to 100%, with
Opacity from 25% (we'll use 51% to see it better) to 50%. To do this, we
will go through the steps shown in the next section of the chapter, seen in
Figures 11-7 through 11-11.

Adding a Gyro Effect Complication

Let's add a Gyro Effect to the top of our watch face design, as shown in
Figure 11-5. Select the top layer in the project, which now has dozens
of layers (a complex project with conditions, complications, gyroscopic

movement, and now a Light_Effect Complication on top of it all!). Click the
Components ➤ Complications ➤ (Gyro) Effect ➤ Light_Effect menu
sequence, and add the Light_Effect image (gray on black) shown in the
middle of Figure 11-5.

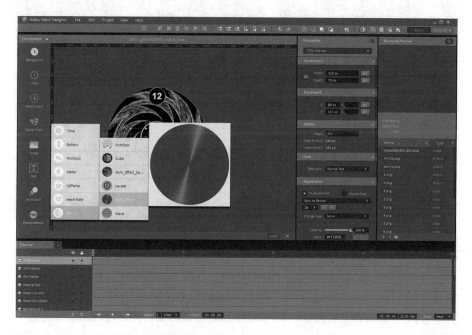

Figure 11-5. *Click the top layer and add a Complication Gyro Effect*
➤ Light Effect

Rename the top layer Light_Effect (Gyro) as is shown in Figure 11-6,
and review the Image Properties ➤ Rotate settings of 15% seen in
Figure 11-6 encircled in red and Properties ➤ Appearance ➤ Opacity ➤
25%, which we will increase to 51% before testing so that we can see the
effect better when testing it in the Run (emulator) in GWD. Scroll down in
the Properties pane (using the middle mouse wheel or right-side scroll bar),
to see the settings in the Gyro Effects section next.

Figure 11-6. *Gyro Light Effect Rotate is 15 degrees and 25% Opacity initially*

As you can see in Figure 11-7, the **Range** goes from **-90 to 90** degrees (the default values), and the XY Dimensions (Scale) and XY Pivot Points (Move) are also left unchanged (default zero values).

Figure 11-7. *Rename Layer Light Effect (Gyro); observe Rotate/ Opacity settings*

The Light Beam Effect image is rotated by the **Properties ➤ Gyro Effect ➤ Rotate** by **-15 degrees**, and **Properties ➤ Gyro Effect ➤ Opacity** is changed by **-25%** in the Y dimension, as the smartwatch user rotates their wrist in both directions.

You can see the results of these settings in the **Run** (emulator) in the GWD, which is now working with Gyro Effect.

To see this Light Reflection image better in the Run (emulator), I also upped the **Properties ➤ Appearance ➤ Opacity to 51%** (Figure 11-7), so that this Light Reflection image compositing could be seen better against your Chapter 8 watch face design when it was being run in the emulator.

You can see the Run (emulator) in Figure 11-8, in which I have tested your new watch face design by using the **Gyro Y Slider**, which is rotating and fading the Light Reflection image as is specified in the Gyro Effect Rotation and Opacity sections.

Figure 11-8. *Increase Opacity to 51% so you can see the Gyro Effect and test it*

I did the screenshot with the watch face compositing Layer setup (image at 51% Opacity is seen encircled in red) and placed it right next to the Run (emulator) so that you could see the effect of pulling the **Gyro Y Slider** to the 79% position. The Light Reflection image on top of the watch face design compositing stack rotates and fades as expected.

I also tested the watch face design Steps % Complication, which we added in Chapter 10, to make sure all of these complex features we have added since Chapter 8 are working together, as one seamless (complex) watch face design.

This watch face design includes Battery Power % Conditions, Hour Numbers Hide/Show Time Conditions, a Steps % Complication, and the Light_Effect Gyroscopic Effect Complication, all working at the same time together. Try it for yourself in the Run (emulator) and see! Even the pinwheel rotates under the Steps % Complication we added!

Let's use a **File ➤ Save As** menu sequence to Save the project as CH11_
Gyroscope2_Watch_Face_LightFX, as seen in Figure 11-9.

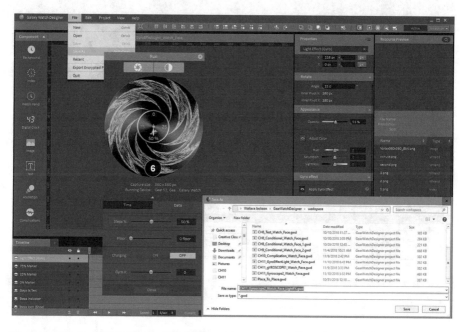

Figure 11-9. *Test Steps Complication to see if it works with Gyro
Effect; Save As*

Pretty cool that you can utilize all of these cutting-edge features
together in one watch face design.

Test the watch face design again using the negative **Gyro Y Slider**
direction, to see the light effect composite over (and affect) the **1 AM**
Hour Indicator, as is shown in Figure 11-10. This happens because it is at
the top of the layer compositing stack in the GWD Timeline. We left the
conditional time logic from Chapter 8 so that the Hour Indicators for each
hour still appear in the watch face design, and their layers are farther down
in the compositing stack. We added this Timeline-based Time Condition in
Chapters 7 and 8, covering the conditional logic setup, using the Timeline
pane, in the Galaxy Watch Designer.

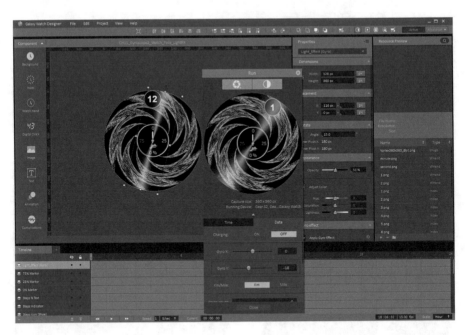

Figure 11-10. *Test the Light Effect in a negative Y direction of -18 and over 1 AM*

Galaxy Watch Designer executes our design from the bottom of the layer stack up, from background vector images and their rotational Gyro Effects, up through the hour and minute and seconds layers and their conditional time settings, up through the Steps % Complication, up through the Gyro Light_Effect on top, as you can see in Figure 11-11.

Figure 11-11. *Light_Effect covers Hour Indicator 8 at -42 Gyro Y Slider setting*

If you have turned a layer (view or eye icon) off, as I have in Figure 11-11 on the lower left (the white X on White Vector Illustration layer), you will not see that layer rendered in the Run (emulator) test pane, so you have the maximum flexibility in testing and building your watch face designs.

In Figure 11-12, I will turn that layer visibility back on, inserting it into the watch face design compositing and programming pipeline. As you can see, it's now visible in the watch face design and does not yet Rotate (as the Gyro Effect settings are not entered in the Gyro Effect section of its Properties Pane as yet), so the Gyro Y Rotation Slider will do nothing at this point in the design.

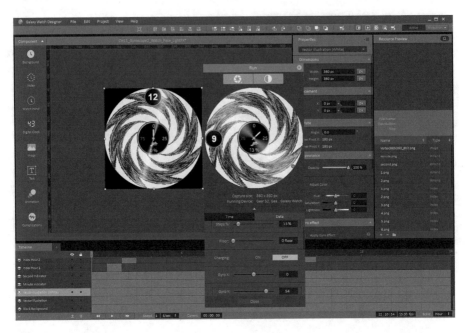

Figure 11-12. *Add White background above Default one and test Light_Effect*

As you can see in the Run (emulator), everything composites and executes as expected in the Galaxy Watch Designer. The Hour, Minute, and Seconds hands are rotating and appearing correctly based on the Time (Tab), and the Steps & Compliment and Gyro Effects are working correctly based on the settings in the Data Tab. You may want to increase Opacity in Light_Effect, to see it better!

Next, since we don't have the time or page bandwidth to create all new digital image assets using GIMP as we did in Chapter 7, let's use the Samples Projects included with Galaxy Watch Designer to look at how to create "Tubular" and "Perspective" isometric 3D effects using Gyroscopic sensors in the smartwatch using 2D images supplied with the software. This work process will let us examine how the Gyro Effect works and learn more about it and get more experience using it without using up too many pages (and figures) within this chapter.

Looking at the Sample Watch Faces

Another great way to investigate how the Gyro Effect works is to dissect the Sample Watch Faces that come with Galaxy Watch Designer. This is a great way to look at all of the GWD Features for new watch designers, so we are going to cover it here, relating to the Gyro Effect, so that the work process is covered in this book. Let's use a **File ➤ New** menu sequence to bring up a **New Project** dialog, seen in Figure 11-13. Click **Samples** at the top left and then the **Vacation** sample.

Figure 11-13. *Open the Vacation Watch Face in the Samples Projects area*

Test the Vacation **Gyro** Sample using the **Run** icon to launch the emulator in Galaxy Watch Designer. As you can see, there are layers for the AM indicator, as well as Hour and Minute text overlayed at the top of the compositing layer pipeline, shadows under that, and a floating person

PNG32 (Alpha) under that, and a PNG24 Pool Line Deformed Grid under
that (to indicate wave turbulence) and a shadow layer PNG32 under that,
and a blue water background color under that.

As you can see in Figure 11-14 in the Run (emulator) Icon pane, the
floating body (inner tube) and the time shadow can be moved using the
Gyro X and **Gyro Y** Sliders in the Data Tab.

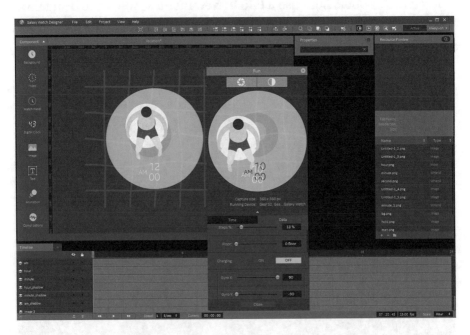

Figure 11-14.   *Test the Vacation sample, to see how the images move*
with Gyro

Notice in Figure 11-15 the Gyro Effect settings for each of the layer
elements, including the white time text and gray time text shadow, as one
must remain fixed, and one must move, to give the proper light source
offset effect shown in Figure 11-14. In fact, a great exercise to learn Gyro
Effect would be to make one move while the other remains fixed; it doesn't
matter which one has the Gryo Effect applied, as long as the Opacity levels
are applied correctly in the compositing pipeline, which is implemented
by the layer Z-order and the Opacity setting in the Properties dialog.

Figure 11-15. *Select the AM layer, and click the Gyro Effect Inner Pivot section*

As seen in Figure 11-15, the Gyro Effects setting for the **AM** indicator is **-137** pixels and **-301** pixels, so the white text is moving relative to the shadows, to create the drop-shadowing offset which can be seen in the **Run** (emulator) icon. You can look at the other layers in the watch face composite and look at GDW's **Properties ➤ Gyro Effect** pane to see which layers are Gyro positioned relative to each other in order to learn about how the Gyroscope effects are implemented for this watch face design.

The next thing that we need to do, all shown in Figure 11-16, is to look at the watch face layers, to see how they are composited, and to observe how each layer (design element) implements the Gyro Effect panel settings.

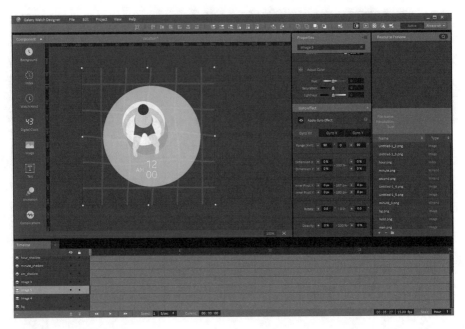

Figure 11-16. *Click Image 5 layer and review the Gyro Effect Inner Pivot settings*

As far as digital image compositing goes, the PNG32 image files include transparency (the inner tube and shadow). There is a Resource Preview pane on the far right of the Galaxy Watch Designer where you can see the image layer, file name (file type), resolution, and data footprint simply by clicking the layer name and the asset will be shown above along with its corresponding data. You can use this feature as well when you are dissecting sample files to see how they have been constructed. Be sure to do this using all of the GWD tools, as this is what we are learning in this section of the chapter. The Image 5 layer shown selected in Figure 11-16 contains the deformed grid which shows the watch face viewer that there is turbulence in the water (pool) that the inner tube is floating on. This is what is moving the inner tube and the shadow around relative to each other. Each layer plays a role in making the effect look more real, moving by using the Gyro Effect.

Fixing a Sample Watch Gyro Face

Let's fix the problem with one of the sample Gyro watch face designs!
Open the **Fly in the sky** sample watch face design project, as shown in
Figure 11-17. This project is in the **Samples** section of the Galaxy Watch
Designer software and also can be opened using the **File ➤ New Project**
dialog anytime you start up the software. Click the **Samples** section
(shown in red) in Figure 11-17, and then scroll right and click the Fly in the
sky 360 x 360 round watch face design and then the OK button to Open it
for closer review, which we will be doing in the final part of this chapter.

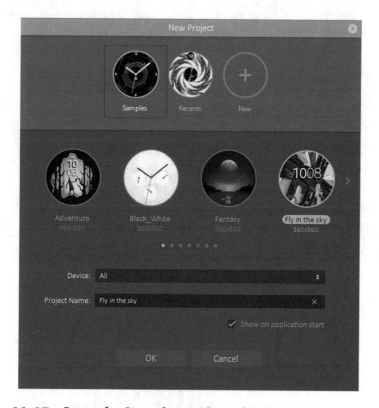

Figure 11-17. *Open the Samples ➤ Fly in the sky project*

Click the Background Image (bg) Layer and the Run Icon (emulator) to test the Sample Project, and see how it works by using the **Gyro X** and **Gyro Y** Sliders under the Data Tab.

As you can see in Figure 11-18, the background layer (i.e., bg) image is set to move **-183 X** pixels in the **Gyro Effect XY Tab** and thus moves slightly in both the X and Y directions when the X and Y Sliders are used (respectively).

Figure 11-18. *Select bg layer; Run (test) the left and right foot image with Gyro*

This is because any values entered in the XY Tab are applied as if they are entered in **both** the X and Y tabs, and this is where entering Gyro values can get very tricky for some advanced projects.

If you want the values applied to both X and Y Tabs equally, enter them in the XY Tab and not in the X and Y tabs. That is, only enter values in **one**

of the three tabs, X (X Only), Y (Y Only), or XY (X and Y Both), for each section of the Gyro Effects Tab.

In this way, advanced special effects can be created using the various sections of the Gyro Effects dialog, using these three different X, Y, and XY tabs, individually. You can only use one section of each tab at a time, so if you want to do something in X and Y, use the XY Tab!

The two dangling foot images (the left and right layers, as can be seen at the bottom-left in Figure 11-18) move separately, based on **Inner Pivot XY** settings, which can be seen in Figure 11-19. This is so that they can "dangle" more realistically in a watch face gyro simulation.

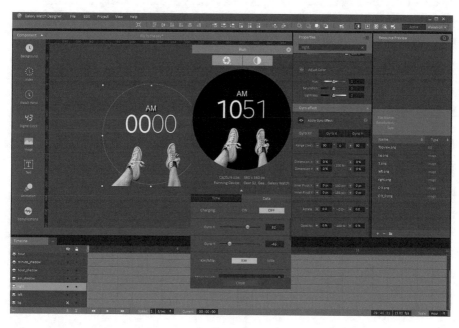

Figure 11-19. *The right foot image Layer Gyro Effect XY Tab is set to -186 pixels*

Both images use the **PNG32** alpha channel, so that they can be composited "over" the background image, which is probably a **PNG24**, and this shows you how this special effect be composited in real time using multiple images within multiple layers inside of the Galaxy Watch Designer.

The gyroscope sensor then attaches itself to each image individually, and moves each image individually, and the effect is then created within the composite, combined with the Z-order layering and alpha channel transparency.

This is why I included the advanced topics on GIMP 2.10 and digital image compositing in this book, because they are necessary to create advanced watch face designs, as you can see looking at these **Samples Projects** in the Galaxy Watch Designer. This work process is an important one to master for watch face designers!

I have clicked the white X in the bg or Background image layer, so that you can see (and test) the foot (left and right) images (layers), as can be seen in Figure 11-19.

Click the right (foot) layer, and take a look at the **Gyro Effect** Tab for the image, which can be seen in Figure 11-20 (notice that your bg or background layer is now hidden using the white X selector in the layer, so that we can better see the two foot alpha channel images).

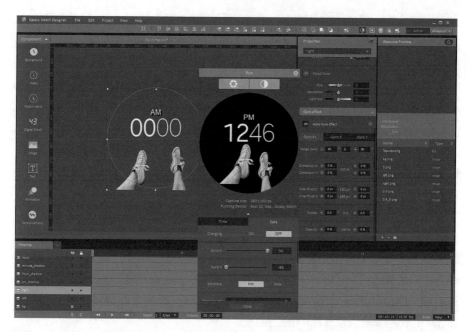

Figure 11-20. *The left foot image has a cutoff mistake, at Gyro X 90, Gyro Y -90*

The **Gyro Effect XY Tab** setting is at **-180 X** pixels and **-186 Y** pixels. When you test this watch face, the edge of the left foot graphic is showing as seen in Figure 11-21. This represents a mistake at **Gyro X Slider 90 degrees and Gyro Y Slider -90 degrees**, as is shown in the Run (emulator) pane in Figure 11-20.

This mistake does not show up in Figure 11-19, as the Gyro Slider X and Y settings are at 32 and -46, respectively, placing the two foot images (intact) in the watch face's field of view.

However, the left foot has been positioned further inside the watch face due to the 90,-90 Gyro X, Y settings, so let's fix this mistake.

As an exercise, and to learn more about **Gyro Effect** settings, try and adjust the Inner Pivot X and Y settings in the Gyro XY Tab, in order to fix this problem, which can be seen in the Run (emulator) Test pane in Figure 11-20.

The fix for this positioning problem turns out to be a relatively simple one. What I did was to drag the right foot image out of the way, as the right foot image overlaps the left foot image, all the way outside of the preview circle, and then I grabbed the left foot image and pulled it downward about the same amount as it protruded into the circle (watch face) which is what showed the mistake in the first place.

This changed the **Gyro Effect Inner Pivot** settings accordingly, which can be seen as -179 degrees and -220 degrees in Figure 11-22 (I encircled it in Red). That was fairly simple, and when I test the Gyro Effect using the Run (emulator) icon pane in Figure 11-21, at the 90, -90 Slider settings, the cut in the left foot graphic is now hidden behind the edge of the watch face design.

Figure 11-21. *Fix the left foot image Layer position by dragging it down, and test*

This is exactly what we were trying to achieve – we have fixed the Sample Fly in the sky watch face design to be perfect! Great job!

The fix for this problem is shown in Figure 11-22 (outlined), and the left foot layer now moves at -179 and -220 and covers up that cut.

Figure 11-22.   *The left foot Layer new setting in Gyro Effects XY Tab:*
-179, -220

As you can see in the GWD **Run** (emulator) testing pane, seen in
Figure 11-21, the two feet are now showing correctly within the watch face
design, at **X 90 degrees (Slider) and Y -90 degrees (Slider)**.

In Figure 11-22, both feet are visible more underneath the edge of
the background, and protrude into the watch face less, thus fixing this
problem, which becomes apparent when the **Gyro X Slider** is set at **90**
degrees and when the **Gyro Y Slider** is at **-90** degrees, as can be seen in
Figures 11-20 and 11-21.

Thus, the mistake in this Sample "Fly in the sky" watch face design has
now been fixed, and the Fly in the sky 2 watch face project has been saved,
using **File ➤ Save As**, so you can reference it along with the other couple
dozen .GWD files included with this book.

In the next chapter, we'll take a look at how to add weather data into
your watch face design, by using a Weather API from an open-source

provider, much as we have been doing with everything else (CC0 or Creative Commons Zero, GIMP 2.10.8, InkScape, Tizen, etc.) within this book, so that everything is readily accessible to the readers and developers.

Summary

In this chapter, we looked at how to incorporate the gyroscope sensor output into your watch face design, using the **Gyro Effect** section of the **Properties pane** in the Galaxy Watch Designer. Gyroscopic effects can be added in any watch face component which includes this sub-section in its Properties pane. We went over the sub-sections of the Gyro Effect in the first section of the chapter, including **Range**, **Dimension X**, **Dimension Y**, **Inner Pivot X**, **Inner Pivot Y**, **Rotate**, and **Opacity**. Next, we looked at how to add Gyroscopic data to a watch face component.

We also looked at how to learn more Gyro Effect features using the watch face design samples which are included with Galaxy Watch Designer, in order to learn new Galaxy Watch Designer features.

CHAPTER 12

Watch Face Weather Design: Using Weather APIs

In this twelfth chapter of the *Smartwatch Design Fundamentals* book, let's get into designing what are called "Weather" watch faces which utilize an open-source weather API, called "OpenWeatherMap" which was a recent feature added in **V.2.0**. There are some complaints from developers online regarding how the OpenWeatherMap API works and support for it in combination with health-related features provided by the S-Health (Samsung Health) Applications.

In this chapter, you will learn how to develop weather-aware watch face designs; how to cover our previous work from any bugs regarding current watch face development (back up all your **.gwd** files); how to sign up for OpenWeatherMap "keys," which allow your watch face designs to pull weather data from an OpenWeatherMap repository; and how often you can pull this data from the weather server before you have to pay the $40 per month ($480 annual) fee, for using this weather data in your watch face designs.

Finally, we will cover how to actually access this data from your watch face design using **dynamic text** weather components, and **not** using compliments or conditions, as we have learned how to implement for Health and Time features, in the first part of this book.

© Wallace Jackson 2019
W. Jackson, *SmartWatch Design Fundamentals*,
https://doi.org/10.1007/978-1-4842-4369-5_12

Weather Data: OpenWeatherMap API

Before you can add weather data to your watch face, you'll need an **API key** from the **OpenWeatherMap.org** website. Let's go to this **https://home.openweathermap.org/** URL, and research the APIs, their developer pricing, and create an account, so we can get a **free API key**.

Figure 12-1. *The OpenWeatherMap.Org site homepage, showing weather data*

Note that due to the different Weather API formats, weather data from OpenWeatherMap.Org might differ from other weather apps! When the Weather function is activated, it **cannot** currently be applied in your watch face design in conjunction with the **S-health** (Samsung Health App, Steps and Heart Rate, among other things) functionality, which may represent a problem for Galaxy Watch Face Designers, as Weather Data goes hand in hand with Health Data. For this reason, this (weather data) display is avoided by many watch face designers.

Still, I thought it best to include a chapter regarding Weather data usage in this book while also covering the problems that arise among watch face designers (which the search engines can readily reveal), including disappearing (blank) GWD files (hope 1.6.2 fixed this).

Samsung is currently working on this issue for future versions of Galaxy Watch Designer, so this limitation is going to be improved, and Samsung promises to be able to support other weather APIs (such as Yahoo Weather and other popular weather APIs) in the near future.

Researching the OpenWeatherMap APIs

Go to the OpenWeatherMap.org website, and click the API button at the top, which will turn **Orange**, as seen in Figure 12-2. There are three primary weather data APIs that each have documentation and allow you to Subscribe to them, a **Current** weather data, **5 day** weather data (with a 3 hour forecast), and **16 day** weather data (with a daily forecast). The first two are available for **FREE**, and the first one (Current weather data) is available in JSON (JavaScript Object Notation), XML (eXtensible Markup Language), and HTML (Hyper-Text Markup Language) formats.

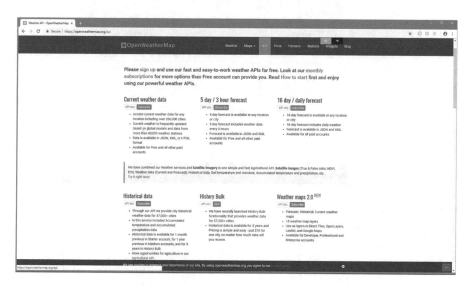

Figure 12-2. *OpenWeatherMap.org website API page, outlining API data plans*

There are **Historical Data** accounts, and new **Weather Maps** available, as shown at the bottom of Figure 12-2, featuring up to **15** weather map layers, which can make for some informative watch faces.

This weather information can cost up to **$24,000** per year at the Enterprise Level, so let's look at those **Weather Data API costs** next!

Researching OpenWeatherMap API Price

The OpenWeatherMap API costs between US**$40** per month for startups and US**$2,000** per month for enterprises to use, if you use any data beyond the **Free API** plan, which we'll be using for this chapter, as you can see in the **Price** Page, shown in Figure 12-3.

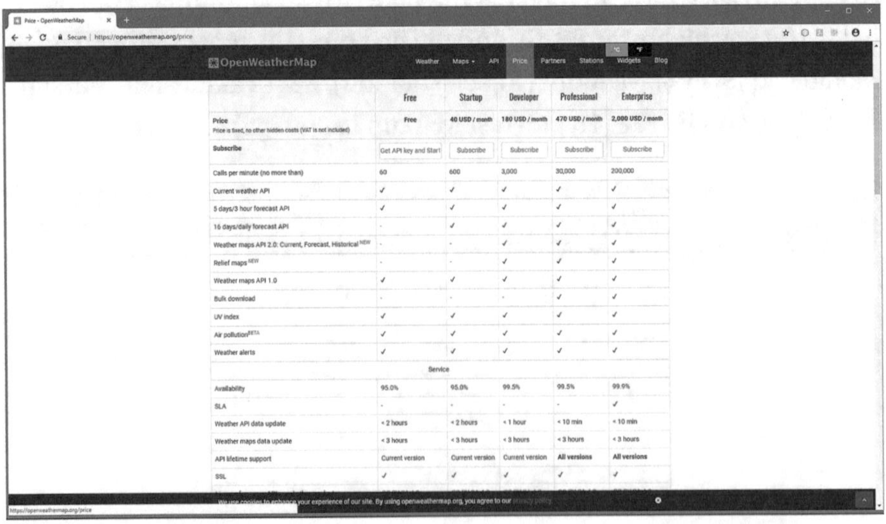

Figure 12-3. *Go to OpenWeatherMap.org site and click Price to review API price*

The Free Plan allows **60** data access calls per minute (one each second), and all other data plans allow weather watch face design users to access between 10 and 3,333 calls each second, around the world.

If you scroll down the Price Page, you will soon find the **Create Your Account**, **Subscribe**, and **Activate Your Key** (as numbered 1, 2, and 3) sections, which we are going to cover in the next section, as this needs to be done correctly in order to create a weather watch face design project. Once you have done this correctly, you will receive a confirmation e-mail for your free service subscription data key.

Sign Up for a Free OpenWeatherMap Key

The instructions for how to sign up for a free OpenWeatherMap.org data key can be found by scrolling down the **Price** Page that we looked at in Figure 12-3 and are shown in Figure 12-4. Under the **1. Create your account** section, the first bullet contains a red "**Signing up**" link, which you should click to get to the correct OpenWeatherMap sign-up page.

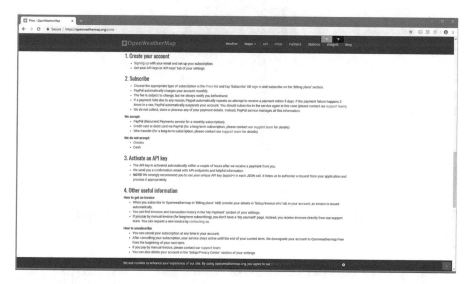

Figure 12-4. *The OpenWeatherMap.org website Price Page (the bottom portion)*

The "Create New Account" Sign-Up form, shown in Figure 12-5, allows you to enter your account name and e-mail address; in my case it is mindtaffy and mindtaffy@gmail.com, as well as a password.

You will also be asked to verify that you are 16 years old, or older, not a robot, and that you agree with the OpenWeatherMap.org Privacy Policy, the Terms and Conditions of Sale, and the Terms and Conditions of Use policies. You can also opt in to News Broadcasts for future updates regarding System News, Product News, and Corporate News regarding OpenWeatherMap APIs, as can all be seen selected using a check mark in Figure 12-5.

Figure 12-5. *Fill out Create Your Account page (top red sign-up link, Figure 12-4)*

After you click the **Create Account** button, you will be taken to a questionnaire that is shown in Figure 12-6. Fill out your Company Name and Purpose for Using OpenWeatherMap, in our case wearables, which indicates watch face design in Galaxy Watch Designer software.

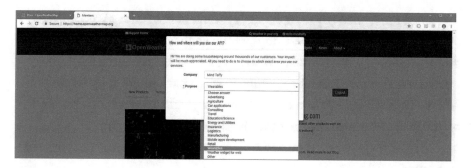

Figure 12-6. *Select the wearables option in the drop-down menu and click button*

I checked my e-mail software and I found that I had received confirmation that I had signed up for the OpenWeatherMap API, which can be seen in Figure 12-7. This confirms that I have signed up for the API and gives sample code for calling the API, from my watch face designs, which we're going to do next, after we back up sample watch face design .gwd files that we've created in previous chapters.

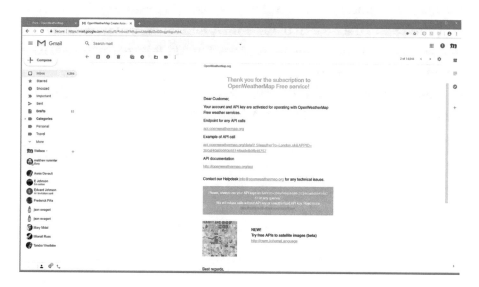

Figure 12-7. *Check e-mail for subscription confirmation from OpenWeatherMap*

Since I searched (by using Google) some of the Galaxy Watch Face Weather issues, I read some things which suggested that there are still some problems with using the Weather API in Galaxy Watch Designer, such as corrupted .GWD files (which is why I backed them up to the / Assets/GWD/ folder before writing this chapter) and weather working in watch faces with some of the other features (conditions, complications, health features) we have learned how to implement during the course of this book.

Creating a New Weather Watch Face

Let's create a watch face design from scratch to use with the weather API just so that you can see the weather features and how to add the API key, as this is the most important part of the process as far as the weather watch face design is concerned. The API key was sent in the e-mail I received after registering on OpenWeatherMap.org as you saw in Figures 12-5 and 12-6. The API Key was sent in the orange block seen in Figure 12-7 at the bottom of the e-mail, and must be entered and then confirmed in order to "Activate" the Weather API features in the Galaxy Watch Designer software.

Create a new 360x360 watch face design, using a **New Project** dialog, seen in Figure 12-8, named **CH12_Weather_Watch_Face**.

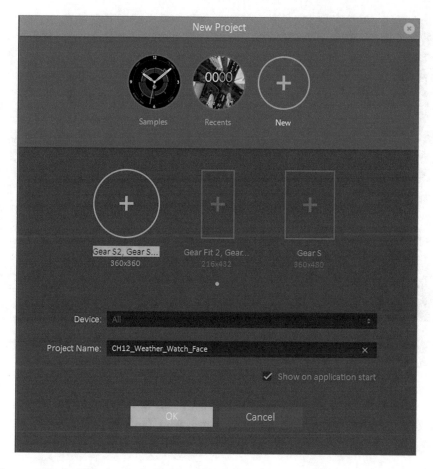

Figure 12-8. *Upgraded Galaxy Watch Designer version 1.6.2, start CH12 project*

Let's use the **360_fashion** watch face **Index Component** for our watch face numbers, as shown in Figure 12-9. Click the Index Component Icon seen on the left, and select the 360_fashion sub-menu as shown selected in blue to access the Plain Index with Ovals and Minutes numbering, as shown in Figure 12-19. This will go on a Black background color, until we create a weather face background image.

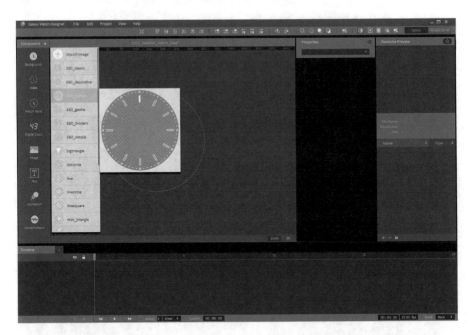

Figure 12-9. *Click the Index Component and select the 360_fashion Index*

As you can see in Figure 12-9, the **360_fashion** has a standard look which will work well with a weather watch face. Let's go into **File ➤ Preferences** to Open the dialog to select **APIs** as seen in Figure 12-10.

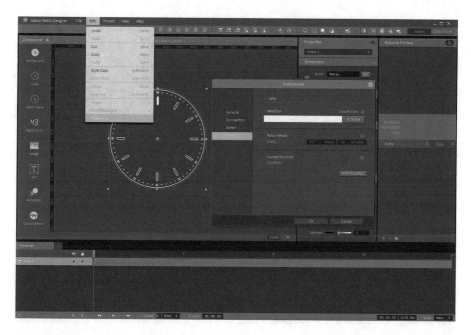

Figure 12-10. *Use the Edit ➤ Preferences menu sequence; then access the APIs*

Enter the OpenWeatherMap.org API Key from the orange area of your e-mail. I initially selected the entire string, including the **&APPID** portion, which is incorrect. The Key is the portion **after the: &APPID=** portion, using a dummy key: "**999xx99xxx999x99999xxxxx9xx99999**." Be sure and get your own API Key (do not use this dummy key)! If you enter the &APPID= portion, you will generate an error when you click the Activate button, which can be seen on the lower-right-hand side of Figure 12-11.

This **Warning** dialog will appear, advising that the server has returned the HTTP error response code of **401**, for this URL: **http://api. openweathermap.org/data/2.5/weather?q=Seoul&APPID=350af40abb980 c55146aabdb9fb48757** .

355

Figure 12-11. *I entered the API Key with the &APPID= Prefix which doesn't work*

As can be seen in Figure 12-12, once I figured out the **&APPID=** part of the API Key was unnecessary, the key was accepted, and this button turned into a **Deactivate** button.

This indicates that the API Key is Activated and that we are ready to move on with the watch face design weather features, which we will add in the next section.

356

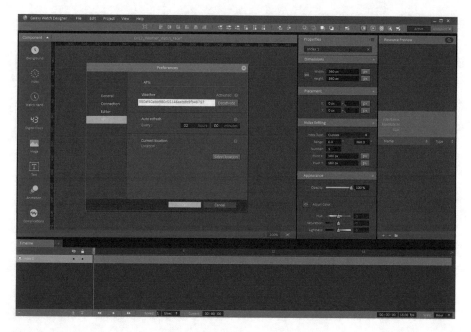

Figure 12-12. *Weather Key dialog shows the Deactivate button when Activated*

The first thing we will want to look for is the **Weather Condition** Icon sub-menu, so let's click the + next to the Timeline Tab, as shown in Figure 12-13, and see if we can find any weather-related conditions.

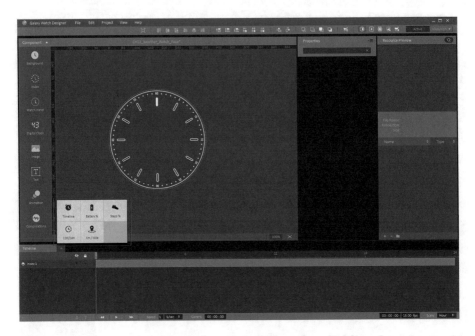

Figure 12-13. *Look for Weather Conditions by clicking the + in Timeline Tab*

The next thing that we would look for is the weather-related complication sub-menu, so click the complication component, as is shown in Figure 12-14, and let's see if there is a weather sub-menu!

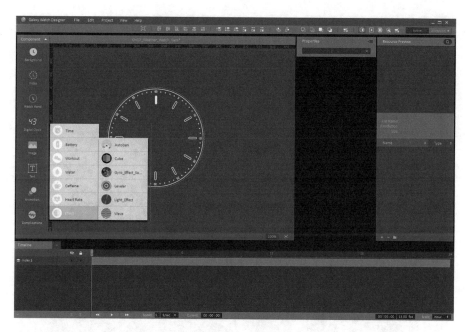

Figure 12-14. *Look for Weather Complication by clicking the complication menu*

The next thing to look at is a **Weather-related Sample Project** area, in the Galaxy Watch Designer **File ➤ New Project** dialog, like we did to explore more about Gyroscopes back in Chapter 11.

Sample Weather Watch Face Design

Let's use a technique we learned in Chapter 11, and open up a **Sample Weather** watch face design to see how to set up weather information access. Open a **New Project** dialog, and click **Samples**, as is shown in the middle of Figure 12-16, and scroll over to the right a couple rows until you hit a Weather watch face, and then select it and Open!

Figure 12-15. *Open Weather Sample Watch Face*

Next, let's investigate how it is getting updates. As is shown in Figure 12-16, this is done in the **Properties ➤ Data Tab** within the **Data Sync** drop-down menu. As you can see, there is a **drop-down menu** that you can access with weather-related options on it. This is how we put weather information on a watch face, by using updatable (dynamic) Text and attaching it to (Syncing it to) the OpenWeatherMap API data.

Now we will know just how to access the Weather API within our own weather watch face designs, which we will be creating here later on in this chapter. We will download a custom background image from open-source Pexels.com website, configure it for use in GIMP 2.10.6, and construct a custom watch face design with an Index, Hour Hand, Minute Hand, and Weather (Temperature) Data Dynamic Text Component, all the while using a nice background image of a girl that is enjoying the weather floating in a pool of water.

After we do that, we will test the weather watch face inside the Galaxy Watch Designer and use the Samsung Remote Test Lab website.

Figure 12-16. *Weather is accessed in Data Sync drop-down menu at the bottom*

When you click the **Current Temperature** option, you will get the **Warning Dialog** which is shown in Figure 12-17, which warns us that "This (Weather Data) Feature cannot be used with the following features: Tag Expressions (Chapter 13), Steps % Percentages, Step Counts, Step Speed, Burned Calories, Moved Distance, Steps Goals, Heart Rate Monitor, Water Intake, Caffeine Intake, Floor and IAP." It further warns that this feature only works on the following devices: The Gear S, Gear S2, Gear S3, Gear Sport and Galaxy Watch, and that to use this feature with Tag Expressions, you must disable Weather Data, or remove objects which have used Weather Data. This is why if you Google Search "Galaxy Watch Designer Weather Data," you will find a plethora of Developer complaints regarding implementing Weather API in watch face designs, which also shows that it is desired (popular) enough to be included as a chapter in this book! For this reason, I am showing you how to do everything that you will need to do to create a Weather watch face design, and get it talking to the OpenWeatherMap.org server, so that they can get the latest Weather info for your designs.

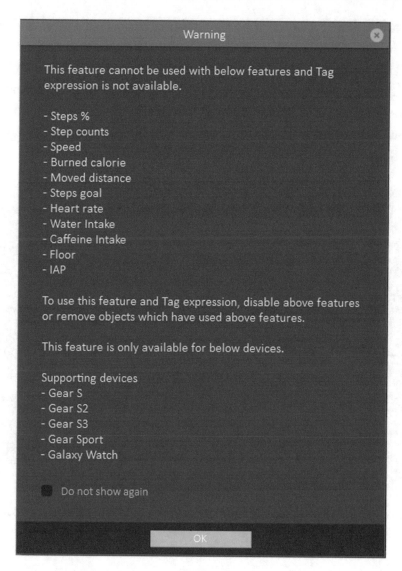

Figure 12-17. *The Weather API Warning dialog in Galaxy Watch Designer*

Next, let's take a look at the CH12 Weather watch face design, and add hour hands and minute hands, which are seen in Figure 12-18.

Click the **Text** Component icon, as shown on the left of Figure 12-18 in Blue, and pop-up grouped boxes of static and dynamic text features, which have a thin gray scroll bar on their right-hand side.

Scroll this down to the bottom, so that you can see all the other icon selections, which hopefully will contain Weather Data API options.

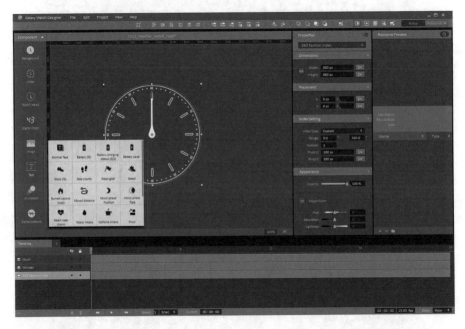

Figure 12-18. *Scroll down to see weather text auto-updating option (bottom)*

As you can see in Figure 12-19, there are five weather-related icons to choose dynamic Text Components from, including **Weather** (type), **Humidity**, **Temperature**, **City Name** (Weather), and **Last Update Time** (Weather).

We will be using the **Temperature** Data, as that is what most people are concerned with these days. Click this icon, encircled in red, and insert a Temperature readout into your watch face design, which will appear at the top-left corner of the watch face design.

Drag this Temperature Data readout into place, in the bottom middle of the watch face analog design, as shown in Figures 12-19 and 12-20.

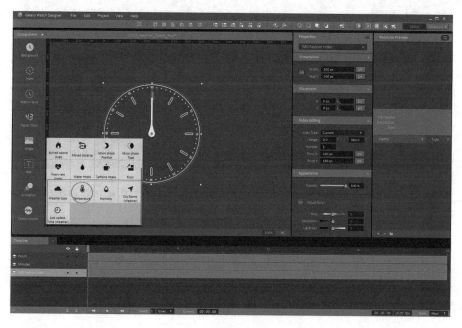

Figure 12-19. *Click (encircled) Temperature Text Auto-Update option in Text area*

Until you rename the new layer, it will be called **Text 1**, as can be seen at the top of the composition, in Figure 12-20.

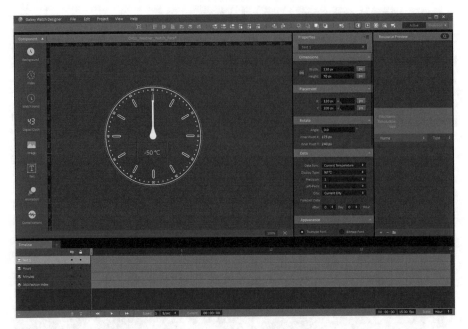

Figure 12-20. *Center Temperature readout under Analog Time watch face design*

At this point the Galaxy Watch Designer software will give you a Warning dialog about required Always-On watch faces having not been generated and ask if you'd like GWD to autogenerate the watch faces.

Figure 12-21. *Have GWD create an Always-On watch face design for you*

Click "Yes" as seen in Figure 12-21, and again as seen in Figure 12-22.

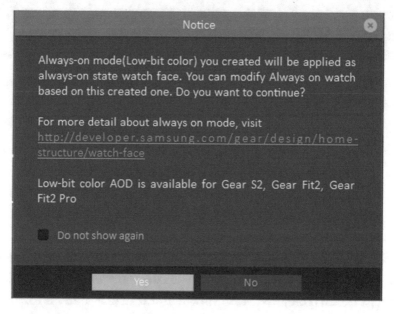

Figure 12-22. *Notice that an Always-On watch face has been applied*

Create a Weather Watch Face Image

Let's create a background image in GIMP to use for the Weather Watch Face we are creating here. Go to PEXELS.com, and find the image of a girl floating in a lagoon, then download it, and open it in GIMP 2.10.6.

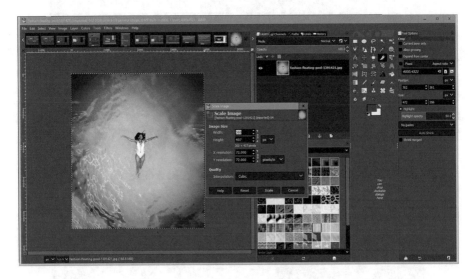

Figure 12-23. *Scale the image down to 360 pixels to fit watch face design*

The first thing to do is to use the **Scale Image** tool to scale the shortest side of the image to **360** pixels, which leaves the other side at around 400 pixels in length. We will then use the **Canvas Size** (Crop) tool to make the image **360 by 360** pixels, so it will fit the weather watch face background perfectly.

This series of moves that will be made using GIMP 2.10.6 can be seen in Figures 12-23 and 12-24, and we will use the tools which are found in the **Image** menu (**Image ➤ Scale Image** and **Image ➤ Canvas Size**). It is important for your watch face design that you learn to use the features of

GIMP in order to make 360 by 360 pixel (or smaller) image assets which can be used within your watch face designs, primarily as PNG8, PNG24, or PNG32 assets. Figure 12-24 shows the **Set Image Canvas Size** dialog creating a **360 by 360** background image for the weather watch face design that we are creating.

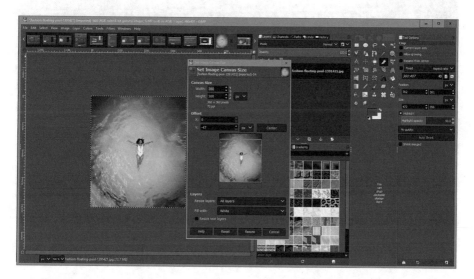

Figure 12-24. *Set Image Canvas size to 360 by 360 pixels (square 1:1 aspect)*

Add this 360 x 360 pixel background image to your weather watch face using this **Float_Image.png** file, and the **Image** Component, seen on the left side of Figure 12-25. Double-click, and then Name, your bottommost (image) layer for this weather watch face: **Float_Image**.

Figure 12-25. *Add an Image Component at the bottom of the compositing stack*

Notice in Figure 12-26 that the **Temperature** readout can be set in degrees Celsius or Fahrenheit using a drop-down menu labeled **Display Type**, which can be seen in Figure 12-26, encircled in red.

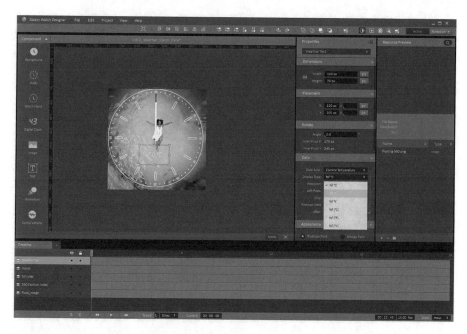

Figure 12-26. *Set the Display Type drop-down menu to degrees Fahrenheit*

Before we can test this weather watch face, we will need to build the project using the Build Icon (the fourth out of five at the top right of GWD). This will first ask us to Save the File as a GWD File, using the **Save As** dialog, as seen in Figure 12-27 at the bottom.

The file will use the **CH12_Weather_Watch_Face.gwd** naming convention that we used when we created the watch face design earlier in the chapter, seen in Figures 12-8 through 12-12.

Click the **Save** button to make sure that the file has the latest watch face design in it, and then the **Build Project** dialog will appear, allowing you to specify the Tizen OS Version to use (Version 4.0 for Galaxy Watches), your developer password, and similar information. This **Save** dialog can be seen in Figure 12-27, and the **Build Project** dialog can be seen in Figure 12-28.

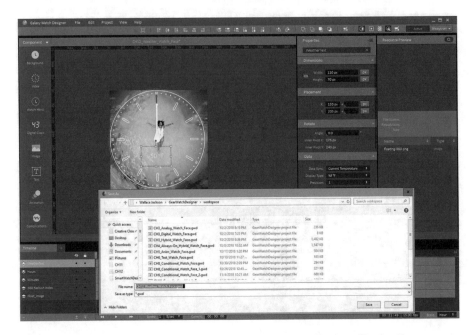

Figure 12-27. *Click the Build Icon to save the GWD File before building .TZ4 file*

Let's build the weather watch face and test it in the next section, so we can see if it talks to the OpenWeatherMap.org server.

Building a Test Weather Watch Face

Let's build and test the weather watch face next, and see if it talks to the OpenWeatherMap.org server. I tried the **Run** (emulator) Icon, and there were no weather-related sliders to test the **Temperature** readout with, so I switched to testing in the Samsung Remote Test Lab (RTL) facility. I was able to get the weather watch face to load, launch, and request the location, which means that it is talking to the OpenWeatherMap server, which means that it is working, and that I have assembled things correctly.

If you Google "Samsung Galaxy weather watch faces," most developers have not yet figured out to look under the dynamic Text for weather, only under complications and conditions, as we did initially, in Figures 12-13 and 12-14, before we looked at the sample weather watch face designs, as we learned to do in Chapter 11.

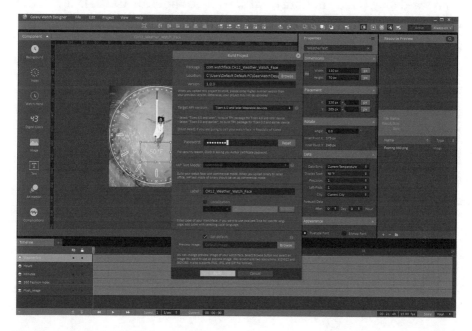

Figure 12-28. *Click the Build icon to save project and open a Build Project dialog*

Click the Build button as seen at the bottom of Figure 12-28, to create the .TZ4 file to test in the Remote Testing Lab, after you have entered your password and configured for Galaxy Watch (Tizen 4.0) as you can see in Figure 12-28.

Go to the Samsung Remote Test Lab website, and select the **Galaxy Watch** and choose **Tizen 4.0** and the **Korea Server** (KR1) and run the JNLP emulator. Right-click the watch face and then load the CH12_ Weather_Watch_Face.tz4 file, and Start it in the dialog that comes up with the emulator. This **com.samsung.clocksetting** dialog can be seen in Figures 12-31 through 12-36 if you want to see it. Select the watch faces app from the dialog (at the bottom) and **start** it, to show the watch faces on the emulator. Scroll over to the Weather Watch Face and click it to select it, so it loads, and goes fullface, as in Figure 12-29.

As you can see, the Minute Hand is still set to Hour Hand Sync, so we will have to start Galaxy Watch Designer, and fix that problem next in the Sync With: drop-down menu for that layer (component) in order to perfect this watch face design. This correction can be seen in Figure 12-30 if you want to look ahead.

Figure 12-29. *Testing the weather watch face in Samsung's Remote Testing Lab*

Let's fix the weather watch face project Minute Hand by setting **Minutes in Hours** instead of Hour in Day from the **Sync with:** drop-down, as can be seen on the right, in Figure 12-30. Be sure and set the **Sync with:** settings correctly for each watch face design component, so that you do not have to go back later and fix things, as we're doing here.

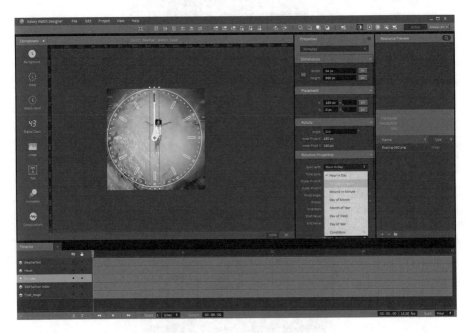

Figure 12-30. *Fix the minute hand by selecting the Minutes in Hours option*

Let's test the weather watch face on the emulator once we have fixed it. Go to the Samsung Remote Test Labs site, as shown in Figure 12-31, and select the OS Tizen 4.0 on the Korea Server (KR1), reserve it for 30 minutes, and then click the blue **Start** button. This will download the JNLP to your workstation, where it will appear on the bottom left, where you will click **Keep**. Then open the JNLP in your browser, and **right-click** it and select **Launch**. The Galaxy Watch Emulator will then load into memory, and appear on the screen, where you can drag it around, and right-click the

watch face, and select **Text ➤ CH12_Weather_Watch_Face.tz4**, to load
the Tizen 4.0 binary created using the Build Icon in Galaxy Watch Designer
(Figure 12-28). Select the **Install** button in the Application Manager dialog
to install it.

Next, highlight and then click the blue **start** (play icon), after
highlighting the **com.samsung.clocksetting** Package Name seen in the
Package Name column, and scroll through the different watches on the
emulator, until you find the **CH12_Weather watch face**, which is shown on
the right in Figure 12-31.

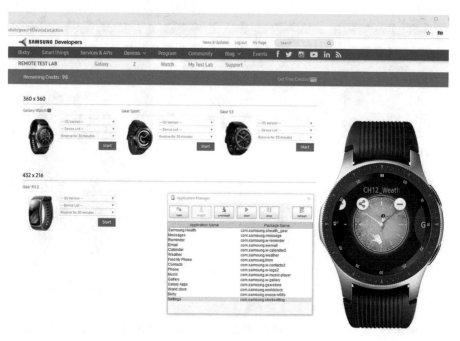

Figure 12-31. *Scroll through watch faces until CH12_Weather watch
face shows*

Next, select the watch face for use by clicking it, and then drag to the
right to access the **Tap to Allow Weather Permission** face, which can be
seen in Figure 12-32. Click the Allow Permission screen, which ostensibly

sends the permission to your smartphone, which is running the Samsung Weather App and tells that App to tell the Open Weather Map server that it is OK to send data to the Galaxy Smart Watch. The only question is if the Samsung emulator has this capability of doing this in the emulator, given that it asks for you to connect to the smartphone using Bluetooth, as is shown in Figure 12-33. That is, does it work beyond this point in testing the watch face design or not? That is the question that we need to answer here.

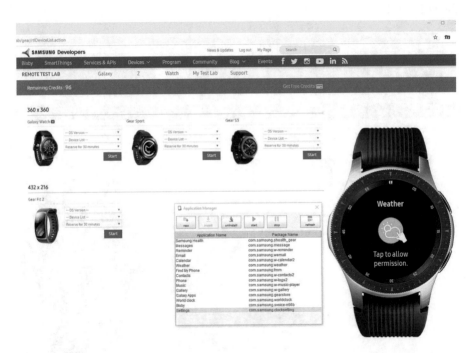

Figure 12-32. *Tap the emulator screen surface to allow the weather permission*

Figure 12-33 shows the Bluetooth request on the watch face.

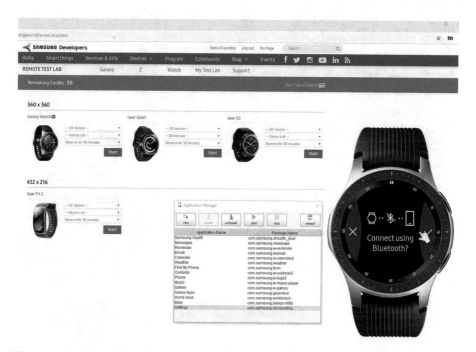

Figure 12-33. *The next screen asks the User: Connect Using Bluetooth?*

If you select the check mark (OK) option, seen in Figure 12-33, for Bluetooth connectivity, the **Connecting...** spinning icon will show on the watch face, as shown in Figure 12-34.

Figure 12-34. *The next screen shows the spinning Bluetooth connection icon*

As you can see in Figure 12-35, the smartwatch emulator is not connecting via the **Samsung Remote Testing Lab**, to the smartphone simulator running the Samsung Weather Application, so you will have to test on one of your own Samsung Galaxy Watches, or on a Samsung Gear 2 or Gear 3 or Gear Sport using a Tizen 3.0 binary generated from the same **Build Project** dialog that we used in Figure 12-28.

This means that if you are serious about developing Samsung watch face designs that you will have to invest in a hardware (physical) smartwatch unit (I use the Gear S3 Frontier myself) and it works on that.

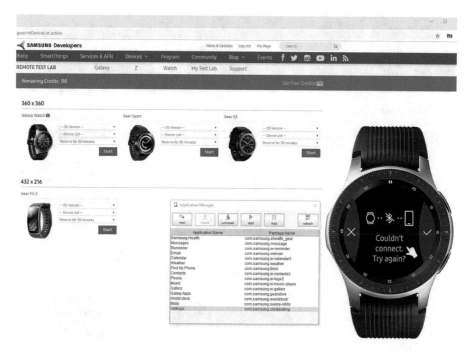

Figure 12-35. *The next screen shows an emulator couldn't connect via Bluetooth*

If you run this watch face project using the **Run on Device** icon at the top of Galaxy Watch Designer and you have the device linked to a smartphone running the **Samsung Weather Application**, then the watch face will talk to the smartphone Samsung Weather App, which will in turn talk to the OpenWeatherMap.org **server**, validate the key you signed up for in Figure 12-5, pass you the **Temperature** data for your locale, and display it using the dynamic Text portion of your Weather Watch Face Design under the analog clock hands.

It should look something like Figure 12-36, only with a higher Temperature readout under (at the bottom of) the watch face.

381

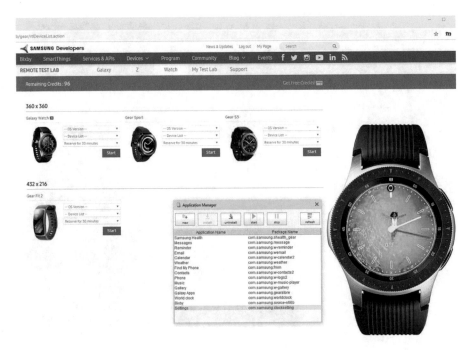

Figure 12-36. *The watch face design is correct but RTL does not talk to OWM*

As you can see, using weather data in a watch face design is a bit trickier than most watch face design, as the data relies on a remote server and requires a developer account and key as well as payments based upon the type of data you are requesting.

If you google search developer's complaints currently regarding this weather data, you will find that some of the developers are finding that the weather data often cannot keep up with the smartwatch request volume, especially if many users of the watch face design exist.

Next, let's get even more advanced with inline coding via the watch face Tag Expression, and get into computer programming constructs in the next chapter.

Summary

This chapter covered adding weather information to your watch face design. This is done using the OpenWeatherMap API, which we covered in detail in the first part of the chapter.

Next, we went through how to create a custom weather watch face design from scratch, using the free API key and dynamic text to access the weather data. This chapter shows you how to incorporate weather data into your watch face design, should you choose to do so, especially after Samsung improves this feature and allows other watch face features to work at the same time as the weather features do!

CHAPTER 13

Watch Face Algorithm Design: Using Tag Expressions

In this thirteenth chapter of the *Smartwatch Design Fundamentals* book, let's get into designing what are called "Algorithmic" watch faces which utilize an algorithmic coding approach, called "Tag Expressions," which was a recent feature added in **V.1.6.0**. There are some complaints from developers online regarding limitations on how these Tag Expressions work and support for Tag Expressions in watch faces with health-related features provided by S-Health (Samsung Health) Applications.

In this chapter, you'll learn how to develop Tag Expression-aware watch face designs, as well as the different types of operations you can use in a tag expression including arithmetic, relational, and conditional. We will also look at the Tags themselves, in two groupings, one for Time-based Tags and a second for Sensor-based Tags, with support for sensors such as altitude (Floor), Speed, Steps, Heart Rate, Water Intake, Caffeine Intake, and the like.

© Wallace Jackson 2019
W. Jackson, *SmartWatch Design Fundamentals*,
https://doi.org/10.1007/978-1-4842-4369-5_13

Finally, we will cover how to actually access the Tag Expression logic equations in your watch face design, by using the **Script** Window, which you can access via a **triangle** icon in most of the **Properties** data fields. We'll use the **Chapter 8 Vector Illustration** watch face to show how you can rotate a pinwheel, based on a number of Tag Expressions.

Arithmetic Expressions

There are five "core" types of mathematical expressions which commonly come under the term "arithmetic," which you can construct in a tag expression. These include additive, subtractive, multiplicative, division, and remainder. Most of you have learned about these in school, and these will allow you to do just about any type of data calculation that you want to in a Tag Expression. We will be covering these operations in this section.

Additive Operations (+)

Additive Conditions in a Tag Expression take two data values and sum them together, just like you learned to do in school.

Subtractive Operations (–)

Subtractive Conditions in a Tag Expression take two data values and subtract them from each other, just like you learned to do in school.

Multiplicative Operations (*)

Multiplicative Conditions in a Tag Expression take two data values and multiply them to each other, just like you learned to do in school.

Division Operations (/)

Division Conditions in a Tag Expression take two data values and divide them between each other, just like you learned to do in school.

Remainder Operations (Modulo or %)

Remainder Conditions in a Tag Expression take two data values and divide them between each other, giving the remainder value of that division, just like you learned to do in school.

Relational Expressions

There are six "core" types of relationship or relational expressions that you can also construct within your tag expressions, and these include **less than, less than or equal to, greater than, greater than or equal to, equal to,** or **not equal to.** Most of you have learned about these relational comparisons in high school as well, and they allow you to do just about any type of data relationship calculation that you would want to do inside of a Tag Expression for your watch face design. We will be covering these in detail in this section before we move on to ternary operations (or conditional comparisons) within the Tag Expressions themselves.

Less Than (<)

The **less than** (<) relational operator compares two different data values and can decide if one of them is less than the other one. If it is less than, something is done, making this a powerful operation for the tag expression.

Less Than or Equal To (<=)

The **less than or equal to** (<=) relational operator compares two different data values and can decide if one of them is less than or equal to the other one. If it is less than or equal to, something is done, making this a powerful operation for the tag expression.

Greater Than (>)

The **greater than** (>) relational operator compares two different data values and can decide if one of them is **greater than** the other one. If it is greater than, something is done, making this a powerful operation for the tag expression.

Greater Than or Equal To (>=)

The **greater than or equal to** (>=) relational operator compares two different data values and can decide if one of them is greater than or equal to the other one. If it is greater than or equal to, then something is done, making this a powerful relational operation for the tag expression.

Equal To (==)

The **equal to** (==) relational operator compares two data values and can decide if they are **equal to** each other. If these two data values are equal to each other, then something is done based on the outcome of this comparison, making this a powerful relational operation for constructing more complex tag expressions.

Not Equal To (!=)

The **not equal to (!=)** relational operator compares two data values and can decide if they are **not equal** to each other. If these two data values are not equal to each other, then something is then done based on the outcome of this comparison, making this a powerful relational operation that developers can use inside their tag expression construction.

Conditional Expressions

The Galaxy Watch Designer also supports conditional programming expressions via a Ternary Operator. These can also be found in many more advanced programming languages, such as Java SE 9 (Android), ActionScript 3 (Flash), ECMAScript 7.0, JavaScript (WebKit), C (Tizen), C++ (Linux), and C# (Windows 7, 8.1, and 10). If you want to research Ternary Operators in more detail, Wikipedia has a great page on them at https://en.wikipedia.org/wiki/Ternary_operation if you are interested.

The primary format for this **Ternary Operator**, often called the in-line if (iif) statement, or broadly termed the **Conditional Operator**, is

`Condition ? A : B`

This statement allows the watch face developer to construct an "if X then Y else Z" type of programming statement for each watch face property, in the place of what would normally be a fixed numeric value.

The ternary operator has three operands in the above form. It returns A if the conditional statement is true, or else it returns B if the conditional statement is false. This gives Galaxy Watch Designers an **If-Then-Else** programming capability inside of a compact, in-line format, to use with their tag expression editor, called the Script Window, as you will soon see.

Time-Based Tags

Let's outline these data tags available for use within the next couple of sections, starting with Time-based tags first and then covering the Sensor-based tags. The Time-based tags are based on common watch face features like Hours, Minutes, and Seconds, as well as Days (of the week) and Dates (which are days of the month), and as such, there are seven of them, which I will outline in Table 13-1.

Table 13-1. *Time-Based Tags*

Tag Name/Type	Tag Format	Tag Range
Hour	[H]	0–23
Minute	[m]	0–59
Second	[s]	0–59
Day of Month	[d]	1–31
Month of Year	[M]	1–12
Day of Week	[e]	1–7
Day of Year	[D]	0.0–11.99

Next, let's take a look at the 13 Sensor-based tags supported in tag expressions in the galaxy watch designer, since we will be looking at how to animate our watch face design later on in this chapter based on sensors such as battery power percentage level, steps goal percentage level, and Floor (altitude) level. This will allow our pinwheel watch face design we created in Chapters 7 and 8 (as well as subsequent chapters) to visually animate based on sensor data and give our users some visual feedback regarding these sensors.

Sensor-Based Tags

Let's outline the sensor tags available for use in the next section, since we covered the Time-based tags first. The Sensor-based tags are based on common watch face sensors like Steps Percentage, Battery Percentage, Floor (altitude), Speed, Distance, Water Intake, and Caffeine Intake. There are 13 of the sensors available to Tag Expressions, which I will outline in Table 13-2.

Table 13-2. *Sensor-Based Tags*

Tag Name/Type	Tag Format	Tag Range
Battery Percentage	[ba]	0–100
Battery Charge Status	[bc]	0 or 1
Battery Level	[bl]	0–4
Steps Percentage	[st]	1–100
Step Counts	[sc]	0 to infinity
Steps Goal	[sg]	0 to infinity
Speed (meters/second)	[sp]	0 to infinity
Burned Calories	[cal]	0 to infinity
Moved Distance	[md]	0 to infinity
Heart Rate	[hr]	0 to infinity
Water Intake	[wi]	0 to infinity
Caffeine Intake	[ci]	0 to infinity
Floor	[fl]	0 to infinity

Next, let's take a look at how you will use what we have covered in the sections in the first part of this chapter regarding how your Tag Expression is composed using operators and tags and show you some samples of how tag expressions can actually be inserted in the **Rotate Angle** property of the Vector Illustration background image for the watch face (the one we did in Chapters 7 and 8) which you have already created.

You could also use the complications watch face design that we created in Chapter 10 if you like, but Tag Expressions don't currently work with weather data, so don't use the Chapter 12 watch face to experiment with tag expressions.

The more you practice using Tag Expressions, the better you will get at it, just like with any other feature covered in this book, and for this reason, we will spin the pinwheel background based on Hours, Minutes, Seconds, Step Goal Percentage, Battery Charge Percentage, and Floor Height (Altitude) as these have sliders and animated testing facilities in the Run (emulator) Icon dialog in Galaxy Watch Designer so that readers can test and see their Tag Expressions at work.

How to Create the Tag Expression

Let's use the **CH8_Conditional_Watch_Face.gwd** that we created in Chapters 7 and 8 and add some Tag Expressions that make the background, a vector illustration pinwheel created using InkScape, and **rotate** based on different Time-based tags such as **Hour**, **Minute**, and **Second** as well as Sensor-based Tags such as **Battery Percentage**, **Steps Percentage**, and **Floor** (altitude). We will do this to give the watch face user a visual (animated) indication of time or of Battery Power Usage, Steps Goals Achieved, Floor (altitude), and the like. Use the **File ➤ Open** menu sequence shown in Figure 13-1 to open the Open dialog, and select the **CH8_Conditional_Watch_Face.gwd** file, and then click the **Open** button to open it in the Galaxy Watch Designer. If you like, you can also use the Complication watch face Design so that the Vector Illustration pinwheel spins behind the complication, as conditions, complications, and tag expressions should all work together within a single watch face design. Pushing this software to the limit is what this book is all about, and there is no reason that you should not try and combine everything you are learning about in this book into your watch face designs as long as Samsung is willing to make it all work together. Weather and Tag Expressions should be working together soon, hopefully sometime in 2019.

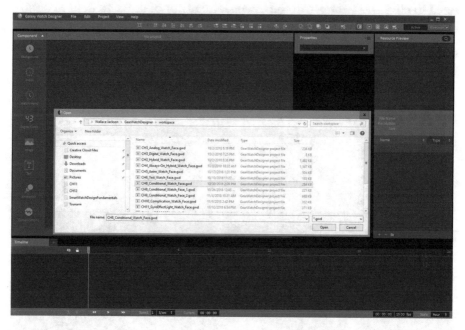

Figure 13-1. *A CH8_Conditional Watch Face Design is the foundation for CH13*

Let's first change the Rotate Properties section to contain a Tag Expression which rotates the Vector Illustration (pinwheel) Background Image that we created in Chapter 7 so it gives animated visual feedback to our watch face users, as to what is going on with their sensors.

Let's start with the Steps Percentage (of goal) Tag, which is **[st]**, so the rotation percentage would be some amount of degree of rotation multiplied by the current **Steps %**, resulting in the **Tag Expression** of

2.0 * [st]

This says: Multiply the Steps Percentage by two, and assign this value to the **Rotation Angle Property**. As the **Steps Goal Percentage** increases, increase the rotation angle by two degrees each time, so that the pinwheel spins based on the value of Steps % Goal as it is achieved.

To enter this Tag Expression into the Rotate Angle data field, you will need to click the **triangle** in the lower-left corner of the data field to open the **Scripts** Window, as is shown in Figure 13-2 encircled in red. You can click the **Steps %** Tag (seen in blue) on the bottom part of the Script Window to insert a Tag into the Expression you're creating.

Figure 13-2. *Click a triangle icon in the Rotate Angle section of Properties pane*

After you create a Tag Expression using the Script window, as is shown in Figure 13-2, with its "blackboard" component and "List of Tags Available for Use" component underneath that, you can close this Tag Expression Editor window by using the **X** (Exit) **Icon** in the upper-right corner. When you do close this Script window, the Warning dialog will open (every time) that warns the developer about the limitations of the Tag Expression (Script window), which we will cover next.

Tag Expression Limitations

As you can see in Figure 13-3, there is a **Warning** dialog that will appear every time you enter a Tag Expression into the Galaxy Watch Designer. This dialog will advise you that the Tag Expression feature will not work with watch face designs which have Weather features such as Weather Type, Current Temperature, Weather Humidity, City Name, Last Update Time, or Sweeps with Update Frequencies Less Than 15 Hz (i.e., slow-moving second hand sweeps).

It also suggests that to use Tag Expressions, you disable any of these features. To acknowledge that you understand these current limitations, click the **OK** button at the bottom of the dialog, and understand as developers that Samsung is working on their watch face design code, so that future versions of the Galaxy Watch Designer after V.1.6.2 will be able to have significantly more of these smartwatch design features all working together in your watch face designs.

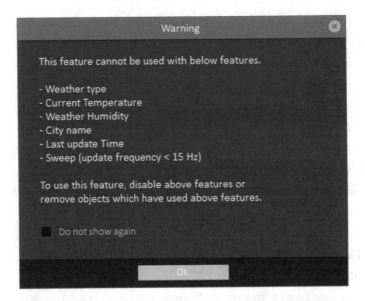

Figure 13-3. *Read the Warning dialog that appears when you exit Script window*

Next, let's see how to use the Galaxy Watch Designer Run (emulator) Icon tool to test the 2.0*[st] Tag Expression we have entered into the Rotate Angle Property field, using the Script window in Figure 13-2. We will use the Run (emulator) dialog to test each of the Tag Expressions in this chapter, so that you can see the result of the Tag Expression in your watch face design. For the Time-based Tag Expressions, we will use the left Time Tab, and for the Sensor-based Tag Expressions (like this 2.0*[st] one), we will use the right Data Tab of the Run (emulator) Icon dialog, as is shown in Figure 13-4.

Testing Tag Expression in Run Data Tab

Notice in Figure 13-4 that you can see the Tag Expression you are testing (as long as the Run dialog does not obscure the Properties pane) which I have encircled in red. I am crafting Tag Expressions in this chapter for Tags which allow using the **Run** (emulator) **Icon** to test the Tag Expression using **Sliders**. If you look at the **Run** (emulator) dialog in Figure 13-4, you will see (encircled in red) that there are sliders in the **Data Tab** for **Battery %**, **Steps %**, and **Floor** (altitude or height), which can be dragged to see the spinning pinwheel that we are creating using the **Tag Expression** feature we are learning about in this chapter. I am setting it up this way so that readers do not need to own a physical smartwatch device in order to learn how to implement these Tag Expressions in their designs.

Figure 13-4. *Look in Rotate Angle field to see the Tag you're testing: Steps % Slider*

Since our first Tag Expression example used 2.0*[st], we will use the **Steps % Slider** shown in Figure 13-4 to rotate our vector illustration pinwheel background which contains the Tag Expression.

Next, let's set up a Tag Expression to rotate the pinwheel vector based upon which **Hour Indicator** is showing, by clicking the triangle icon to open the **Script** window, as shown in Figure 13-5. Change the Steps % [st]

tag, to be the Hour [H] tag, and change your number of degrees rotated from **2** to **5** because 5 times 12 (Hours) is 60 (degrees), and this will give us more visible pinwheel rotation each Hour so that users will see that it is rotating, and you can use 10.0, if you like to get 120 degrees of rotation, or 15.0 if you like to get 180 degrees of total rotation for the Vector Illustration (pinwheel) background graphic.

Therefore, the new Tag Expression is **5.0*[H]**, as can be seen, encircled in red, in Figure 13-5. You can insert this **[H]** tag, by selecting it from the bottom of the Script window, as shown, encircled in red, in Figure 13-5.

Close the script window and then the Warning dialog, and you will be ready to test this new Tag Expression using the **Run** (emulator) **Icon** next. After you test the Hour-based Tag Expression using the Time Tab, let's change Hours [H] to Minutes [m], and then Seconds [s], next, so that we can use the Play button in the Run (emulator) to animate our test. This will allow you to see the Tag Expression in action without having to drag a Slider Bar to create the pinwheel movement.

Figure 13-5 shows the 5.0 * [H] Tag Expression being created in the Script window. Notice that the **Rotate Angle** field still contains the older **2.0 * [st]** Steps % Tag Expression, because the new Hour-based Tag Expression has not been "entered" into that data field as yet, by closing the **Script** window using it's **Close** Icon in the upper-left corner.

Once you do close the **Script** window, your Tag Expression will be entered into the Rotate Angle field, and the **Warning** dialog will again be displayed, as you saw in Figure 13-3. To finish the process, click the **OK** button, to close the Warning dialog, and you will be able to Test the Hour-based Tag Expression by using your **Run** (emulator) **Icon,** located at the top right of the Galaxy Watch Designer software.

Figure 13-5. *Create 2.0*[H] Tag Expression: spins background based on Hours*

I have encircled the **Play to animate by time** feature in the **Run** (emulator) dialog in Figure 13-6, so that you can see a Tag Expression that uses Minutes and Seconds, which we are going to create next, which will rotate your pinwheel background vector image as time (minutes or seconds) goes by.

As you can see in Figure 13-6 (encircled in red), the Tag Expression is currently using [H] Hours, so you will be able to see the rotation better by moving the Slider Bar, which will change the Hour Indicators (and the pinwheel rotation) more rapidly than the Play button will. The Play button can be used to automate the testing of the Minute- and Seconds-based Tag Expressions, as these will allow your watch face users to better see the pinwheel rotate based on minutes or seconds.

We will change this [H] Hour Tag to a Minutes Tag next, so that you can see the vector illustration pinwheel background graphic rotation better when testing with the Play transport button. We'll use 5 degrees to multiply by minutes, as there are 60 minutes. Five times 60 equals 300 degrees (nearly a full rotation), so feel free to use 6 degrees if you wish!

Figure 13-6. *Use the Run (emulator) Icon and Slider to test [H] Tag using Time Slider*

Let's change the [H] Hour tag in your Tag Expression to be the [m] Minutes tag, as is shown in Figure 13-7.

You will do this by clicking the triangle button or icon if you wish to look at it that way, in the lower-left corner of the **Rotate Angle** field, and open up the **Script** window, so you can replace the [H] Hour Tag with the [m] Minute Tag, as you can see in Figure 13-7.

This will rotate the background image with a Tag Expression of **1.0*[m]**, or using one degree each minute, according to the new Tag Expression, as seen in Figures 13-7 and 13-8.

To test this new Tag Expression, launch the **Run** (emulator) **Icon**, and click the **Play** transport button on the left end of the Time Slider, seen encircled in Red in Figures 13-6 and 13-8. This will make the Run (emulator) dialog function as if it were an actual running watch face, and you will be able to see your Minutes-based Tag Expression rotate the Vector Illustration background image (a pinwheel) based on the seconds data, which essentially uses the Tag Expression to change those seconds into pinwheel rotation for visual feedback for your user to see the seconds go by via the pinwheel background image rotation.

Figure 13-7. *Create Tag Expression that rotates a background based on minutes*

Test the **1.0*[m]** Tag Expression in Run, as seen in Figure 13-8.

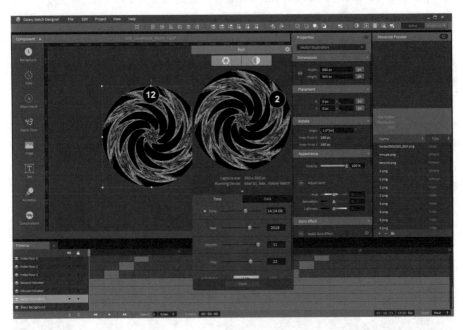

Figure 13-8. *Use the Run (emulator) to Play (test) a Minutes-based Tag Expression*

Next, let's change the Tag Expression so that it rotates the pinwheel background one degree each second, so that it acts like a second hand. As you can see in Figure 13-9, we again click the triangle in the **Rotate Angle** field to open up the **Script** window and edit the Tag Expression, so that it reads **1.0*[s]**, or multiply one degree by the Seconds value to Rotate the Vector Illustration and then use the **Run** (emulator) **Icon** to access the **Play** transport feature and use that to animate the background image which is now based on the Tag Expression of 1.0*[s] so that it will visualize the ticking seconds of the watch face using the pinwheel background Vector Illustration image.

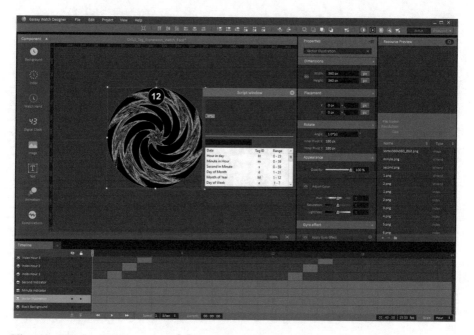

Figure 13-9. *Write a 1.0*[s] Tag Expression that rotates based on seconds*

As you can see in Figure 13-10, clicking the Play transport icon in the Run (emulator) Time Tab now sets your pinwheel background vector illustration graphic in motion visualizing the seconds ticking away for the user. Next, let's switch back to using Sensor-based Tag Expressions and replace the Seconds [s] tag with the Battery Power % Percentage Tag **[ba]** which is shown in Figure 13-11.

Figure 13-10. *Test the Seconds Tag Expression 1.0*[s] by using the Play Icon*

Next, let's rotate your pinwheel watch face background image one degree for each percentage of battery power usage in order to create a visual representation of how quickly the Battery is draining on the smartwatch.

This can be done with the Tag Expression of **1.0*[ba]** as can be seen in the Script window in Figure 13-11. To have this **[ba]** Tag inserted into the Tag Expression for you, click the lower part of the Script window on the Battery (%) Percentage Tag (shown in Blue) as seen in Figure 13-11.

To replace the previous 1.0*[s] Tag Expression as seen in the Rotate Angle field in the Properties pane, close the **Script** window using the "X" icon at the top right of the window, and click the **OK** button in the **Warning** dialog that appears next (see Figure 13-3). This will then enter the 1,0*[ba] Tag Expression in the Rotate Angle data field.

Next, let's create a Tag Expression that uses the Floor [fl] Tag so that the pinwheel spins the higher the Floor level becomes. Since there is a Floor Slider Bar in the Data Tab in the Run (emulator) dialog, we can easily test this Tag Expression as well and make sure that the pinwheel is animating correctly based on the Floor Sensor data.

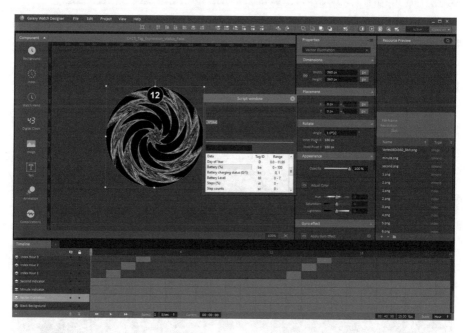

Figure 13-11. *Write a Tag Expression that rotates based on Battery % (1.0*[ba])*

As can be seen in Figure 13-12, I have changed the [ba] Tag to be a Floor (altitude) [fl] Tag so that the pinwheel now rotates as the Floor changes in height levels.

This can be tested in the Run (emulator) as it has a Slider under the Data Tab for Floor, which as you drag it from left to right should rotate the pinwheel background, as shown in Figure 13-13.

As you can see in Figure 13-12, I had been previously testing the Speed [sp] Tag, which does not have a Slider under the Data Tab, before I created the [fl] Floor-based Tag Expression 1.0*[fl] which is shown in the Script window in Figure 13-12.

I finished the Floor-based Tag Expression by closing the Script window shown in Figure 13-12 and then acknowledged the Tag Expression limitations in the Warning dialog that follows by clicking the OK button at the bottom of the dialog.

I then tested this Floor Tag Expression, by using the **Run** (emulator) Icon, and clicked the Data Tab and dragged the Floor Slider to the right to make sure the pinwheel background spun around due to the Tag Expression changing the Rotate Angle based on the Floor Tag.

Figure 13-12. *Write Tag Expression 1.0*[fl] that rotates the vector based on Floor*

Test the Floor **[fl]** Tag Expression in the **Run** (emulator), by dragging the **Floor Slider** under the **Data Tab** to the right, and see if the pinwheel spins in the background in response to the Floor sensor data.

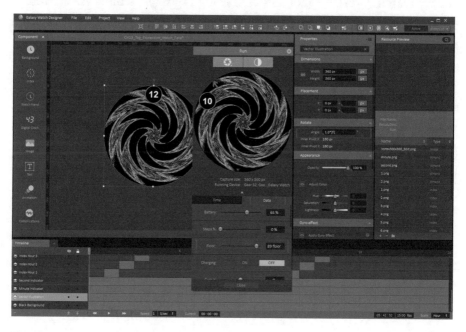

Figure 13-13. *Use the Run (emulator) to test Floor Tag Expression in Data Tab*

We have now created half a dozen Tag Expressions, three Time-based (Hour, Minute, and Second) and three Sensor-based (Battery, Steps, and Floor) which change the Rotation Angle of your Vector Illustration (pinwheel) background image, giving your users a visual representation of time, steps, battery, and floor movements over time.

In the next chapter, we'll take a look at how to publish your watch face designs in the Samsung Galaxy Watch storefront, since we have now covered all of the major features of smartwatch design that are available in the Galaxy Watch Designer software package.

Summary

In this chapter, we took a look at how to add algorithms (code) to the Galaxy Watch Face Designer software using Tag Expressions. We started out learning the syntax used in Galaxy Watch Designer tag expressions, along with the allowed symbols and keywords which represent the sensor- and time-related data.

Next, we learned how to access the Tag Expressions dialog via the triangle icon under the Property that you want to evaluate a Tag Expression, as well as how to test Tag Expressions using the Run (emulator) Icon. Then we tried a variety of tag expressions to show you how they work.

CHAPTER 14

Watch Face Publishing

In this final chapter of the *Smartwatch Design Fundamentals* book, let's take a look at how to publish your watch faces in the Samsung store. There are two types of Seller Office Accounts, the **Private Seller** Account, which allows **Free** watch faces to be published, and the **Corporate Seller** Account, which allows for **Paid** watch faces. The Private Seller Account can be **upgraded** to the Corporate Seller Account at any time by submitting some paperwork. We will be focusing on the Private Seller Account in this chapter, as most readers will be starting with this, as getting into doing corporate paperwork is not an option for most readers, who are not going to be corporations.

In this chapter you'll be learning how to sign up for the basic Private Seller Account, which anyone can do. I will take you through the screens that I went through to sign up for this Private Seller Account in the first section of the chapter, in Figures 14-1 through 14-7, so that you can see what I did, and we'll discover information about Samsung Themes Magazine and the Themes Creation Service, which you can use to create, and even sell, themes for the Galaxy (6.0 and onward) Smartphones and Galaxy Watches worldwide in 185 countries.

© Wallace Jackson 2019
W. Jackson, *SmartWatch Design Fundamentals*,
https://doi.org/10.1007/978-1-4842-4369-5_14

Finally, we will cover how to **Build** Watch Face TPK4 files, and how to **publish** these directly to the Samsung Store, from your Galaxy Watch Designer software, so that you can immediately offer the free version of your watch face design on the Samsung Galaxy Watch store.

Private Seller: Sign Up Online

Before you can distribute your watch face, you'll need to sign up as a seller on the Samsung Developers website. Let's go ahead and sign in (sign up) now by using the `https://developer.samsung.com/galaxy-watch/distribute/how-to-distribute` URL. Click the blue **Sign In** button, seen in the middle of Figure 14-1.

Figure 14-1. *developer.samsung.com/galaxy-watch/distribute/how-to-distribute*

Once you click the **Sign In** button, you will be taken to the Sign-In with your Samsung Account page, shown in Figure 14-2, with images of the Samsung Galaxy Phone and Samsung Galaxy Watch.

There are also links for Samsung Z and Samsung Smart TV, which is the Samsung Trademark **SmartTV**™ for Interactive Television Sets (iTV Set), much like **AndroidTV**™, **AppleTV**™, or **ConnectedTV**™ (a trademark registered by Matsushita, also known as "Panasonic").

If you click Samsung Z, you will be taken to the Tizen Store Seller Office page, which has links for Smart TV, Galaxy (Smartphone), and Galaxy Watch at the bottom as well. You would use this if you were developing apps by using Tizen Studio 2.5, which is also free to use.

Once you click this Blue "**Sign In with Samsung Account**" button, you'll be taken to Samsung's Account page, seen in Figure 14-3.

Figure 14-2. *Sign in with a Samsung Account on a Samsung Galaxy Apps page*

Fill in your **e-mail address** and **password**, and click the **Sign In** button. This signs you into a Samsung Account, as seen in Figure 14-3.

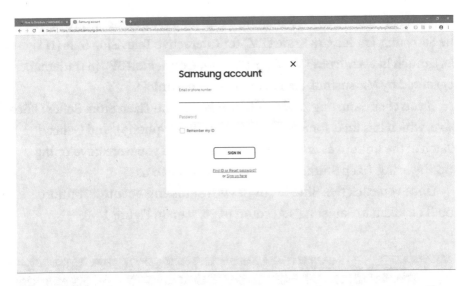

Figure 14-3. *Log in to your Samsung account, by using an e-mail and password*

Once you have signed into your Samsung account, as is shown in Figure 14-3, next, you'll be taken to Samsung's **Seller Sign Up Now** page, shown in Figure 14-4. It is here that you will decide which type of Seller you are going to become, and if you are a Samsung **Partner**, or if you are a Samsung **Developer** Seller Type.

Figure 14-4. *Select the Private Seller Member Type and Developer Seller Type*

To complete this form, you will be required to check boxes which say that you have read, and agree to, the various **Samsung Terms and Conditions** regarding your use of these Samsung Seller Services and that you have also read, and agree to, the Samsung **Privacy Policy**.

Once you have selected these checkboxes, you will click the dark blue **Next** button, shown at the bottom right of Figure 14-5.

There is also an "Agree to All" checkbox, at the very bottom of the form (page), as seen in Figure 14-5. Selecting this is equivalent to selecting both of these "I have read and agree to the Terms and Conditions" and "I have read and agree to the Privacy Policy" checkboxes.

This is simply a shortcut way to complete the form's legal compliance requirements before clicking the dark blue Next button at the bottom right of the form. Do this now, and complete the Seller Sign-Up Process, so we can proceed.

Figure 14-5. *Agree to Samsung Terms and Conditions and to the Privacy Policy*

This will take you to the **Sign Up Now** page, which is shown in Figure 14-6. Fill out your **E-mail**, **Password**, **First Name**, **Last Name**, and **Address** information and **Phone Number**, as I have done in the yellow fields seen in the screenshot. Be sure to fill out all of the fields as I have blanked a few of them in this screenshot for privacy purposes. I left my Name, Title, State, Country, and Password and blanked the rest.

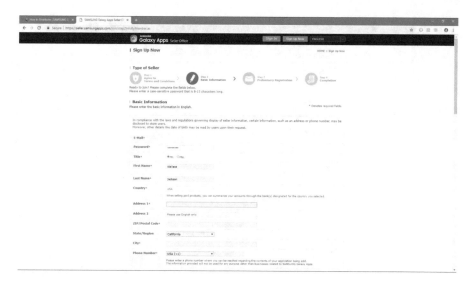

Figure 14-6. *Sign Up to be a Seller by completing the Basic Information Form*

Scroll down and expose more key information, regarding your **Seller's Home** URL and **Help** URL, as well as any Background Images, Profile Images, and Banner Images you may upload, as can be seen in Figure 14-7. If you do not want to provide your own imagery, Samsung will provide a default image for you to use.

This bottom section allows you to put more information, such as links and images, onto your seller page, in order to customize it.

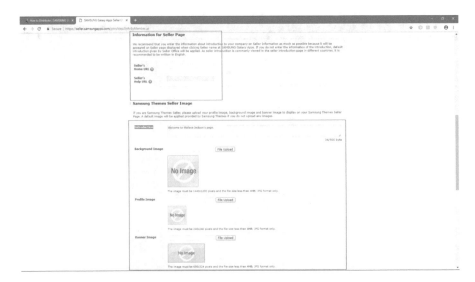

Figure 14-7. *Enter your Home URL and Help URL, Introduction, and Images*

As you may have noticed, the caption for the imagery upload section of this form, shown in Figure 14-7, reads "**Samsung Themes Seller Image**." This suggests that it might be a good idea as a watch face designer if you are also a Samsung Themes Seller. Let's take a closer look at what these Samsung Themes are, in the next section of the chapter, in case you want to also become a Samsung Themes Seller, just so that you are fully prepared to maximize your presence.

You may want to develop themes for Samsung devices, as your Galaxy Watch page has references to these and because these can also be sold to Samsung Smartphone and Smartwatch users. It is also not that complex to provide themes to the public, and they are in 185 stores across the world, so this creates great exposure for your brand.

Samsung Themes

Notice that at the bottom of Figure 14-7 there are Samsung Themes Seller Images. You can click the **Get Access** button seen in Figure 14-8 to get the website shown in Figure 14-10, where you can sign up to create your own themes. This is called a **Theme Partnership Service Request** where you enter your Company Name, Company Website, and E-Mail address. Themes include Home screen and Lock screen wallpaper, application icons, smartphone backgrounds, other design elements for default applications (Phone Dialer, Contacts, Messages, E-mail, Calculator, Alarm Clock, etc.), sounds (Ringtones, Alarm Sounds, Touch Sounds, Dial Pad Tones, Keyboard Sounds, Device button press sounds, and Delete button press sounds), and some Custom Fonts. Figure 14-8 shows the **Samsung Developer Themes** page, at https://developer.samsung.com/theme which tells us that there is a premium decorative content service available in **185** countries around the world. I'm sure Samsung is adding more countries to this number currently, just as they are updating the Galaxy Watch Designer software package versions over time as well.

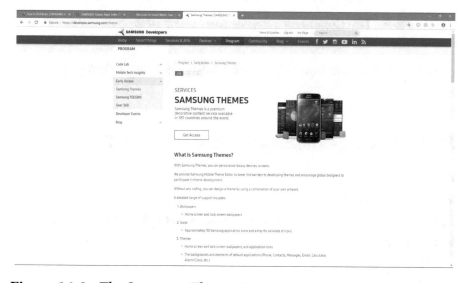

Figure 14-8. *The Samsung Themes Services website and Get Access button*

Samsung Themes Magazine

Samsung is so into their Themes that they have created the **Samsung Themes Magazine** website located at samsungthemesmagazine.com which can be seen in Figure 14-9.

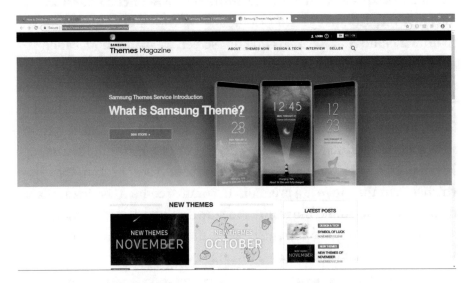

Figure 14-9. *The Samsung Themes Magazine website*

Let's take a look at how to become a Samsung Theme Designer in the next section.

Becoming a Samsung Theme Designer

As you can see in Figure 14-10, you can sign up to become a **Samsung Theme Designer** by clicking the white **Get Access** button shown in Figure 14-8, which will take you to the **Themes Service Partnership request** page.

Simply enter your **Corporate Name**, **Corporate Website**, and **E-mail address** into the form found at the Themes Service Partnership Request page, as shown in Figures 14-10 and 14-11. This will sign your brand (corporation) up to be a Samsung Themes Development Service.

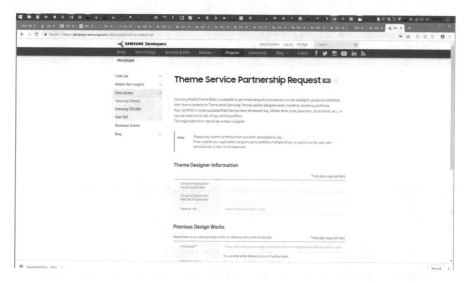

Figure 14-10. *Themes Service Partnership Request Form for Theme Designers*

Figure 14-11 shows how I filled out this **Theme Service Partnership Request** and then clicked the **Continue** and **Next** buttons.

Figure 14-11. *Enter Your Information, Concept, and Samples and click Next*

Next, let's take a look at how to actually generate (Build and Publish) the watch face packages (.TPK4 and .TPK3) that contain the watch face designs and which live in the Samsung Smartwatch Store.

Once these are downloaded onto your user's smartwatch, these Tizen 3.0 (Gear S, Gear S2, Gear S3, Gear Fit, and Gear Fit 2) and Tizen 4.0 (Galaxy Watch) **packages** contain your watch face **code** and **assets**. As you now know, these comprise your watch face and are executed by the Smartwatch.

Building Watch Face Designs (TPK4)

Next, let's take a look at how to build Galaxy Watch Tizen 4.0 (TPK4) package files, which will allow us to distribute our watch face design in the Samsung Galaxy Watch Face Store. If you generate a Tizen 3.0 watch face (TPK3) file, and upload that to the store as well, you will then add support for the Gear S, Gear S2, Gear S3, Gear Fit, and Gear Fit 2 smartwatch devices in the store. The way to do this is the same as the way that you will create the Tizen 4 watch face design file, including Always-On watch faces, so, to support more smartwatches, you would go through the same work process outlined over the rest of this chapter for both the Tizen 3.0 (TPK3) and Tizen 4.0 (TPK4) package types.

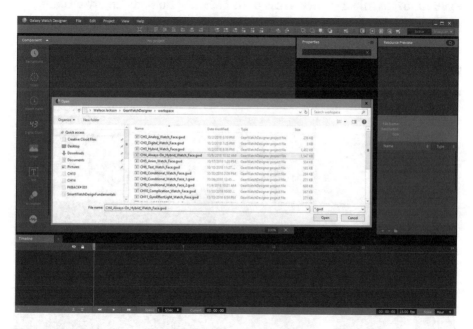

Figure 14-12.   *Open the CH4_Always-On_Hybrid_Watch_Face.gwd project file*

Since we have already created a watch face design which has the Always-On watch face components in place, back in Chapter 3, let's use the **File ➤ Open** menu sequence to access this Analog Watch Face called **CH3_Analog_Watch_Face.gwd**, and see how this project is published to the Samsung Watch Face Store. As you can see in Figure 14-13, if you click the **Build Icon**, which shows a solid wrench in the middle of a dotted face (shown encircled in red at the top right), the **Build Project** dialog will

open, where you can set the **Target API** version in a drop-down as "Tizen
4.0 and later wearable devices." Enter a Samsung Developer password in
the Password field (shown encircled in red), and click the **Build** button
at the bottom of the dialog (shown in blue), which will trigger the **Run
(emulator) Icon**, as Galaxy Watch Designer wants to make sure you have
Always-On watch face design states in place and check their OPR (On
Pixel Ratio) to make sure it is less than **15%**, or you'll get an error dialog
informing you that your OPR is too high for you to post your watch face
design in the Samsung Galaxy Watch store. If you like, you can change
the **Label** for the watch face design, away from the file name (I like to use
descriptive file names, for this reason).

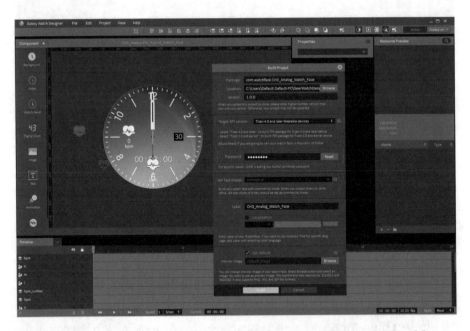

Figure 14-13. *Enter your password and create a Tizen 4.0 Build to
create a .TZ4*

Once you click the **Build** button, you'll see the **Run** (emulator) dialog, as shown in Figure 14-14, which means that your Galaxy Watch Designer is running the project in order to test it, and make sure it runs, and that the **OPD** for the watch face design is within the **15% "ceiling"** that Samsung has set for Galaxy Store listing. If the OPD is greater than 15%, you will see an error dialog appear over the Run (emulator) dialog, informing you your OPD is too high, and the watch face won't be listed!

Figure 14-14. *Use the Build Icon to Test (Run) and Build the Watch Face Design*

The next thing to do is to create a **Preview Image** of the Watch Face, to add to your build. This can be done in GIMP 2.10.10, and added via the **Build Project** dialog, shown in Figures 14-13 and 14-17. This can be done using the **Run** (emulator) dialog image or the **Remote Testing Lab** image (see Figure 12-36, for instance). Simply screenshot the image (as I have done for this book), and then use the latest version of GIMP 2.10 to crop it out to either 360 by 360 or 512 by 512, and then export it as a PNG8 or PNG24 image, and then import it into the Build Project dialog's Preview Image field, which we will be doing in the next section so that you can see how to do this step.

Adding a Preview Image to the Build

I used GIMP to crop to a 360 by 360 pixel image, seen in Figure 14-15, and used the GIMP 2.20.8 **File ➤ Export As** menu sequence to export it as **Preview.PNG** so that I had an image asset to use in the **Preview Image** field in the **Build Dialog** in Galaxy Watch Designer, so that I had a Preview Image of the Watch Face to use in the Samsung store. You are allowed to use Preview Images of 360 by 360 or 512 by 512 in the Samsung store in .PNG, .GIF, or .JPG (JPEG) digital image formats.

Figure 14-15. *Use GIMP to create a 360 pixel PNG preview of Watch Face*

Figure 14-16 shows a screenshot of the GIMP 2.10.8 File ➤ **Export As** dialog, saving this 24-bit **Preview.PNG** file into the GWD's **C:/Users/ Default.Default-PC/GearWatchDesigner/screenshot** folder.

Figure 14-16. *Save .PNG as Preview.PNG in GearWatchDesigner/ screenshot/*

The next thing to do is click the Build Project ➤ Preview Image field, and select the **Preview.PNG** image asset using the Browse button as is shown encircled in red in Figure 14-17, to define your preview image.

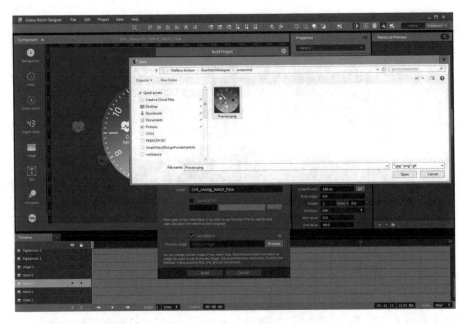

Figure 14-17. *Add Preview.PNG to Tizen 4 Build using Preview Image ➤ Browse*

Figure 14-18 shows the **Preview Image** defined (encircled in red) in the Build Project dialog, along with your **Label**, **Target API Version**, and **Password**. Click the (lights up as blue on mouse-over) **Build** button to create the **CH3_Analog_Watch_Face.TPK4** file, which you will **Publish (Project ➤ Upload)** to the Store later on in the chapter.

Figure 14-18. *Preview.PNG added to Tizen 4.0 Build File will display in the Store*

As you can see in Figure 14-19, you are now ready to use the **Project ➤ Upload** menu sequence to upload your watch face design to the Samsung Store.

After you do this, the Galaxy Watch Designer will open your default browser application (as you can see mine is Google Chrome) and then reference the Samsung Galaxy Apps Seller website, which can be seen in Figure 14-19.

Sign in by clicking the blue "Sign In with Samsung Account" button. The website pages that you see next will be very similar (if not identical) to the web pages that you saw in Figures 14-2 through 14-7 at the beginning of this chapter when you signed up to be a Samsung Seller. You will be using these same pages to register your watch face.

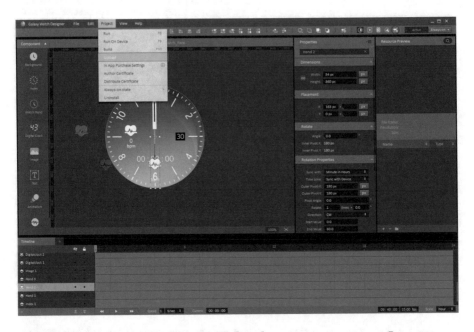

Figure 14-19. *Use a Project ➤ Upload menu sequence or Icon to upload to store*

Galaxy Watch Designer will send you to the **Samsung Seller Office** for Galaxy Apps using your default browser, mine is Chrome, as is shown in Figure 14-20. Sign in to your Samsung Seller Account.

Figure 14-20. *Click blue "Sign in with Samsung Account" button on the web page*

At this point you will confirm what type of Member (Private Seller or Corporate Seller) you are, as well as what type of Seller (Partner or Developer) you are, as you did in Figure 14-4. Once you have selected these options and your Country, click the blue **Next** button seen at the bottom center of the page in Figure 14-21, so you can proceed.

Figure 14-21. *Select your Member and Seller Type and Country and click Next*

Click "Next" as seen in Figure 14-22 after selecting "Agree" checkboxes.

Figure 14-22. *Check the "I have read and agree" checkboxes and click Next*

Make sure you are signed up as a Galaxy Apps Seller in Figure 14-23 as you did in Figure 14-6 earlier in the chapter.

Figure 14-23. *Make sure your information is correct in the Sign Up Now website*

Enter your Seller Page **Brand Name**, **Description**, **Imagery**, and **Logo**, and click the blue **Confirm** button shown in Figure 14-24.

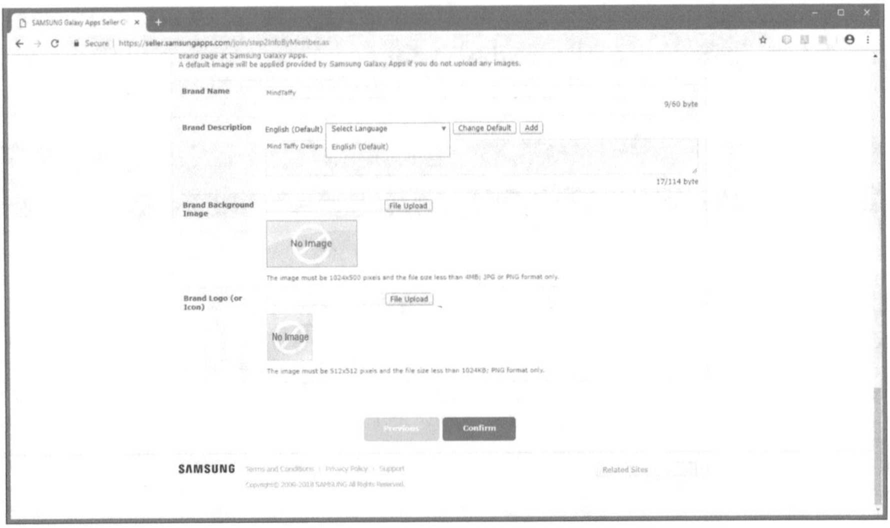

Figure 14-24. *Enter your Seller Page Brand Name, Brand Description, and Imagery*

Once you've completed all of this, you will get the **"Welcome to Samsung Galaxy Apps Seller Office"** page, shown in Figure 14-25, which confirms your upload to the Samsung Galaxy Watch Face Seller Store. This page informs you that a **confirmation e-mail** has been sent to your registered e-mail address, and asks you to use the confirmation link in that e-mail to complete the registration process.

You also have a blue button, seen at the bottom of Figure 14-25, that you can use to resend the confirmation e-mail.

Figure 14-25. *The Welcome to Samsung Galaxy Apps Seller Office web page*

Notice in Figure 14-26 that I then went into my Gmail account and retrieved the Welcome to Samsung Galaxy Apps Seller Office e-mail and the included link (seen in blue) and clicked that link to complete the watch face apps registration process.

I was then directed to another web page, seen in Figure 14-27, which welcomed me as a registered Samsung Seller.

At the bottom of that website was a drop-down menu which included some other Samsung links in it to Samsung Galaxy Apps as well as to Samsung Developers, in case I needed them.

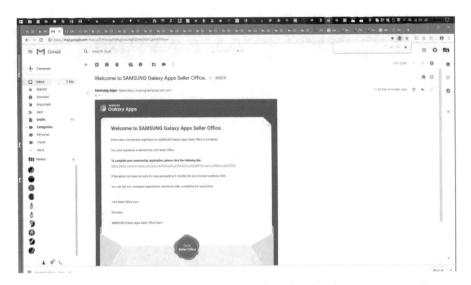

Figure 14-26. *The Welcome to Samsung Galaxy Apps Sellers Office page*

Once you click the confirmation link that comes in your e-mail, you will see the **Welcome!** web page, as shown in Figure 14-27.

Figure 14-27. *Watch Face Developer Seller Welcome! website from Samsung*

Congratulations! You have published your watch face design. I hope you have enjoyed this book on the Galaxy Watch Designer 1.6.2 software package (the current version at the time of writing this book).

Summary

This final chapter takes a look at how to publish your watch face designs on the Samsung Galaxy Watch Storefront. We took a look at the difference between a free account (where your watch face designs are free for public download) and a commercial account (where you can charge money for your watch face designs). We looked at how to set up the free watch face developer account, since this is what the majority of the readers of this book will do, since you have to have corporate and similar legal documents in place to become a commercial developer account. You can upgrade a **Free Developer** account to a **Commercial Developer** account at any time on the Samsung Developer website; simply follow the instructions on their website to accomplish this.

Next, we covered those steps (screens) that you must navigate through in order to set up a **Samsung Galaxy Watch Seller** account, as well as took a much closer look at the **Samsung Galaxy Theme Services** website and **Themes Magazine**, which Samsung has tied in closely with Galaxy Watch Development Seller accounts. Needless to say, if you maximize this themes development, you will maximize your Samsung Galaxy Watch downloads. For this reason, we looked at how to become a Samsung Theme Developer, and after that we looked at how to generate a Galaxy Watch Design (**.TP4 Tizen 4.0 binary**) for publishing on the Samsung Galaxy Watch Face Store. After that we looked at how to upload that TP4 Tizen Package to the Galaxy Watch Store using your free account information. Now smartwatch users around the world can get a smartwatch from $50 to $250 and sport one of your watch face designs for all of their friends! I hope that you enjoyed this book as much as I enjoyed writing it!

Index

A

© Wallace Jackson 2019
W. Jackson, *SmartWatch Design Fundamentals*,
https://doi.org/10.1007/978-1-4842-4369-5